Gender a[nd]
Culture in Britain
since 1600

Gender and History
Series editors: Amanda Capern and Louella McCarthy

Published

Ann Taylor Allen	*Women in Twentieth-Century Europe*
Paul J. Bailey	*Women and Gender in Twentieth-Century China*
Trev Lynn Broughton and Helen Rogers (eds)	*Gender and Fatherhood in the Nineteenth Century*
Ana Carden-Coyne (ed.)	*Gender and Conflict since 1914: Historical and Interdisciplinary Perspectives*
Krista Cowman	*Women in British Politics c.1689–1979*
Shani D'Cruze and Louise A. Jackson	*Women, Crime and Justice in England since 1660*
William Henry Foster	*Gender, Mastery and Slavery: From European to Atlantic World Frontiers*
Rachel G. Fuchs and Victoria E. Thompson	*Women in Nineteenth-Century Europe*
Hannah Greig, Jane Hamlett and Leonie Hannan (eds)	*Gender and Material Culture in Britain since 1600*
Lesley A. Hall	*Sex, Gender and Social Change in Britain since 1880* (2nd edition)
Laurence Lux-Sterritt and Carmen Mangion (eds)	*Gender, Catholicism and Spirituality: Women and the Roman Catholic Church in Britain and Europe, 1200–1900*
Perry Willson	*Women in Twentieth-Century Italy*
Angela Woollacott	*Gender and Empire*

Forthcoming

Beatrice Craig	*Women and Business since 1500*
Jacqueline DeVries	*Women, Religion and Social Change in Britain since 1795*
Natasha Hodgson	*Gender and the Crusades*
Jane Martin	*Gender and Education in Britain since 1770*
Marianna Muravyeva	*Sexual Variations in Europe since 1600*
Corinna Peniston-Bird and Emma Vickers (eds)	*Gender and the Second World War*

Gender and History Series
Series Standing Order ISBN 978–1–4039–9374–8 hardback
Series Standing Order ISBN 978–1–4039–9375–5 paperback
(*outside North America only*)

You can receive future titles in this series as they are published by placing a standing order. Please contact your bookseller or, in the case of difficulty, write to us at the address below with your name and address, the title of the series and the ISBN quoted above.

Customer Services Department, Macmillan Distribution Ltd, Houndmills, Basingstoke, Hampshire, RG21 6XS, UK

Gender and Material Culture in Britain since 1600

Edited by

HANNAH GREIG
JANE HAMLETT
AND
LEONIE HANNAN

 palgrave

First published 2016 by
PALGRAVE

Palgrave in the UK is an imprint of Macmillan Publishers Limited, registered in England, company number 785998, of 4 Crinan Street, London, N1 9XW.

Palgrave Macmillan in the US is a division of St Martin's Press LLC, 175 Fifth Avenue, New York, NY 10010.

Palgrave is the global imprint of the above companies and is represented throughout the world.

Palgrave® and Macmillan® are registered trademarks in the United States, the United Kingdom, Europe and other countries.

ISBN 978–1–137–34065–8 hardback
ISBN 978–1–137–34064–1 paperback

This book is printed on paper suitable for recycling and made from fully managed and sustained forest sources. Logging, pulping and manufacturing processes are expected to conform to the environmental regulations of the country of origin.

A catalogue record for this book is available from the British Library.

A catalog record for this book is available from the Library of Congress.

Printed in China

Contents

List of Figures

Introduction: Gender and Material Culture

Hannah Greig, Jane Hamlett

and Leonie Hannan

In June 2011 the pen manufacturer BIC launched a new range of its famous disposable pens. Branded as 'For Her', the line offered pens in an 'elegant design – just for her!' The designs that BIC hoped would entice the female market included casing the pens in pastel pinks, purples and florals, and offering 'slim line casing' with a 'comfort grip' to ensure the product would 'fit comfortably in a woman's hand'. The marketing was serious but the eventual response from some of its intended audience was one of derision. By the end of the following year the 'For Her' pens were subject to a deluge of sarcastic Amazon reviews. 'Thank goodness someone has finally noticed that for years women have struggled with pen usage,' read one, 'what is the point of being allowed to vote, when ordinary pens have been just far too uncomfortable and downright heavy to grasp in our teeny tiny porcelain hands?' 'This pen will help me list all my household chores and record my calorie consumption in my diary.' 'It is a truth universally acknowledged that a single woman in possession of a vacuous mind must be in want of a Bic for Her pen' noted another.[1]

BIC's marketing strategy, and indeed the response it generated, highlight how intimately conceptions of gender inform our current material culture. Of course, the overtly gendered presentation of goods not only applies to products aimed at female consumers. Action men, spaceships and replica guns also crowd shop shelves. Advertising campaigns for beer, cars and shaving paraphernalia are often unambiguously gendered male. Shared ideas of what men and women are, or should be, are at the heart of contemporary British culture. And, despite the irate reaction it provoked, the BIC strategy tells us that there must be some success in such marketing approaches, otherwise why are they so pervasive?

If we look at the objects that we own, that we covet and which surround us in our everyday culture it is very evident that ideas about gender and the material world are closely connected. Gender informs things and, in turn, the things people own inform conceptions and perceptions of gender in wide-ranging ways. As in the BIC case, marketing is often a tool that is used to shape both these relationships. Such close connections, though, are not new.

Material objects have always shaped people's interactions with the world around them. The number and types of things that people have owned have certainly changed dramatically over time, but things have always mattered. Moreover, just as the items that make up our material environment today betray the norms, codes, anxieties, possibilities and restrictions of our contemporary culture, so too can material objects inform us about history and the conditions of the past. For this reason, and as this book explores, studying the material culture of the past (or a 'material history') can help us think afresh about particular types of historical experiences and identities. And in this volume we are particularly interested in exploring the marked and longstanding interrelationship between material culture and ideas about gender. This book considers what material culture tells us about gender in history and also what gender tells us about material culture.

Written by scholars in a range of history-related disciplines, the essays in this book are intended to be read as exercises in discovery. They offer exposés of current research methods and interests with the aim of demonstrating to students, and other researchers new to the field, how a relationship between material culture and gender is being addressed. All the contributors work on early modern and modern British history but specialise in different periods from the sixteenth to the mid-twentieth centuries. All share an interest in gender and material culture. However, the authors also define, approach and interrogate such broadly shared interests in diverse ways. Most focus on a particular kind of gendered or sexual identity – masculinity or femininity, queer or straight – rather than gender in its entirety. When brought together, though, such diversity testifies to the nuanced ways in which the category of 'gender' in history can be approached. The reader will also find that each author explores the interrelationship of material culture and gender from a different methodological and intellectual starting point. For instance, some essays deal with a very specific type of object, such as an eighteenth-century jug or a twentieth-century powder puff; others look at broader material environments, such as the sixteenth-century guild and the interior of a twentieth-century pub; and some focus on constellations of goods such as those associated with the paraphernalia of letter-writing or maintaining eighteenth-century men's hair.

Representing their individual academic perspectives, each author also places different weight on the relationship between gender and material culture. For some a longstanding interest in gendered experiences in the past has subsequently led them to investigate material histories, whereas others have found that an engagement with object histories and design histories has in turn led them to engage with questions of gender. Many of the contributors work within university humanities disciplines but have also participated in research projects and teaching initiatives that involve close collaborations with national and regional museums. The intellectual diversity inherent in this collection is important to its purpose – which is to offer a series of methodological case studies rather than a comprehensive study of the relationship between gender and material culture in British history. Primarily aimed at undergraduate and postgraduate students, this book showcases the range of possible intellectual approaches and research methods available to the researcher in this field.

Gender and Culture

The study of gender identities, that is, how men and women were treated and how their roles were understood, is now a familiar part of history. Histories of women and gender line library shelves and feature on many undergraduate courses. But this has not always been the case.[2] In the 1970s, inspired by new social histories of working people, historians started to pay more attention to women's lives.[3] This new trend was strongly influenced by Second Wave Feminism. Feminist scholars argued that in order to understand women's lives, it was essential to look at the patriarchal power structures that dictated them. This led to a flowering of studies of women in different times and places.[4] Uncovering 'herstories' or 'hidden histories' showed that women were surprisingly active in the supposed affairs of men. Queens, wives and widows were often powerful. Looking closely at women also made historians realise the importance of the home, family and private life. Some even argued that history should be given a different periodisation, structured around childhood, marriage, death and the human lifecycle rather than being categorised according to monarchs, governments or regime changes.

The recovery of 'herstory' as distinct from history, however, generated a new set of concerns that the study of women might be 'ghettoised' or 'hived off' as a sub-discipline of mainstream historical enquiry.[5] Despite the raft of energetic new scholarship published in the 1970s, for the most part professional historians (who were then mainly male) went on much as before, leaving women's history to one side, and viewing it as a niche interest. In response, some historians of women sought to demonstrate how gendered values were an essential part of historical societies, howsoever conceived, and not just relevant to the study of women. Joan Wallach Scott articulated this new approach in her famous article 'Gender: A Useful Category of Historical Analysis'.[6] Instead of focusing exclusively on women, Scott argued that the broader social construction of gender should be at the centre of historical enquiry. A study of gender would, she suggested, allow historians to interrogate the building blocks of power and thereby better understand the subjection of women within historical processes. Importantly, Scott drew attention to the unevenness of the gendered power dynamic, and its constituent parts. Gender, in such an analysis, is understood as a product and expression of culture rather than sex. Ideas of gender are both created by and represented in a society's cultural products, for example in magazines, novels or advertising. These symbols are then perceived and sometimes understood in different ways by individual men and women, who proceed to construct their own gender ideas and identities, which might adhere to these norms, or challenge them. As Scott so persuasively argued, studying gender is thus a means of understanding the operation of power within culture.

Gender history and cultural history are therefore closely intertwined. Miri Rubin characterises cultural history as 'an approach that considers the domain of representation and struggle over meaning as the most fruitful areas for the pursuit of historical understanding'.[7] In British women's history, one of the first books to offer a deep exploration of the cultural formation of gender was Leonore Davidoff and Catherine Hall's *Family Fortunes*.[8] They mapped how ideals of masculinity and femininity were articulated in novels, poetry and advice manuals, and also how these influenced individual families through looking at personal documents such as letters and diaries. Not everyone agreed with this picture, however. Amanda Vickery, for example, argued that Victorian conduct manuals can be read as evidence that many people did not live up to contemporary moral standards, hence the need for books of advice.[9] What is clear though, is that gender history has been driven forward by arguments about the way in which gender ideals are represented in culture, and how this relates to their performance and articulation in everyday life.

Approaching gender as a cultural construct allows us to see that masculinity and femininity are not fixed qualities, rooted in biological essentials. Instead they are socially constructed categories, framed in different ways in different times and places. Seeing gender as an identity encouraged historians to explore intersections with other forms of social identity. In the 1980s, Marxist Feminist historians looked at the relationship between gender and class. More recently historians of race and empire have stressed the need to see how class, race and gender work together.[10] The awareness that gender can be unfixed or fluid also has implications for how we see sexuality in history. The study of sexuality has paralleled gender studies, with historians such as Karen Harvey demonstrating that there are no fixed sexual identities, rather a number of possible variants at any given historical moment.[11] Historians of gender and sexuality are constantly trying to find the means by which gender identities are forged. As these identities are not static, and are created by an ongoing process, they can never be entirely pinned down. Nonetheless, as some of the essays here will show, we can certainly attempt to uncover the processes by which they are made.

The turn towards gender has generated a new history of men as well as of women. In recent decades there has been an outpouring of work on the cultural construction of masculinity.[12] Examining how male identities are constructed according to contemporary ideas of manhood has led gender historians to enter new territories such as politics. Matthew McCormack, for example, has demonstrated how fundamental elite men's roles as householders and fathers were to their political rights in the Georgian period.[13] Explorations of masculinity have also transformed how we see some areas of women's history. Understandings of the home, traditionally perceived as woman's domain, have been radically unsettled. John Tosh's seminal book, *A Man's Place*, shows that men could be central to Victorian domesticity.[14] Many of the chapters in this book are a product of this new focus on masculinity, and look specifically at male identities and practices.

An unintended consequence of the emphasis on masculinities is that the study of femininity as a cultural construct has been left rather to one side. Some historians have called for more attention to be paid to femininity so it can 'catch up' with masculinity.[15] In a recent overview of the history of masculinity, John Tosh called for a more relational history of gender that directly compares men and women.[16] Trying to balance the focus between men's and women's lives, to bring ideas of masculinity and femininity into a more coherent history, and work out the consequences for both men and women, is one of the major challenges that gender historians continue to wrestle with today.

Historians constantly reflect on how they and their peers have written about culture in the past. In the 1990s, many studies looked at how gender identities were represented in public culture, in books, prints, paintings and other visual sources. However, some historians became dissatisfied with this approach, arguing that it side-lined how gendered culture was experienced. Michael Roper, for example, has criticised the excessive preoccupation of such histories with cultural codes and public representations, arguing that these do not, on their own, reveal what such codes meant to individuals.[17] For Roper, cultural history needs to consider the relationship between culture and lives lived, or in other words, the subjective experiences of men and women. In a similar vein, Peter Mandler has argued that it is not enough to simply identify a particular cultural construction. We also need to examine the 'reach' or 'throw' of that idea.[18] So if we find a particular book or magazine article that promotes feminine domesticity, we also need to think about how many were published, who bought them, and if we can find out what their readers thought about them. This can be a difficult task but, increasingly, social and cultural historians are constructing histories that deal with culture in a complex way. Lucy Delap's recent history of twentieth-century domestic service, for instance, examines the relationship between experience and culture by looking at the representation of servant–mistress relationships in advice literature, and examining jokes about servants in *Punch* cartoons, as well as the experience of service in oral history.[19] In this book, we suggest that studying material culture is an attractive proposition for historians who want to explore the operation of gender ideals in society. Looking at the gendering of the material world can allow us to connect cultural ideas of masculinity and femininity with the everyday practices of everyday life and individual experience.

Material Culture

So what exactly is 'material culture' and how does it relate to ideas about gender and culture? Before looking at the relationship between material things and gender, it is helpful to briefly review what historians understand by the phrase 'material culture'. For the purposes of this book, we define material culture as objects or physical structures that had a particular use or meaning, or set of values attached to them. The use of the term 'culture' signifies that we are not simply interested in surviving objects (although they can be the focus of our analysis), but rather their role in contemporary society both in creating meaning and in acting as a force for historical change in their own right. The field that has come to be known as 'material culture studies' is by its nature interdisciplinary, incorporating the efforts of archaeologists, anthropologists, historians, art historians, design historians, geographers, sociologists, scholars of literature and many more. It is a diverse field, which encompasses researchers who ask very different questions of the material world. Nevertheless, there are shared and significant intellectual concerns and approaches within this kaleidoscope of practice that have helped to shape the discipline.

For example, the fundamental question of how people and things relate to one another has been a determining concern, with historians asking questions such as: 'What did things mean to people in the past? How were they used? Why were they made? Who sold them? Who bought them? Who kept them and why?' In fact, a central criticism of scholarship on material culture has been that objects are often recognised only in terms of their relevance to human action. In other words, things are mere supplements to human activity – perhaps the product of human endeavour, or the route by which an action is achieved, but nonetheless secondary. This is an important point to acknowledge for those of us who analyse material artefacts in order to answer questions about the social, economic or cultural worlds of the past. As Frank Trentmann has highlighted, 'historical material culture studies have been more about culture than about material'.[20] By viewing the objects of the past as inanimate and inactive as compared with the living, breathing humans who made, exchanged and used them, we can miss the dynamism of the object–person interactions that took place many decades or centuries ago.

Philosophers have offered a useful corrective to this person-centric view of the world and provided illuminating examples of where objects have agency. As one example, Pierre Bourdieu, the French anthropologist and philosopher, showed how everyday goods are capable of socialising the young.[21] Bourdieu focused especially on the way in which objects were arranged within the home and the influence these spatial and material arrangements had on childhood development. More recently, Bruno Latour contributed his influential Actor Network Theory, which takes the argument further by stating that agency is shared between humans and things, each one capable of acting upon the other.[22] This philosophical concern with the agency of things is strongly evident in anthropological studies of material culture. Anthropology as a discipline has always focused on human society and culture; early work on the gift and on commodity usefully emphasised the role of the object in this picture and ensured that research remained alert to the importance of the material in constructing the cultural.[23] In fact, some of the most influential texts for historical material culture studies hail from anthropology, a notable example being Arjun Appadurai's *The Social Life of Things* – which brought the concept of objects having their own (manifold) biographies to a much broader academic audience.[24]

One way to navigate the different ways that scholars have studied material culture is to roughly divide the approaches into three: the study of the object as an end in itself, the study of the object as a means to shed light on its context, and the study of how material things are constructed through other sources. In general, curatorial work tends to make the object central, whereas academic historians are more likely to engage in the second and third kinds of research. There is a much greater prevalence of the second and third kinds of research in our field today. But when first approaching historical objects, there are some basic exercises that can be employed to help develop analytical skills in relation to the material properties of the sources you encounter. Over thirty years ago, Jules Prown elucidated an approach that worked through a close analysis of the object itself in order to get to a better understanding of the object's social and cultural context.[25] Acknowledging that many researchers felt de-skilled in the detailed examination of things as opposed to texts, Prown suggested a protocol that moved from description, through deduction and, finally, on to speculation – forcing the researcher through a process of close looking and describing before allowing consideration of the object's context to come to the fore. This is certainly one way to engage with material culture as historical evidence, and a useful exercise for the textually trained historian. However, as the chapters in this book show, studies of material culture use the artefacts themselves to a greater or lesser extent and, often, it is the more purely object-focused studies that are in the minority. After all, historians regularly deal with a class of object that no longer exists. Many elements of material culture are ephemeral and do not survive through time. This material world is only made manifest through textual and visual sources. Even where relevant artefacts come easily to hand, historians will, for the most part, seek to combine material evidence with other sources. The key to making the most of material culture as a source for historical enquiry is to recognise the new avenues it can offer the historian but, at the same time, to apply all the same critical skills employed in the choice and analysis of more traditional primary sources.

Historical artefacts that do survive are often encountered far removed from their original social or cultural contexts, preserved and displayed in a museum space. The act of encountering an object in a museum brings its own cultural conditions, but these are likely to be very different conditions from the way in which the object was encountered in a past culture that was usually complicated and often changing. By stopping to consider the ways in which objects were made, used, exchanged, lost, adapted and even destroyed, we can reinvigorate our view of historical artefacts otherwise disassociated from human action by the distance of time and place. As Susan Vincent's chapter illuminates, the extensive use of a razor blade by eighteenth-century men resulted in the development of a tactile, physical competency. Through repetition the act of shaving could become a professional practice or a personal habit. Instead of looking to human actors for all the answers about objects, identifying the places where human hand, object and sensory experience came together has the potential to open up new and exciting historical questions.[26]

In recent years, influenced by cultural geography, many historians have begun to study 'space' and 'place'. These broad terms have been used in a huge variety of ways and can refer to imagined realms as much as real physical spaces. Feminist geographers have found the concept particularly helpful in understanding the operation of gender. Doreen Massey, for example, argues that looking at the way in which space is constructed by social interactions illuminates how place is experienced.[27] Historians too have found space useful, particularly when it comes to interpreting how real, physical spaces and architectural structures are actually used by people on a daily basis. The chapters in this book mainly focus on the idea of space in relation to real physical worlds, and as a means of understanding how men and women in the past interpreted material structures. Clark's exploration of the barber shop in Chapter 7 is a case in point: in order to understand the significance of changes in the use and presentation of objects relating to male grooming, we need also to place these goods in their broader spatial context and look at how that was changing too. Likewise, Stella Moss's chapter on mid-twentieth-century male drinking practices considers both the spatial arrangements of the public house and the objects present in order to understand the social behaviours that operated within that place. By connecting analysis of material things to their equally material environments, it is possible to gain a new vantage point from which to explore elusive human experiences.

In recent years, historians have been drawn to the study of material culture in ever-increasing numbers, and some commentators have even described this as a 'material turn' in history. Karen Harvey's introduction to her edited collection *History and Material Culture* succinctly outlines the variety of approaches and kinds of objects that are currently in use.[28] However, a particular challenge for students seeking to understand this field and take a material approach in their own work is that the definition and use of material sources is not evenly distributed across periods and genres of historical research. In fact some of the most frenetic activity in the field has come from social and cultural historians working on the early modern period. As an era of rapidly increasing production of domestic goods, eighteenth-century Britain has been extensively examined as a burgeoning consumer culture and domestic furnishings and personal effects have been particularly closely scrutinised. Within literary studies, the book historian Peter Stallybrass has also played a pioneering role in promoting interest in 'material texts',[29] enhancing our understanding not only of cultural history, but also of literary culture. Design historians – focused on the nineteenth and twentieth centuries – have a longstanding interest in material things, often looking far beyond the designer's drawing board and into the realm of everyday life.[30] Urban specialists have also recently become preoccupied with the agency of the material world of the modern city.[31] And a recent trend in both modern and early modern studies has been to see the passage and transmission of objects as a means by which different societies and economies were connected, moving towards global histories of the movement of objects.[32]

Whilst the development of material culture studies across different disciplines, and for diverse purposes, means it can sometimes be difficult to categorise 'material culture' as a distinct field of historical scholarship, what clearly emerges from the historiography is that objects matter. What people made, owned, used, sold, inherited, lost and destroyed have the potential to reveal rich histories of past experiences and societies. And, as we will now discuss, gender is one such area of history that material culture has the power to reveal.

Historians, Material Culture and Gender

The last twenty years have seen a groundswell in historical studies that draw connections between gender and material culture. For the early modern period, scholars such as Maxine Berg, Tara Hamling, Lisa Jardine, John Styles and Amanda Vickery have all contributed key texts and many of these works have dwelt strongly on themes pertinent to this volume including the production and consumption of goods, the cultural construction of identities, and material cultures of home.[33] Here we will examine the ways in which gender and material culture have become aligned in historical scholarship, and move on to consider the criticisms that have been made of this field.

There are many scholars who develop connections between practices of production and consumption and the construction of gendered identity. Amanda Vickery, for example, has scrutinised eighteenth-century account books revealing different terrains of male and female consumption,[34] but she has also worked on the operation of taste within the domestic sphere, bringing to the fore complex relationships between gender, status, family relationships, identity and the exercise of authority.[35] Whilst Vickery's work emerged from a concern with gender and consumption, another key strand of gender and material culture scholarship is work that focuses specifically on the house and home, but there are contrasting views on how gendered power dynamics played out in domestic space. Historians do not always agree on how this worked. In a feminist reading of the Victorian drawing room, Juliet Kinchin proposes that this space reinforced the subjection of women in the domestic sphere.[36] In contrast, Deborah Cohen argues that the late nineteenth century saw a significant growth in female power, as wives seized control of home décor from their husbands.[37] These differences can in part be explained by a focus on different source materials, Kinchin's being confined to advice literature while Cohen offers a broader reading of everyday practices through a range of texts including diaries and autobiographies. Notwithstanding disagreement amongst historians in this field, scholarship focusing on histories of home has become an important force within historical research in British history across a range of periods.[38]

Another strand of scholarship has focused its energies on the ways in which people constructed identities through material culture. A good example of this is Dena Goodman's work on gender, material culture, and social and intellectual life in eighteenth-century France.[39] By focusing on the gendered 'self', Goodman deploys the evidence of material culture and text to explore how women negotiated prescribed forms of behaviour and took an active role in the development of 'modern' French society through the practice of letter-writing.[40] Material goods are often seen to have specific gendered associations. Pat Kirkham's *The Gendered Object* seeks instead to trace the gendering of things across different societies and cultures.[41] How people deployed objects can also be used to question the purchase of gendered restrictions and identities. Sometimes we can use the material world to question the pervasiveness of gendered ideas in past cultures. Jane Hamlett takes this approach in her study of rooms belonging to late nineteenth-century female students. She argues that the display of hunting trophies, which were usually to be found in masculine areas of middle-class homes, such as studies and billiard rooms, suggests that these students were not bound by gendered conventions.[42] This is important, as the first women in higher education have often been seen as under siege, forced to conform to exacting social standards of femininity in order to avoid censure.

Despite this wealth of scholarship, gender and the material world are not always considered companionable bedfellows. Historians of modern urban Britain such as Patrick Joyce emphasise the role of material things in shaping historical change.[43] These historians are, however, almost solely concerned with the construction and extension of new forms of governance. For the most part, they rarely engage with histories of gender, sexuality and private life. Other historians argue that material history thus far has placed too much emphasis on women and the world of goods. Trentmann argues, for example, that many material histories of the eighteenth century focus too readily on the domestic, the 'soft' and the personal, leaving much room for the development of histories of the 'hard', the 'public' or the institutional.[44] The discussion of the relative merits of 'soft' and 'hard' subjects, itself implicitly gendered, reveals a longstanding fissure in approaches to the material world. As Vickery points out, women and their things, shopping, consumerism and so on, have often been viewed as inconsequential frills and frivolities.[45] This book highlights recent work that begins to bridge this divide. Matt Houlbrook's re-working of his important article connects structures of governance and policing with the making of sexualised identity through the powder puff, an object that became strongly associated with queer sexuality in 1920s Britain. Karen Harvey, meanwhile, examines the emergence of the association between masculinity and 'hard' aesthetics, exploring the longer-term origins of the perceived divide between the feminine world of soft furnishings and the masculine world of industrial tools. She selects a series of objects that can be seen to relate to both, significantly complicating the way that we understand this divide.

In many ways it is unsurprising that the study of gender and material culture have become closely aligned in certain studies. The parallels evident in the development of these fields as areas of historical enquiry are likely to have contributed to their integration. A marked area of common ground is the inherent interest, in both fields, in people and histories on the periphery of grand narratives. At the outset, the overarching intention of women's history was to carve out a place for women in male-dominated histories written from male-orientated records. This focus on the periphery can be ascribed to gender history too, which (whether under the banner of queer histories, masculinities or femininities) has purposefully foregrounded people and identities previously obscured or entirely absent from mainstream narratives. The early theoretical framework for studies of material culture was similarly rooted in the need to find different sources and different methods in order to recover histories of people and places otherwise lacking mainstream historical recognition. Within the American institutions that pioneered historical material culture studies, material sources were an essential route (and often the only route) to recovering histories of native and slave communities.[46] In this regard, using material culture as an historical source was seen as a way to challenge and nuance the written record, a means of subverting narratives preserved in, and privileged by, text.

Perhaps most strikingly, from their origins the fields of both gender and material culture studies looked primarily to culture – to the fluid and complex ways in which both people and things were shaped and challenged by multi-faceted cultural associations and contexts. As discussed in the previous section, it is the *culture* in material culture as much as the *material* that has in many ways been the defining concern. The study of material culture involves more than just an acknowledgement of a world of goods and a physical existence of things. Rather it is the ways those things both define and are defined by a cultural nexus that inform many of the intellectual underpinnings of the field. Indeed, if anything, the cultural side of material culture studies has become ever more pronounced in more recent waves of scholarship which look for peripheral materialities – at things that no longer survive as things, ephemeral items that might, ironically, only be evidenced in written rather than extant material records. In Chapter 1, Helen Smith uses textual evidence of the material culture of early modern guilds to reveal the widespread participation of women in guild life, but her analysis also illuminates the way masculine identity was forged through membership of a guild. Moreover, Smith's analysis uses an expanded notion of material culture to access gender identities and relationships, taking into account the operation of finance and the embodied nature of labour, alongside the objects and spaces of the early modern guild. Much as certain critics feared that gender history represented a challenge to women's history, one might argue, then, that the cultural focus of material culture studies has led to a move away from materiality. This book puts the cultural and the material on a more even footing. The studies here try to weigh up both, although they take different approaches and use varied source material. Vivienne Richmond, for example, puts a surviving object at the heart of her analysis. Her piece explains how the chance find of a hand-worked, prize-winning piece of underwear propelled her on a journey of discovery, uncovering the lives of two working-class sisters. As we have seen, historians of gender are always searching for new ways of understanding the complex operation of culture. The creation of identity in culture is a process that is always in flux. Looking at material culture can help us understand this. Studying the material is a way of overcoming the problems Roper et al. have raised with the 'over culturing' of gender history, which we discussed earlier on. Looking at the material allows us to see how broad shared cultural ideas are actually played out in everyday life. It offers us a means to connect those ideas to the physical world and to human experience.

The chapters that comprise this book have been organised chronologically for ease of reference. Helen Smith leads with her investigation of the material culture of the early modern guild, exploring its relationship not just to the masculinity of the craftsmen organised within it, but also (more unexpectedly) its relationship to femininity and the material contributions and expressions of guild-associated women. Gender and eighteenth-century materiality are then addressed in chapters by Leonie Hannan (on women's letter-writing) and Susan Vincent (on men's hair). Karen Harvey's study of masculinity and craft – as revealed through an unusual collection of ceramic jugs – takes us from the eighteenth and into the nineteenth century. Vivienne Richmond's essay moves the focus back to women's material worlds with her study of Victorian clothes, whilst Jessica Clark revisits men's hair but this time from the perspective of the nineteenth-century barbershop. The closing chapters deal with the twentieth century. Matt Houlbrook explores the powerful significance ascribed to the powder puff in the policing of homosexuality in twentieth-century London, and Stella Moss's closing chapter draws on the Mass Observation archive to recover the materiality and masculinity associated with the 1930s pub.

This chronological span brings into sharp relief enormous historical variations, even within a relatively confined geography and culture. Putting a chronology or precise dates to everyday material practices, such as men's and women's roles in purchasing certain goods or cleaning and maintaining them, is a challenge for students and professional researchers alike. Yet, as historians, we must somehow deal with fluctuations in what people did with things over time. The approach of the chapters in this book is to look at certain activities and practices over a longue durée, or else to locate them at a particular point in time. Susan Vincent's and Leonie Hannan's chapters both address gendered behaviours and material practices over the 'long eighteenth century', which starts after the Restoration in 1660 and ends in 1830.[47] Others focus on specific historical periods: Karen Harvey addresses a shift in ideas of masculinity produced by changing working patterns; Matt Houlbrook pinpoints the 1920s as a time when a certain kind of queer sexual identity became commodified; Vivienne Richmond, meanwhile, centres her chapter on the production of a piece of clothing that probably took place in the 1880s. What such approaches suggest, however, is the way in which objects – through their changing look, function and significance – illuminate historical change in material form. An object-driven historical chronology might share some of the broader features of other forms of historical chronology. Technological innovation, for instance, has a dramatic impact on the appearance of a material world. Yet objects might also indicate unexpected turning points and previously obscure moments of change that have the potential to challenge chronologies and teleologies inherent in other histories.

The focus of this book is more on local than global histories, but it nonetheless presents a range of British localities over a period of 400 years. The chapters also include men and women from a wide range of classes and groups, from the very well off to the working poor. London features heavily in these accounts, from the capital city's early modern guilds and barbershops, through to the activities of its early twentieth-century police courts. That said, the collection also attends to regional gendered identities – most especially in Karen Harvey's study of Sheffield and Stella Moss's exploration of working-class drinking habits in the public houses of Bolton. The book, therefore, provides a range of points of entry for the reader in terms of period, location and social status. Moreover, taken together, these chapters present a wide range of approaches to the study of gender and material culture that can be used, adapted and developed by future researchers drawn to this exciting and growing field.

Notes

The editors would like to thank the Scouloudi Foundation, in association with the Institute of Historical Research, for supporting this book with a Scouloudi Publication Award. Gratitude is also owed to *The Historical Journal* for granting permission for the reproduction in this volume of Matt Houlbrook's 2007 article, 'The Man with the Powder Puff in Interwar London'. We are also indebted to Giorgio Riello, John Styles and the anonymous readers for their assistance, critical comments and suggestions.

1. Many hundreds of reviews have been posted on Amazon. Those quoted above were posted by anonymous reviewers 'Purpleprose' and 'Siobhan' on 20 August 2012 and 'Jehodgson' on 27 August 2012 relating to the BIC 'For Her' box of 12 medium pens. At the time of writing this introduction, over 800 critical and satirical reviews of the BIC 'For Her' range have been posted on Amazon.

2. Apart from some isolated studies by pioneering female scholars, including A. Clark, *Women's Working Lives in the Seventeenth Century* (London: G. Routledge and Sons, 1919), and I. Pinchbeck, *Women Workers in the Industrial Revolution, 1750–1850* (London: G. Routledge and Sons, 1930).

3. E. P. Thompson, *The Making of the English Working Class* (London: Victor Gollancz, 1963).

4. M. Vicinus (ed.), *Suffer and Be Still: Women in the Victorian Age* (Bloomington: Indiana University Press, 1972).

5. J. Bennett, 'Feminism and History', *Gender and History*, 1:3 (1989), pp. 254–253.

6. J. W. Scott, 'Gender: A Useful Category of Historical Analysis', *The American Historical Review*, 91:5 (1986), pp. 1053–1075.

7. M. Rubin, 'Cultural History I – What's in a Name?' Institute of Historical Research, Making History Site. Available at: http://www.history.ac.uk/makinghistory/resources/articles/cultural_history.html.

8. L. Davidoff and C. Hall, *Family Fortunes: Men and Women of the English Middle Class 1780–1850, Revised Edition* (London: Yale University Press, 2002).

9. A. Vickery, 'Golden Age to Separate Spheres: A Review of the Categories and Chronology of English Women's History', *Historical Journal*, 36:2 (1993), pp. 383–414.

10. C. Hall, *White, Male and Middle-Class: Explorations in Feminism and History* (Cambridge: Polity Press, 1992), pp. 20–21.

11. K. Harvey, 'The Substance of Sexual Difference: Change and Persistence in Eighteenth-Century Representations of the Body', *Gender and History*, 14:2 (2002), pp. 202–223.

12. M. Roper and J. Tosh (eds), *Manful Assertions: Masculinities in Britain since 1800* (London: Routledge, 1991).

13. M. McCormack, *The Independent Man: Citizenship and Gender Politics in Georgian England* (Manchester: Manchester University Press, 2005).

14. J. Tosh, *A Man's Place: Masculinity and the Middle-class Home in Victorian England* (London: Yale 1999). For an introduction to the recent work on Victorian fatherhood that has followed this, see H. Rogers and T. Lynn Broughton, *Gender and Fatherhood in the Nineteenth Century* (Basingstoke: Palgrave Macmillan, 2007).

15. J. Hamlett and S. Wiggins, 'Introduction: Victorian Women in Britain and the United States: New Perspectives', *Women's History Review*, 18:5 (2009), pp. 712–713.

16. J. Tosh, 'The History of Masculinity: An Outdated Concept?' in J. H. Arnold and S. Brady (eds), *What is Masculinity? Historical Dynamics from Antiquity to the Contemporary World* (Basingstoke: Palgrave Macmillan, 2011), pp. 17–34.

17. M. Roper, 'Slipping Out of View: Subjectivity and Emotion in Gender History', *History Workshop Journal*, 59 (2005), pp. 57–72.

18. P. Mandler, 'The Problem with Cultural History', *Cultural and Social History*, 1:1 (2004), p. 96.

19. L. Delap, *Knowing their Place: Domestic Service in Twentieth-century Britain* (Oxford: Oxford University Press, 2011).

20. F. Trentmann, 'Materiality in the Future of History: Things, Practices, and Politics', *Journal of British Studies*, 48:2 (2009), p. 288.

21. P. Bourdieu, *Outline of a Theory of Practice* (Cambridge: Cambridge University Press, 1979).

22. B. Latour, *Reassembling the Social: An Introduction to Actor-Network-Theory* (Oxford: Oxford University Press, 2005).

23. The classic text being M. Mauss, *The Gift: The Form and Reason for Exchange in Archaic Societies* (London: Routledge Classics, 2002). For a good overview of this literature, see D. Miller, 'Consumption and Commodities', *Annual Review of Anthropology*, 24 (1995), pp. 141–161.

24. A. Appadurai (ed.), *The Social Life of Things: Commodities in Cultural Perspective* (Cambridge: Cambridge University Press, 1986).

25. J. D. Prown, 'Mind in Matter: an Introduction to Material Culture Theory and Method', *The Winterthur Portfolio*, 17:1 (1982), pp. 1–19.

26. Trentmann, 'Materiality', p. 290.

27. D. Massey, *Space, Place and Gender* (Cambridge: Polity Press, 1994), p. 168.

28. K. Harvey, *History and Material Culture: A Student's Guide to Approaching Alternative Sources* (London: Routledge, 2009).

29. See A. Jones and P. Stallybrass (eds), *Renaissance Clothing and the Materials of Memory* (Cambridge: Cambridge University Press, 2000).

30. J. Attfield, *Wild Things: The Material Culture of Everyday Life* (Oxford: Berg, 2000).

31. Patrick Joyce and Tony Bennett emphasise the agency of objects, and their role as a shaping force in history: 'the social ... is seen to be performed by material things as much as by humans', P. Joyce and T. Bennett, 'Material Powers: Introduction', in Joyce and Bennett (eds), *Material Powers: Cultural Studies, History and the Material Turn* (London: Routledge, 2010), p. 4. While Chris Otter argues: 'at certain points specific materials have played a pivotal role in constituting particular forms of the western urban system', C. Otter, 'Locating Matter: the Place of Materiality in Urban History', in Joyce and Bennett, *Material Powers*, p. 46.

32. Telling global histories through an analysis of the movement of objects has become increasingly popular, as demonstrated by Giorgio Riello's recent work on the inter-continental exchange of commodities in the early modern period: A. Gerritsen and G. Riello (eds), *The Global Lives of Things: The Material Culture of Connections in the First Global Age* (London: Routledge, 2015). Also see Margot Finn's research project on the East India Company in eighteenth- and nineteenth-century Britain, which places the decoration and furnishing of country houses in the context of trade and the burgeoning British Empire. See http://blogs.ucl.ac.uk/eicah/.

33. M. Berg, 'Women's Consumption and the Industrial Classes of Eighteenth-Century England', *Journal of Social History*, 30:2 (1996), pp. 425–434; M. Berg and E. Eger (eds), *Luxury in the Eighteenth Century: Debates, Desires and Delectable Goods* (Basingstoke: Palgrave Macmillan, 2002); M. Berg and H. Clifford (eds), *Consumers and Luxury in Europe 1650–1850* (Manchester: Manchester University Press, 1999); J. Styles and A. Vickery (eds), *Gender, Taste and Material Culture in Britain and North America* (London: Yale University Press, 2006); T. Hamling, *Decorating the Godly Household: Religious Art in Protestant Britain, c. 1560–1660* (London: Yale University Press, 2010); T. Hamling and C. Richardson (eds), *Everyday Objects: Medieval and Early Modern Material Culture and its Meanings* (Farnham: Ashgate, 2010); L. Jardine, *Worldly Goods: A New History of the Renaissance* (New York: Doubleday, 1996); L. Jardine, *Ingenious Pursuits: Building the Scientific Revolution* (London: Little, Brown, 1999).

34. A. Vickery, 'His and Hers: Gender, Consumption and Household Accounting in Eighteenth-Century England', *Past and Present*, 1 (supplement 1) (2006), pp. 12–38.

35. A. Vickery, *Behind Closed Doors: At Home in Georgian England* (London: Yale University Press, 2009); Styles and Vickery, *Gender, Taste and Material Culture*.

36. J. Kinchin, 'Interiors: Nineteenth-Century Essays on the "Masculine" and the "Feminine" Room', in P. Kirkham (ed.), *The Gendered Object* (Manchester: Manchester University Press, 1996), pp. 12–29.

37. D. Cohen, *Household Gods: The British and their Possessions* (New Haven, CT, and London: Yale University Press, 2006), p. 90.

38. An example of this is the Centre for Studies of Home at Queen Mary University of London. Available at: http://www.studiesofhome.qmul.ac.uk/.

39. D. Goodman and K. Norberg (eds), *Fashioning the Eighteenth Century: What Furniture can Tell Us about the European and American Past* (London: Routledge, 2006), and D. Goodman, *Becoming a Woman in the Age of Letters* (New York: Cornell University Press, 2009).

40. Goodman, *Becoming a Woman.*

41. Kirkham, *The Gendered Object.* Also see Penny Sparke's consideration of the emergence of a feminine form of taste: P. Sparke, *As Long as It's Pink: The Sexual Politics of Taste* (London: Pandora, 1995).

42. J. Hamlett, '"Nicely Feminine, yet learned": Student Rooms at Royal Holloway and the Oxbridge Colleges in Late Nineteenth-century Britain', *Women's History Review*, 15:1 (2006), pp. 137–161.

43. P. Joyce, *The Rule of Freedom: Liberalism and the Modern City* (London: Verso, 2003), p. 2.

44. Trentmann, 'Materiality', pp. 286–287.

45. Vickery, 'His and Hers', p. 13.

46 For example, Winterthur Museum, Garden and Library, see http://www.winterthur.org/.

47. Various definitions of the long eighteenth century are in use, see for example, F. O'Gorman, *The Long Eighteenth Century: British Political and Social History, 1688–1832* (London: Bloomsbury Academic, 2012).

1
Gender and Material Culture in the Early Modern London Guilds

Helen Smith

Between the thirteenth and the end of the eighteenth centuries, guilds, or livery companies, were central to the economic, administrative and social structures of Europe's towns and cities. In major cities, craftsmen grouped themselves in companies defined by a common occupation, whilst in smaller towns, artisans and merchants came together in heterogeneous alliances designed to protect their social, economic, and (prior to the Reformation) religious interests. Guilds were central to urban life and ceremony, sponsoring and participating in dramatic performances, royal entries, and civic events. With close ties to local and national government, companies benefitted from rights, privileges and protection, but were in turn required to support and implement the interests of town and crown, not least through financial contributions to civic and royal projects.[1]

The livery companies were instrumental in the production, quality control and distribution of a wide range of consumer goods, foodstuffs and materials. Objects made by craftsmen, and sometimes women, embodied not only company values and hierarchies, but the 'skilled identities' of the artisan.[2] The companies possessed extensive powers of search, licensing them to enter homes, shops, and warehouses to seek out unauthorised workers, illegal tools, or poorly crafted goods. The Weavers' ordinances of 1577, for example, empowered the company to conduct searches four times a year, and to view 'all manner of works, stuff, and wares whatsoever made or to be made ... whether the same is well and workmanly wrought and of good, sufficient, and lawful stuff'.[3] Moreover, the guilds were themselves possessed of a rich material life, articulated in civic pageantry, costly funeral processions, elaborate halls and social rituals.

Given that the guilds were central to the practical and legislative operation of the majority of early modern English trades, it is surprising that they feature only occasionally in work responding to the current 'material turn' in literary and historical study.[4] Recent work on gender and material culture has concentrated overwhelmingly on the representation and, to a lesser extent, the experiences of women.[5] The livery companies, however, offer a rich site for the study of masculinity and material culture, not least as existing scholarship on the guilds emphasises the increasingly exclusive homosociality of company transactions and rituals. This chapter takes a dual approach to the study of gender and material culture, asking first how manhood was expressed, displayed and constituted in material forms, before going on to reveal women's shaping presence in spaces hitherto assumed to be almost exclusively homosocial. My definition of material culture – or, rather, of materiality – is capacious, embracing not only individual artefacts but spaces and the built environment; institutions; ritual, ceremony and feasting; financial transactions; and embodied labours, including gardening, cooking and cleaning.

Gender and the Livery Companies

Within the City of London – by the end of the seventeenth century the largest city in Europe – masculine identity and guild membership were tightly linked. Company membership was a pre-requisite for full citizenship (possession of 'the freedom'). The right to engage independently in economic activity, like the right to hold municipal office, was restricted to freemen. When a man completed his apprenticeship, usually after seven years, he was sworn in as a member of his Company, becoming a journeyman who hoped to ascend through the ranks to become master of his own establishment. Marriage to a prosperous widow, often possessed of considerable business skills as well as her husband's stock and trade connections, was one route to promotion. By the middle of the sixteenth century, around three-quarters of adult males in the City of London were freemen, and members of a livery company. Whilst some Londoners became free by patrimony (as the son of a London freeman) or redemption (purchase), apprenticeship 'was the route through which nine of every ten men in the capital became citizens and companymen in the sixteenth century'.[6]

Among the numerous companies of early modern London, the 'twelve great companies' – the Mercers, Grocers, Drapers, Fishmongers, Goldsmiths, Skinners, Merchant Taylors, Haberdashers, Salters, Ironmongers, Vintners and Clothworkers – were the richest and most powerful.[7] As the city's population grew, however, London's informal economy expanded rapidly.[8] The seventeenth century has been described by historians as a period of decline for the livery guilds.[9] They faced a series of challenges, including an extended period of civil war, and the great fire of London in 1666, which destroyed forty-four livery halls, resulting in years and even decades of temporary accommodation, and ruinously expensive rebuilding projects.

Recent scholarship has begun to reveal the extent to which women participated in guild life, and to uncover the patterns of women's employment at different historical moments and in diverse local and national contexts.[10] England was unusual in that women were not officially barred from obtaining the freedom, though the numbers who did so were relatively low. In London, twenty women were admitted to the freedom of the Carpenters in the last twenty years of the seventeenth century; their professions included sempster, milliner and child's-coat-seller.[11] Many women worked alongside their husbands, while, in the capital, customary law allowed married women to run their own businesses.[12]

Writing of the marginalisation of women, Ian Archer concludes that 'women possessed very weak occupational identities; denied participation in guild structures, save as widows carrying on their husbands' businesses, they lacked institutional means of expression'.[13] Recent research, however, as well as taking a nuanced view of women's involvement in guild life, has begun to attend more fully to the influence of women's work within London's informal economy. Natasha Korda in particular has argued that attention to diverse modes of work allows us to redefine 'all-male' sites as 'network[s] of commerce between active economic agents of both genders', an insight that this chapter extends to the material structures and practices of the London Companies.[14]

If much work on the guilds has neglected women's impact upon their economic, material and social structures, so too, guild historians, though describing transactions and relationships between men, have paid little attention to questions of masculine identity. It is only recently that scholars have begun to investigate the importance of work, guilds, and fraternities in shaping the experience of manhood. James R. Farr, for example, argues that artisans in early modern Dijon cultivated 'a form of worker solidarity' in 'the growth of journeyman brotherhoods', which offered a distinctly masculine culture and identity rooted in work.[15] 'Manhood' was an aspirational, and often tenuous, condition. As John Tosh points out, masculinity distinguishes 'not only between men and women, but between different categories of men – distinctions which have to be maintained by force, as well as validated through cultural means'.[16] In the early modern period, full manhood depended on age, economic security, temperament, and the ability to maintain a household. Admission to the freedom was an important part of the life-cycle: few men in the sixteenth and early seventeenth centuries achieved citizenship before their twenty-sixth year, and since most delayed marriage and establishing a household until after they were made free, 'that was also the minimum age at which most males became adults in Tudor London'.[17] For Merry E. Wiesner and Cynthia Truant, it was journeymens' insecure gendered status within the companies that led to the exclusion of women from the realm of male corporate labour.[18]

Whilst Company membership was 'a crucial component of a citizen's identity, and the companies generated ... institutional loyalties', those loyalties could be stretched or tested.[19] A majority of men could not expect to achieve the mature masculinity manifested in the office of warden or under-warden, and divisions existed within the guilds: between apprentices, who had a reputation for unruly behaviour, journeymen, masters and members of the livery. As Paul Griffiths points out, a 'deep sensitivity to age and authority could shatter the peace of institutions', especially when members of the 'younger sort' were alleged to have been elevated or privileged above the 'ancients'.[20] The tensions between social and economic groups and individuals surfaces periodically in company court records. The very fact that the Haberdashers saw the need to agree, in November 1659, a penalty of ten shillings payable by any member who 'by any abusive and uncivill words or gestures shall affront or iniure any other member' suggests the urgency of possible disagreements.[21] In Coventry, Daniel

Whitehead, waiting for the award of his freedom, went to Stourbridge fair and purchased grocery wares to resell. The masters and wardens threatened to refuse him the freedom for his anticipation of its privileges, but quickly commuted their sentence to a fine 'by Reason that the yongr men had theire voyces razzid', a clear example of the power of potentially unruly youthful masculinity.[22] In these examples we see how men who 'did not have access to patriarchal manhood (such as the journeyman who never moved beyond dependence on wage labour), nonetheless found plenty of ways in which to assert their manhood'.[23]

Manhood and Material Culture in the Livery Companies

The guilds were central to trade regulation, ensuring that workmen did not trespass on others' rights, and that goods were produced according to agreed standards. In 1650, for example, the Tylers and Bricklayers' Company found that Abell Barton had used 'very bad mortar and insufficient workmanship', whilst in 1663, its searchers instructed John Wallis to rebuild seven chimneys in a 'workmanlike fashion'.[24] Joseph Ward argues that 'the language company officers used when disciplining members reveals ... the importance of reputation to freemen'.[25] It also uncovers the ideal of 'workmanship' – a phrase that possessed clear connotations of skill and artistry in this period – as a constitutive category of masculinity. This form of manhood was both achieved through, and epitomised in, craft and the material processes of production.

The practice of search and seize could bring conflicting models of masculinity to the fore. The stationer Simon Stafford described an occasion in 1598 upon which Cuthbert Burby, Thomas Dawson, and others 'did very riotously and wantonly and unlawfully enter into yor sayd subiect Simon Stafford his workinge howse in the parish of St Peters aforesayd within foure days after his wife was [...] in childbirth', opposing the allegedly unruly masculinity of the searchers with the responsibilities of a husband and new father.[26] In 1584, another stationer, John Wolfe, complained about a violent search in which, he claimed, John Day and several other stationers, 'beinge in moste ryotous manner accompaned [*sic*] wythe sworde and daggers and othere such ... vnlawfullie and most ryotouslye assembled themselves together' and broke into Wolfe's house, 'wresting his poore oulde father by the throate beatinge and threatnynge his men'.[27] Implicitly counterposing his orderly domestic space to the 'riotous' behaviour of the searchers, Wolfe draws upon the vulnerability of aged manhood and the importance of family ties in objecting to this violent incursion into household space.

The relationships between gendered identity and the spaces of urban and civic life, most notably the guildhalls, were complex: urban sites 'were never simply physical locations but continuously invented and reinvented by their myriad users'. In turn, the places of congregation, business, and display conferred 'attitudinal and even behavioural aspects onto their users'.[28] Within the halls, objects and furnishings – from wainscotting to windows – announced the largesse and perpetuated the memory of Company members and benefactors.[29] The interior spaces of the livery halls were mutable, rearranged to suit the changing circumstances of the companies. Fishmongers' Hall, for example, was often let out as a private residence, bringing in an income, but reshaping the availability and function of the Company's property.

As Jasmine Kilburn-Toppin points out, 'within the late-medieval craft fraternities and early modern guilds of London, the gifting of material culture for display in livery halls, and use in company rituals, was a significant means for guildsmen to establish reputations in life and uphold memory within the craft community after death'.[30] In 1606, for example, Richard Wyatt, George Isack, John Reave and William Wilson donated an octagonal table bearing the date and their initials to the Carpenters' Company. This object at once celebrated the skilled trade of the Company, and commemorated the men's service as Master and Wardens, giving a material and persistent form to their association.[31] In 1632, Mr Avenon donated a silver cup and cover to the Goldsmiths' Company. Its inscription emphasised its convivial and memorial functions, both recording and promoting masculine bonding: 'When at your hall doth shine with plate, / and all your dishes served in state, / When mirth abound, and wine is free, / then (freely drinking) think on me'.[32] Some guildsmen left tools and materials to the Company. Master Masons, for example, frequently bequeathed tools and instruments, alongside building 'plots' (plans), books and designs, creating a 'cumulative resource' of both use and symbolic value to succeeding generations.[33]

Towards the end of the sixteenth century, a new fashion for civic portraiture emerged. In July 1598, the Haberdashers' Court ordered the Wardens to commission and display ten paintings of the company's 'ancient benefactors'.[34] The Ironmongers and Merchant Taylors imitated their example in the first decade of the new century, whilst the Drapers, Brewers, and Grocers did likewise in the 1610s. During the 1620s portraits were commissioned by the Barber-Surgeons, Painter-Stainers, Carpenters and Goldsmiths; in the 1630s, the Leathersellers and Salters followed suit, as did the Ironmongers, Merchant Taylors and, once again, the Painter-Stainers.[35] The emphasis placed by the Haberdashers upon the antiquity of their benefactors suggests that these portraits had a dual purpose: they expressed the wealth and status of the company, but also invested it with a sense of its own history. In a sometimes uncertain economic and political climate, the creation of a genealogy of benefactors and masters not only operated as a prompt to morality and beneficence for members – the Merchant Taylors' portrait of Robert Dowe reminded viewers that 'A vertuous lyfe is the fairest passage to a blessed death'[36] – but established the companies as long-standing elements of the civic fabric.

Portraits of male masters and benefactors detail the clothing and accessories of office, reminding us of the distinctions of rank and hierarchy conveyed by livery and aldermanic gowns. The portraits emphasise the 'gravity and sagacity' of their sitters,[37] not least through the depiction of luxurious facial hair: in the sixteenth and early seventeenth centuries, 'the beard made the man', and full beards were markers of age and wisdom.[38] The gloves that many men hold in their portraits signify full membership of the freemanry: a newly elected freeman frequently celebrated his elevation by giving gloves to his fellows.

Paintings did not only make statements about the position and prestige of their subject: they took on new meanings as they were incorporated into the existing material milieu of the Company hall. Equally, the display of portraits and objects could serve to reinforce hierarchy. Towards the end of his life, John Vernon, a former master and generous benefactor of the London Merchant Taylors, had his portrait painted. In July 1616, he donated the picture 'to the end that his faythfull true love borne to the Company might be had in remembrance'.[39] Vernon suggested in performatively self-deprecating fashion that the Merchant Taylors might hang a portrait of 'a lesse deserving' man (himself) in the parlour – a more withdrawn and hence prestigious space than the main hall.[40]

Company charity formed a crucial strand in the 'informal network of social organisations and individuals which provided support for many of the poor people who lived in early modern London' and beyond.[41] Members' charitable acts were frequently commemorated and incorporated into the companies' culture of ceremony and display. In 1652, the Haberdashers' Assistants ordered that details of the Company's diverse charities should be hung on tables (framed boards) around the Hall, 'whereby the memory of their worthy deeds may bee preferred and made knowne in honor to themselves and encouragement to and example of others whose hartes God shall stirr upp and incline to workes of this nature'.[42] Bequests might also be the objects of elaborate display at the moment of benefaction. The gift and charitable economies of the guilds helped to perpetuate ideals of brotherhood and masculine collaboration, but also allowed men to testify to the extent to which their identities were interwoven with Company structures and rituals, and display their status and legacy within Company space.

The livery halls were also the setting for annual and quarter-day dinners, which served 'to solemnize and give legal weight to [companies'] most mundane business decisions'.[43] The elaborate material culture and expressive hierarchies of feasting made a powerful statement to members and guests about the status and prosperity of the Company, and served to reinforce ideals of brotherhood and fellowship. In 1633, the Salters' Assistants decided to invite liverymen to the quarter day dinners, for the 'increase and continuance of love'; in the same year, the Vintners, who had earlier introduced two quarter-day dinners to increase 'love and affection' among their members, punished Raphael King for his 'rude and unbrotherly behavior' towards a fellow Assistant, which included bad language, throwing food, and 'many uncivil touches with his knife and trencher'.[44]

Company feasts were elaborate and frequently, particularly in the earlier part of the period, excessive occasions. They were also one of the moments at which social differentiation was most overtly expressed: the dinners were usually restricted to the livery, and 'the obligations of individuals to the corporate body were underlined by the table service of the younger members and the part financing of the feasts by the wardens'.[45] The busy dinners served to reinforce ideals of brotherhood, but also to mark out space between the livery and the yeomanry. In 1614, for example, the Fishmongers recorded that 'the yonger lyverey ... sete downe in the parlor', separated from their more senior associates; in 1617, one hundred and seventy six members ate in the great hall, whilst eighty dined in the parlour.[46]

Distinctions between Company members were also played out at funerals and in civic pageants and processions. When the Haberdashers processed to celebrate one of their members becoming Lord Mayor, the progression was fronted by up to one hundred and forty poor men followed by between ninety and one hundred yeomen bachelors, then the livery, with the younger members in front and the 'ancients' behind. Each group was differentiated by dress, and music, banners and whifflers (ushers) marched between each group and the next to fully articulate these social and economic distinctions.[47] The procession thus announced the inclusiveness and beneficence of the brotherhood at the same time as it reinforced its hierarchies.

The rich round of dinners, bequests, and funeral pomp was largely limited to the livery; Ian Archer argues that 'among the wills of the artisans there is much less evidence of this kind', and far fewer 'material demonstrations of their loyalty'.[48] The material culture of the livery companies thus articulated an ideal of masculinity that was inaccessible to the majority of guild members, but which nonetheless served to shape those members' identity through a careful balance between aspiration and exclusion.

Women's Work

Women were routinely among the guests at company feasts; their presence marking the mature masculinity of the married livery, as well as, on occasion, the status of the Company in playing host to gentry and nobility. In 1638–1639 Thomas Steed, Renter Warden of the Founders' Company, recorded numerous payments for laundry, including nine shillings for washing of linen the day after the Lord Mayor's feast, 'having all the Livery & wifes'.[49] In 1640, John Falkener spent eighteen pounds and three pence on 'the Lord Maiores dinar, having all the Company & there wives at dinar and the Master and Wardens & Stewards there wives at supar nex day at night'.[50] The Vintners' 1622 resolution to establish quarter-day dinners specified that the events would include the Assistants and their wives, as well as the widows of Assistants. In 1595 'much speech was used' as the Fishmongers' Company debated how to make their great chamber 'fit to receive gentlewomen at any time of assembly'.[51] Women are routinely mentioned in accounts for the Fishmongers' dinners, especially in the earlier part of the period; in 1596, the Clerk took particular note of 'some Gentlewomen in [unfashionable] frenchoods at the high table'.[52]

Though dinners were curtailed by most livery companies as the sixteenth century progressed, in part because of royal and neighbourly complaints about their excesses, and then because of the expense of rebuilding after the Fire, some regained their social energies early in the eighteenth century: in 1735, for example, Fishmongers' court members invited their wives to a 'diversion on the river' in the Company's elaborately decorated barge, followed by a supper at the Hall.[53] Yet ideals of civility and good order, expressed through the display of marital prowess, were always uneasy. Gender divisions were both enacted and, to some degree, subverted at the Fishmongers' election dinners during the seventeenth century, where the 'wyves and widdowes' of the Company were seated at a side table, emphasising their separate and subordinate role; the women evidently exploited the opportunity for gendered sociability, as recurring complaints noted that they grew 'very disorderlye'.[54]

Women as well as men contributed to the Companies' material goods, whether as executors passing on the gifts of their deceased husbands, or exercising their own agency through gift-giving. In October 1605, for example, Eustatia Skelton gave a pair of gilded silver spoons to the Founders.[55] Two years later, 'Mistres Grethed and hir daughtor', the surviving family of Oswald Grethed, a former under-warden and auditor, gave sixteen shillings towards the cost of a new carpet, a valuable and prestigious item to be prominently displayed on a cupboard or table.[56] In 1608, the Stationers' Court records note that 'Mystres Bysshop', widow of the bookseller George Bishop, 'hathe of her owne motion & voluntary good will freely gyven to the Company. A table cloathe, A towell, and Twoo Dozen of napkyns, wrought with white Lady woorke / The whiche were Delyuered to mr Seton and mr Standish Wardens, at a court holden this daye /'.[57]

When Mary Bishop's will was read out on 4 October 1613, she 'did give and bequeath to the Company of Staconers in London being at her funerall, ten poundes foure arras wrought cushens a cubberd cloth and two long flaxen table-clothes of her owne spinning'.[58] The entry insists that these gifts are the products of Bishop's own labour, distinguishing them from comparable presentations by male stationers. They were also valuable: in her study of the Drapers' Company, Lena Cowen Orlin notes that 'the most valuable of the Company's goods were textiles – napery, table carpets, and cushion covers'.[59] Moreover, these goods suggest that Bishop established herself as an enduring presence through the presentation of gifts which had both a useful and a livery function, proclaiming the status of both giver and Company.

Ian Archer notes that 'it is striking how many donors arranged for the distribution of their requests to the [Haberdashers'] Company's poor at the St Katherine feast at which the election of the new Master and Wardens was published before the Livery'.[60] Florence Caldwell timed her gift of six gowns for poor members of the Haberdashers' Company so that they were ready for the recipients to wear when they waited on the Master and Wardens as they progressed to church on the day of the election feast, a very public statement of her own generosity and her material incorporation into the life and ceremony of the Company.[61]

Women's work had a profound effect upon the shape, and hence practices, of the livery hall. When the Fishmongers repaired their hall in 1639, they employed the widowed Anne Barsey as their master plumber.[62] Twenty-seven years later, the hall was destroyed by the great fire, and the Company employed another woman as master plumber for their new premises: the widow Elizabeth Heard.[63] Margaret Pierce, 'widow, the painter' was paid one hundred and forty six pounds for painting the new woodwork inside and outside the hall, whilst Isabell King, another widow, was in charge of rubbish disposal; the contract for leadwork was held by the widows Peirce and Heard.[64] The employment of women as master craftsmen in the building trades continued into the next century, when five of the nine masters employed to build a beadle's house for the Company were women.[65] In 1627, officers of the Grocers' Company permitted Mary Stroude, a plumber's widow, to 'continue the plumber's work to this Hall during her widowhood and for so long time as she shall carefully, honestly, and at reasonable rates perform the said work'.[66] Each of these cases suggests the probability that husbands and wives worked together to organise and run their trades, leaving the widow fully qualified to take over the business.

Though the Carpenters were fortunate in that their hall survived the fire, it still required redecorating by the late seventeenth century. The Company borrowed three hundred pounds from one of their tenants, Mrs Purefoy, to help meet the costs of the project; a reminder that materiality in the sense of objects and buildings is inextricably linked to material concerns in the sense of finance and embodied labour. Purefoy, in return, was assured of an annuity for life of thirty-six pounds, making this a mutually beneficial arrangement, and one that ensured close ties between the Company and a benefactor who also occupied their property.[67]

Women's rights in property could clash with the interests of the companies, especially given the 'dense social lives' of buildings in the capital 'with its urgent issues of proximity and jurisdiction'.[68] The guild halls, which usually consisted of an agglomeration of buildings and properties, especially before the fire, overlapped with and extended into domestic space. For some employees, especially the Beadle, the hall was home as well as workplace. When the Lady Dawes, widow of the former Prime Warden, moved out of Fishmongers' Hall, she left the Company thirty-six chairs, gilded and tin-plated sconces for candles, and iron firebacks, contributing significantly and visibly to the furnishing of the great chamber and great parlour.[69] But the overlap between company and domestic space could lead to tensions: in 1644 the Beadle's wife refused to leave her home in Carpenters' Hall, after it was alleged she had been in contact with a plague victim; in 1653 she, her husband and son were threatened with eviction if they engaged in any further 'disorderly and uncivil behaviour' towards the Clerk.[70]

Such 'uncivil' behaviour was closely tied to ideologies of gender, contradicting the ideals both of feminine obedience and of masculine civility. In the late sixteenth century, the Fishmongers employed Widow Garland as their garden-keeper, and periodically complained about her 'disorderly' behaviour, including allowing 'the common drying of clothes' and games of bowling by strangers.[71] Negotiations over the use of the garden, and the newly-built garden parlour, in 1644–1645, reveal more of the social and behavioural distinctions between men: Alderman Penington, newly elected as Governor of the Turkey Company, whose own house was not suitable for court meetings, requested the use of the garden house, with the important assurance: 'those who would come being civil men'. The following year, the bowling alley was closed, due to the 'great disorders & abuses' surrounding its use; the keeper and his wife (suggesting a marital working partnership) were to open the gate each day for the 'civil' recreation of walking, and the keeper himself was warned against being 'taken drunke'.[72]

Family and company loyalties could come into conflict: in 1626, the Carpenters applied to the Court of Chancery for a decree confirming that lands at Bramshott bequeathed by their former Master, Richard Wyatt, were intended to support almshouses for ten poor men. Wyatt's career had been advanced by marriage to his own Master's daughter, Margaret, in the early 1580s, and his generous legacy also included land at Henley-on-Thames to support thirteen poor women. Wyatt's son, Henry, challenged the Company's title to the Bramshott lands, but was proved to have withheld rent from the Company. It was Richard's widow, Henry's mother, who stepped in to reimburse some of his debts, and gave a further forty pounds 'to provide ten new coats once in every three years for the Almsmen, with the letters R. W. on each coat'.[73] The widow Wyatt's material commitments took two forms: her financial largesse was celebrated and memorialised on the bodies of the almsmen, who would have been required to take part in Company processions on ceremonial occasions.

Portraits of women as well as men hung in the livery halls. In 1616, the Merchant Taylors acquired a portrait of Elizabeth I, an intriguing statement of nostalgia for a previous age and monarch. The Cutlers acquired a portrait of Margaret Crathorne, widow of one of their members, in 1569,[74] whilst in 1640 the Ironmongers' Court commissioned a portrait of their benefactress Margaret Dane,[75] and the Brewers displayed a portrait of Dame Alice Owen, from c. 1610.[76] Owen, a wealthy widow, two of whose three husbands had been Brewers, established a school at Islington. The rules and orders governing the school, drawn up on 20 September 1613, shortly before her death, left the governance of the school in trust to 'My trusty and well-beloved friends the Master, Wardens and Assistants of the Company of Brewers of London', suggesting Owen's close identification with the Company.[77]

In 1571, at the beginning of a substantial project to rebuild their hall, the Carpenters' Company commissioned a series of paintings celebrating 'the story': biblical scenes which highlight the role of carpentry.[78] Alongside figures in traditional biblical costume, the frames include representations of 'full-bearded senior male figures' wearing contemporary livery dress, inserting the carpenters as witnesses of the biblical past, whilst insisting upon the antiquity of their trade. Celebrating the 'artisanal masterpiece' that was the newly-modelled Hall, these paintings drew attention 'to the senior craftsmen who had undertaken the rebuilding project and commissioned the wall paintings'.[79] The third of these images, however, includes a woman, watching Joseph's work and holding a spindle.[80] Her dress situates her somewhere between the biblical figures and contemporary costume, and her work equally stresses the centrality of biblical tradition to women's domestic work: according to Proverbs, frequently cited in discussions of women's behaviour in the early modern period, the virtuous woman 'seeketh wool, and flax, and worketh willingly with her hands. ... She layeth her hands to the spindle, and her hands hold the distaff' (Proverbs 31.13, 19).

This figure, less overt than a portrait of a female benefactor, or an initialled carpet, nonetheless makes women present within the scene of manufacture, positioning carpentry within a productive domestic economy. Masters were responsible for the material well-being of their apprentices, providing food, clothing and lodging: tasks which very frequently involved the labour of the master's wife and other female members of the household. When two apprentices complained to the Weavers' Company that they had 'lain in one pair of sheets three months or more', the Court of Assistants ordered the master to provide clean sheets every month.[81] For the purposes of this chapter, the Carpenters' 'story' stands in for the forgotten labours of women, which worked to efface their own materiality (particularly in the case of the 'invisible' work of cleaning and laundry), but nonetheless structured and maintained the spaces and ceremonies of the livery hall, as well as of the household.[82]

The Founders' Company accounts contain numerous payments for domestic work. These range from 'cleenenge the halle' (evidently a major annual undertaking) to 'skouringe the brasse & pewter' and 'washing lynnen for the Courte dynner laste'.[83] In 1612, Upper Warden Ezekiel Major recorded a payment of four shillings 'to Widdo Judrey for skowringe the vessel, & bromes'.[84] In 1614, Judrey received payment 'for makinge the hall (cleane) the yere past'.[85] A similar payment was made in 1615, and again in 1616, when the Company also paid to mend the windows in the hall, parlour and 'Goodwyfe Juderis howse', and paid a shilling and fourpence for the widow's communion bread and wine. In 1620, her diverse tasks included cleaning, providing candles for lanterns, and washing linen for the Company quarter-day and Lord Mayor's day dinners.[86] Judrey's status as the widow of a former Beadle suggests the complexity of relationships between the guilds and their domestic workers, with the payments occupying a space somewhere between wages for work done and charitable support, even as Judrey's diverse efforts maintained and shaped the physical and social fabric of the hall.

Such tasks were not always women's work: in 1622, after Judrey's death, John Falkener began to receive payment for cleaning the hall.[87] From 1628 to 1629, the work of Mrs Falkener was also acknowledged and remunerated. The entries are usually vague: she received payment 'for heer paines', or 'for hier extreordinary paines this yeare'.[88] In 1633–1634, the nature of those pains is made more explicit: Mrs Falkener was paid one pound 'for heere paines for dressing of sartaine diners for the Master & Wardens at myttinges' (her maid received two shillings 'for heer paines'), and in 1644, she received a pound 'for dressing of dinars the hole yeare'.[89] In 1641, the Grocer's Company granted Mary Knight the same allowance that had previously been given to her late husband for polishing the company's pewter.[90]

From 1617, Mistress Tiffin took on the job of Founders' Company cook, succeeding her husband John Tiffin until her own death in 1630. This rare instance of a woman employed as a professional cook in this period, prompts the question of how many women were engaged in culinary employment alongside their husbands, as Mrs Tiffin probably was, gaining the knowledge and experience to continue alone in the role. More humble fare was provided by Mrs Mitchell in 1678–1679: she was paid one pound eight shillings and seven pence 'for beere, ale, bread and cheese at severall tyme'.[91] This may well be evidence of catering for Company members beyond the livery, asserting the inclusiveness of the brotherhood, whilst reiterating the distinctions between livery and yeomanry.[92]

The kinds of labour described above are routinely ignored in Company histories and in more recent critical work on the guilds, in part thanks to a longstanding bias that separates the productive and public work of making and regulation from the self-effacing 'domestic' or 'private' work of cleaning, maintenance and repair. Women's work, however, constituted part of the essential rhythm of operations of the guilds and their memberships, and underpinned the companies' capacity for the civic and social display of 'brotherhood'.

Conclusion

Broadening the purview of 'material culture' to include the overlapping operations of finance, embodied labour and physical objects and structures, this chapter has briefly surveyed how masculinity was constructed and expressed through material engagements, whether in 'workmanlike' building, elaborate clothing or the donation of an engraved silver spoon. Yet it has also demonstrated that women were more active, and more visible, in the material lives of the guilds than previous scholarship has acknowledged. Gifts, objects and spaces at once enacted ideals of brotherhood and community and reinforced hierarchies and exclusions, whilst women's labour was instrumental in shaping and maintaining the declaredly 'masculine' space of the livery halls. The performance of economic and guild status, and of mature, civic masculinity, was structured by and depended upon the effaced labours of numerous women and men, whose material contribution to the smooth running and to the ceremonial existence of the guilds remains to be fully recovered.

Notes

1. For a useful overview, see I. Anders Gadd and P. Wallis, 'Introduction' to Gadd and Wallis (eds), *Guilds, Society and Economy in London 1450–1800* (London: Centre for Metropolitan History, 2002), pp. 1–14. G. Unwin, *The Guilds and Companies of London*, 4th edn (London: Cass, 1963), remains a valuable guide.
2. J. Kilburn-Toppin, 'Material Memories of the Guildsmen: Crafting Identities in Early Modern London', in E. Kuijpers, J. Pollmann, J. Müller and J. van der Steen (eds), *Memory before Modernity: Practices of Memory in Early Modern Europe* (Leiden: Brill, 2013), pp. 165–181, at p. 178. For a series of objects that celebrate the craft identity of the consumer, see Karen Harvey's chapter in this volume.
3. S. Rappaport, *Worlds within Worlds: Structures of Life in Sixteenth-Century London* (Cambridge: Cambridge University Press, 1989), p. 187.
4. For a thoughtful assessment of material culture studies, see D. Hicks and M. C. Beaudry, 'Introduction: Material Culture Studies: a Reactionary View', in Hicks and Beaudry (eds), *The Oxford Handbook of Material Culture Studies* (Oxford: Oxford University Press, 2010), pp. 1–21.
5. In an influential collection, V. de Grazia and E. Furlough (eds), *The Sex of Things: Gender and Consumption in Historical Perspective* (Berkeley and Los Angeles: University of California Press, 1996), two of thirteen chapters address questions of masculine identity. For recent work on women and material culture, see especially J. Batchelor and C. Kaplan (eds), *Women and Material Culture, 1660–1830* (Basingstoke: Palgrave Macmillan, 2007). Much work on material culture sidesteps questions of gender or sexed identity altogether. Giorgio Riello, for instance, calls for 'a type of historical analysis that gives as much space to materiality as has previously been given to economic or political forces, kinship or gender', implicitly suggesting that these fields do not coincide. See G. Riello, 'The Material Culture of Walking: Spaces of Methodologies in the Long Eighteenth Century', in T. Hamling and C. Richardson (eds), *Everyday Objects: Medieval and Early Modern Material Culture and its Meanings* (Farnham: Ashgate, 2010), pp. 41–56, at p. 42.
6. Rappaport, *Worlds within Worlds*, p. 24. J. P. Ward, however, notes the extension of City and guild interests into the suburbs and liberties, arguing that 'livery companies were metropolitan by nature', Ward, *Metropolitan Communities: Trade Guilds,*

Identity, and Change in Early Modern London (Stanford, CA: Stanford University Press, 1997), p. 4.

7. A 1501–1502 list of 'the Crafts of the City' includes 78 livery companies.

8. N. Korda, *Labors Lost: Women's Work and the Early Modern Stage* (Philadelphia: University of Pennsylvania Press, 2011), p. 22.

9. Rappaport suggests that by the end of the seventeenth century, 'economic and other restrictions imposed upon the unfree population – then the majority of the city's inhabitants – became unenforceable. The freedom lost much of its meaning and the system of privileges based upon it collapsed,' Rappaport, *Worlds within Worlds*, p. 60. See, however, Ward, who argues for 'the ability of London's livery companies to evolve in response to economic and social change', Ward, *Metropolitan Communities*, p. 3. P. Gauci argues that in the mid- to late eighteenth century 'the livery retained its appeal as a prerequisite for advancement up the civic ladder, and as the qualification for the parliamentary vote in the City' and that the guilds 'provided the clubbable atmosphere in which professional and personal ambition could be advanced in a semi-public fashion', Gauci, *Emporium of the World: The Merchants of London, 1660–1800* (London: Hambledon Continuum, 2007), pp. 74–75.

10. For a recent overview, see C. Crowston, 'Women, Gender, and Guild in Early Modern Europe: an Overview of Recent Research', *International Review of Social History*, 53 (2008), pp. 19–44. See also, H. Deceulaer and B. Panhuysen, 'Dressed to Work: a Gendered Comparison of the Tailoring Trades in the Northern and Southern Netherlands, 16th to 18th Centuries', in M. Prak et al. (eds), *Craft Guilds in the Early Modern Low Countries: Work, Power, and Representation* (Aldershot: Ashgate, 2006), pp. 133–156; A. Schmidt, 'Women and Guilds: Corporations and Female Labour Market Participation in Early Modern Holland', *Gender and History*, 21 (2009); and S. D. Smith, 'Women's Admission to Guilds in Early-Modern England: the Case of the Merchant Tailors' Company, 1693–1776', *Gender and History*, 17 (2005), pp. 99–126.

11. B. W. E. Alford and T. C. Barker, *A History of the Carpenters Company* (London: Allen & Unwin, 1968), p. 117.

12. On the legal rights of women, see especially A. Erickson, *Women and Property in Early Modern England* (London: Routledge, 1993).

13. I. Archer, 'Material Londoners?' in L. Cowen Orlin (ed.), *Material Londoners, ca. 1600* (Philadelphia: University of Pennsylvania Press, 2000), pp. 174–192, at p. 187.

14. N. Korda, 'Labour's Lost: Women's Work and Early Modern Theatrical Commerce', in P. Holland (ed.), *From Script to Stage in Early Modern England* (Basingstoke: Palgrave Macmillan, 2004), pp. 195–196. See also, H. Smith, *Grossly Material Things: Women and Book Production in Early Modern England* (Oxford: Oxford University Press, 2013).

15. J. R. Farr, *Hands of Honor: Artisans and their World in Dijon, 1550–1650* (Ithaca, NY: Cornell University Press, 1988), pp. 75, 63. For the earlier period, see C. M. Fitzgerald, *The Drama of Masculinity and Medieval English Guild Culture* (New York: Palgrave Macmillan, 2007).

16. J. Tosh, 'What Should Historians Do with Masculinity? Reflections on Nineteenth-Century Britain', *History Workshop*, 38 (1994), pp. 179–202, at p. 192.

17. Rappaport, *Worlds within Worlds*, p. 49.

18. M. E. Wiesner, 'Guilds, Male Bonding and Women's Work in Early Modern Germany', *Gender and History*, 1 (1989), pp. 125–137; and C. Truant, *The Rites of Labor: Brotherhoods of Compagnonnage in Old and New Regime France* (Ithaca, NY: Cornell University Press, 1994).

19. I. W. Archer, *The Pursuit of Stability: Social Relations in Elizabethan London* (Cambridge: Cambridge University Press, 1991), p. 100.
20. P. Griffiths, *Youth and Authority: Formative Experiences in England, 1560–1640* (Oxford: Clarendon Press, 1996), p. 99.
21. I. W. Archer, *The History of the Haberdashers' Company* (Chichester: Phillimore, 1991), p. 120, citing Guildhall Library MS 15842/1 f. 69v.
22. R. M. Berger, *The Most Necessary Luxuries: The Mercers' Company of Coventry, 1550–1680* (University Park, PA: Pennsylvania State University Press, 1993), p. 228.
23. A. Shepard, *Meanings of Manhood in Early Modern England* (Oxford: Oxford University Press, 2003), p. 6.
24. Guildhall Library MS 3047/2, cited in Ward, *Metropolitan Communities*, p. 49.
25. Ward, *Metropolitan Communities*, p. 45.
26. The National Archives (TNA) TNA: STAC 5/27/22.
27. TNA, Star Chamber Proceeding, 26 Eliz., Bundle W 34, no. 23; cited in H. Hoppe, 'John Wolfe, Printer and Publisher, 1579–1601', *The Library*, 4th series, XIV (1933), 256–257.
28. A. Bailey and R. Hentschell, 'Introduction: Gendered Geographies of Vice', in Bailey and Hentschell (eds), *Masculinity and the Metropolis of Vice, 1550–1650* (New York: Palgrave Macmillan, 2010), p. 5.
29. See I. W. Archer 'The Arts and Acts of Memorialization in Early Modern London', in J. F. Merritt (ed.), *Imagining Early Modern London: Perceptions and Portrayals of the City from Stow to Strype, 1590–1720* (Cambridge: Cambridge University Press, 2001), esp. p. 98.
30. J. Kilburn-Toppin, 'Material Memories', p. 165.
31. Alford and Barker, *A History*, p. 109.
32. Ibid., pp. 156–157.
33. J. Summerson, 'Three Elizabethan Architects', *Bulletin of the John Rylands Library*, 40 (1987), pp. 202–228.
34. Haberdashers' Company, Court Minutes, Guildhall Library MS 15842/1, f. 102r; cited in R. Tittler, *The Face of the City: Civic Portraiture and Civic Identity in Early Modern England* (Manchester: Manchester University Press, 2007), p. 55. On the 'articulacy' of tools, and their relation to the public performance of labouring identity, see Harvey's chapter in this volume.
35. Tittler, *The Face of the City*, p. 56.
36. F. M. Fry, *A Historical Catalogue of the Pictures, Herse-Cloths and Tapestry at Merchant Taylors' Hall: With a List of the Sculptures and Engravings* (London: Chapman and Hall, 1907), plate 38.
37. Tittler, *The Face of the City*, p. 123.
38. W. Fisher, *Materializing Gender in Early Modern English Literature and Culture* (Cambridge: Cambridge University Press, 2010), p. 128.
39. Court minutes of the Merchant Taylors' Company, Guildhall Library microfilm, 328/7, ff. 244–246. See also Fry, *A Historical Catalogue*, pp. 67–68.
40. Court Minutes of the Merchant Taylors' Company, Guildhall Library microfilm, 328/7, ff. 244–246, cited in Tittler, *The Face of the City*, p. 154.
41. Rappaport, *Worlds within Worlds*, p. 200.
42. Archer, *History of the Haberdashers' Company*, p. 74.
43. Berger, *The Most Necessary Luxuries*, p. 204.
44. SHA DI/I/I, fol. 95r, and GL MSS 15201/3, p. 74, cited in Ward, *Metropolitan Communities*, pp. 95–96.
45. Archer, *The Pursuit of Stability*, p. 116.

46. P. Metcalf, *The Halls of the Fishmongers' Company* (London and Chichester: Phillimore, 1977), p. 30.
47. Archer, *History of the Haberdashers' Company*, pp. 120–121.
48. Archer, *The Pursuit of Stability*, p. 112.
49. Founders' Company, *Wardens' Accounts, 1497–1681*, ed. G. Parsloe (London: Athlone Press, 1964), p. 309.
50. Ibid., p. 313. A similar payment occurred in 1642 (p. 315).
51. Metcalf, *Halls*, p. 26; citing Fishmongers' Company Court Minutes, 27 October 1595.
52. Ibid., p. 33.
53. Ibid., p. 81.
54. Ibid., p. 33.
55. Founders' Company, *Wardens' Accounts*, p. 235.
56. Ibid., p. 238.
57. W. A. Jackson (ed.), *Records of the Court of the Stationers' Company, 1602–1640* (London: Bibliographical Society, 1957), p. 33.
58. Ibid., p. 62.
59. L. C. Orlin, *Locating Privacy in Tudor London* (Oxford: Oxford University Press, 2007), p. 121.
60. Archer, *History of the Haberdashers' Company*, p. 75.
61. Ibid., p. 75.
62. Metcalf, *Halls*, p. 80.
63. Ibid., p. 71.
64. Ibid., pp. 71, 80.
65. Ibid., p. 80.
66. GL MS 11588/3, p. 62, cited in Ward, *Metropolitan Communities*, p. 51.
67. Alford and Barker, *A History*, p. 119.
68. Orlin, *Locating Privacy*, p. 131.
69. Metcalf, *Halls*, p. 83.
70. Alford and Barker, *A History*, p. 110.
71. Metcalf, *Halls*, p. 40.
72. Ibid., p. 42.
73. See Alford and Barker, *A History*, pp. 102–104.
74. C. Welch, *History of the Cutlers' Company of London and of the Minor Cutlery Crafts*, 2 vols (London: Privately printed, 1916–1923), I, plate opp. p. 213.
75. J. Nicholl, *Some Account of the Worshipfull Company of Ironmongers*, 2nd edn (London: Privately printed, 1851), p. 465.
76. E. Wedlake Brayley, J. N. Brewer and J. Nightingale, *London and Middlesex, or, an Historical, Commercial, & Descriptive Survey*, 4 vols (London: W. Wilson, 1810–1816), II, p. 405. For a list of portraits owned by London Livery Companies, see Tittler, *The Face of the City*, pp. 174–175.
77. M. Ball, *The Worshipful Company of Brewers: A Short History* (London: Hutchinson Benham, 1977), pp. 67–68.
78. Kilburn-Toppin, 'Material Memories of the Guildsmen', p. 178.
79. Ibid., p. 179.
80. The original paintings do not survive, but they were drawn by John Wykeham Archer when discovered in 1846. See drawing of the paintings in Carpenters' Hall, London, available at: http://www.britishmuseum.org/research/collection_online/collection_object_details/collection_image_gallery.aspx?assetId=673034&objectId=3191808&partId=1.

81. CLRO Jour. 16, 162v, cited in Griffiths, *Youth and Authority*, p. 222; GL MS 4655/, f. 80, cited in A. Plummer, *The London Weavers' Company, 1600–1970* (London and Boston, MA: Routledge & Kegan Paul, 1982), p. 95.

82. D. Callaghan reminds us that: 'the invisibility of women's work as well as the creation of an absolute distinction between aesthetic and productive labor is a relatively new phenomenon, and one which certainly postdates the Renaissance', 'Looking Well to Linens: Women and Cultural Production in *Othello* and Shakespeare's England', in J. Howard and S. Shershow (eds), *Marxist Shakespeares* (London: Routledge, 2000), p. 78.

83. These examples are found together at Founders Company, *Wardens' Accounts*, pp. 240–241, but recur throughout in different forms.

84. Founders' Company, *Wardens' Accounts*, p. 250.

85. Ibid., pp. 256–257.

86. Ibid., pp. 260, 263, 273. Further payments occurred in 1617 (p. 266); 1618 (p. 269); 1619 (p. 271).

87. Ibid., pp. 278, 282, 321.

88. Ibid., pp. 291, 316, 318.

89. Ibid., p. 300.

90. GL MS 11588/4, p. 39, cited in Ward, *Metropolitan Communities*, p. 161, n. 29.

91. Founders' Company, *Wardens' Accounts*, p. 401.

92. See also Archer, *The Pursuit of Stability*, pp. 118–119, on the provision of bread and cheese for the yeomanry.

2

Women's Letters: Eighteenth-Century Letter-Writing and the Life of the Mind

Leonie Hannan

Historical letters are usually studied solely for the words that appear on the page. Here, the material qualities of the letter and the paraphernalia required for letter-writing will be explored for the insights they provide into women's lives in the past. By considering the material realities of correspondence, the ways in which women moved beyond the home to connect with a wider social sphere can be more fully appreciated. For example, the social practice of letter-writing was central to women's participation in the intellectual culture of the late seventeenth and early eighteenth centuries. Women made use of correspondence to exchange ideas, but in doing so the material processes of writing, sending and receiving letters shaped their experience of the life of the mind. In other words, correspondence as a technology played a critical role in women's engagement with intellectual life. Whilst men could engage in intellectual discussion in a wider variety of locations, letter-writing provided a key point of access for women who were committed to learning.[1] As such, the interrelation between the material realities and the cerebral possibilities of this method of communication were of particular importance to women in this period.

In contrast to other forms of life writing, such as journals or diaries, letters expect a reply and generate exchange. Described by correspondents as 'paper visits', letters were the material realisation of a personal conversation. But the letters themselves, as we find them in archives today, are just partial remnants of the powerful social practice that was correspondence – a form of communication that entranced the literate population of eighteenth-century England with its peculiar rhythms of exchange and its tools of delivery: the pen, ink and page. Correspondence was commandeered to meet the full range of society's needs. Letters fostered familial ties, negotiated political allegiance, brokered marriage, facilitated trade, broke bad news and celebrated good news.

Of course, before a woman could correspond, she must be able to write. Whilst not everyone was literate, by 1720 literacy rates for female Londoners had reached 50 per cent.[2] In fact, the level of female literacy amongst the middling and upper sorts in seventeenth- and eighteenth-century England was high, and amongst 'the top social categories' likely to be 100 per cent.[3] Jacqueline Eales has recently illuminated the exceptionally high rates of literacy amongst women from clerical families in the seventeenth century, demonstrating that there was in fact a substantial population of women of the middling sort who enjoyed the freedom of pen and page.[4] Susan Whyman has also shown that 'epistolary literacy' was detectable across the social scale – from ordinary tradesmen to privileged courtier – and she identifies letter-writing as a training ground for more adventurous forms of writing.[5] Low rates of female literacy have been consistently blamed for women's silence on intellectual matters, but archival letter collections tell a different story – one of widespread written literacy and participation in correspondence culture. Moreover, these collections emphasise the expansive use women made of the letter as a form of expression, perhaps ill-spelled or clumsily printed on the page but nonetheless personal, thoughtful and historically important.

The examples of women's letter-writing explored here hail from the first half of the 'long eighteenth century'.[6] This chapter uses archival collections of manuscript letters as well as examples of writing equipment, deliberately combining the evidence of textual sources (used in both material and textual ways) with the evidence of material culture. Whilst the written content of letters has been given much scholarly attention,[7] the material technologies of correspondence have typically been treated separately. These different historiographies reflect the traditional rift between studies that consider text versus those that look primarily at material things. For example, Michael Finlay's detailed study of western writing implements documents the material processes by which individuals and manufacturers produced and used the tools of writing, but reflects less fully on the social, economic and cultural ramifications of writing as a technology.[8] On the other hand, many of the most significant publications on letter-writing – such as Clare Brant's *Eighteenth-Century Letters and British Culture* – spend very few lines considering the material realities of epistolary culture.[9] This traditional division between the material and the textual is being bridged by recent studies that attend to the 'materiality of text', and work by scholars concerned with the history of the book have been at the forefront of this new marriage of object and text.[10]

Letter-writing was an activity that both men and women engaged with and so the act of cutting a quill or sealing a letter was not in itself a gender-specific experience. There was, of course, plenty of contemporary published guidance concerning the writing of letters, much of which reinforced a sense of gendered norms within epistolary culture. In reality women wrote letters for a vast range of purposes, and sent them to diverse people, according to their own needs. So whilst women's writing was certainly subject to gender-specific cultural prescriptions and connotations, the experience of putting pen to page was one that both men and women held in common. Where male and female experiences of letter-writing differed was in their broader spatial, social and cultural context. For many women, letter-writing formed a legitimate part of their daily work, but was an activity firmly rooted in the spaces of home. In other words, women were a lot less likely to conduct epistolary activities in a non-domestic environment dedicated to business or leisure. Men, of course, also wrote in the home,[11] but their lives often had alternative loci for writing and intellectual practices. Moreover, the times of the day when women put pen to paper were framed by the competing demands on their time and energies, which commonly differed greatly from those of their male counterparts. Whilst the other chapters in this volume primarily discuss non-domestic spaces, the differences that existed in men's and women's use of space is a prominent theme throughout. The construction of social and commercial spaces like the hair salon or public house had a strong relationship with domestic space – nineteenth-century London salons might ape the 'comforts of home' in their décor, whilst the vault in twentieth-century pubs deliberately dispensed with such comforts to create an alternative, exclusively 'male' social space. Whilst great diversity existed in individual women's freedoms to read and write for their own intellectual satisfaction, most women experienced the intellectual in the context of the household and the family and as part of that complex matrix of domestic life.

As historians seeking to understand letter-writing at several hundred years' remove, we do so from a position of only semi-familiarity with the pursuit itself. Increasingly, the moments when we pick up a pen are becoming few and far between and, soon, will be relegated to the narrow confines of the shopping list or a message in a greetings card. Moreover, the pen we take in hand does not require of us the skills of cutting and shaping a quill, the act of dipping its nib in ink, nor the procedure of fixing the ink to the page. 'Epistolary' culture such as we know it exists largely through electronic means and has, consequently, changed in its conventions and habits. Even the briefest reflection on our own epistolary practice provides yet more evidence that tools, technology and process fundamentally shape the way we communicate. Just as we recognise the deep influence that communication technologies have on our social and professional lives today, we must also pay appropriate attention to the technologies that framed early modern communication.

Here, the materiality of letter-writing will be discussed in four sections: the first focusing on the tools of writing themselves; the next on the prerequisites and pressures of the system of carriage (which embodied the acts of constructing, posting, and receiving letters); the third considers the letter as an object; and the final section investigates the spaces of letter-writing as they were evoked by letter-writers. The chapter, therefore, considers materiality in its broadest sense, taking in the material realities of the carriage of letters and the material environments of letter-writing. Whilst it is important to focus on artefacts as historical sources, this is best achieved when the object is not separated from its environment. By recognising the inter-connected nature of things and spaces, a fuller material history of writing can be constructed.

The Materials of Writing

During the period in question, the primary tools of the letter-writer changed very little (Fig. 2.1). The quill remained popular despite the invention of metal-nibbed pens, and paper continued its dominance for ordinary use, relegating parchment to a role as a specialist writing surface. Other vital substances for writing were ink and pounce. The powder used both to condition the paper and dry the ink on the page, pounce was variously composed of sandarach,[12] cuttlefish or pumice stone. Sandarach gave its name to the pots that were manufactured to contain the

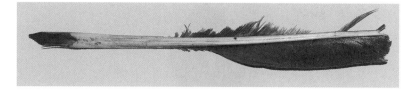

Figure 2.1 A quill dating from 1769, which was found in a bundle of newspapers. From the Museum of Writing Collection at the Institute of English Studies, School of Advanced Study, University of London.

pounce and they are still referred to in museum catalogues as 'sanders' (Fig. 2.2).[13] When reading eighteenth-century letters today, the glittery effect that often appears in the thicker lines of ink is the result of the combination of ink and sandarach, a remnant of the material process behind the writing of a letter.[14]

In the seventeenth century, recipes for ink commonly appeared in letter-writing manuals, suggesting that correspondents could feasibly have been producing their own ink at home.[15] As the period progressed, these references to home production largely disappeared from published manuals and it is possible that the growing reach of stationers' shops allowed most letter-writers to purchase ready-made inks along with paper. But ink and page only got the correspondent so far, and before a letter could be sent another substance was usually employed: sealing wax. Despite its name, this was not made of wax. Since the sixteenth century, shellac (an early modern varnish or lacquer) was the main material used in the creation of sealing wax.[16] The melted wax could just

Figure 2.2 A sander dating from 1756, Derby porcelain. From the Museum of Writing Collection at the Institute of English Studies, School of Advanced Study, University of London.

Figure 2.3 A seal dating from 1750–1754 with an image of a wedding: body. From the Museum of Writing Collection at the Institute of English Studies, School of Advanced Study, University of London.

be deposited in a dollop on the paper, but most letter-writers pressed into the semi-liquid substance a seal to demarcate the sender and diminish the possibility of opening and re-sealing the letter without detection (Figs. 2.3 and 2.4). Seals were made out of a variety of decorative materials and had imprinted designs,

Figure 2.4 A seal, as above: matrix. From the Museum of Writing Collection at the Institute of English Studies, School of Advanced Study, University of London.

Figure 2.5 A quill knife and wax lifter in mother of pearl and gold. Made from expensive materials, these implements were produced for an elite market, but simply made quill knives were cheap to purchase and within the reach of even the poorest letter-writer. From the Museum of Writing Collection at the Institute of English Studies, School of Advanced Study, University of London.

which were intended to represent the sender, ranging from calligraphically entwined initials to the sender's profile. In this way, the wax, the process of fixing, and the small ornamental instrument with which the letter was personalised, were all referred to by the same term.

These were the materials of writing but a letter-writer needed some specific skills in order to create and maintain such tools. Quill pens, for example, could be bought 'in the rough' as unfinished quills, semi-prepared or as finished pens (Fig. 2.5).[17] The tool we still call a 'pen-knife' received its name from the need to cut and re-cut quill nibs, a skilled task but a necessary one for a prolific writer. Whilst the Coventry school master Philemon Holland (1522–1637) boasted that he had written a whole book with just one pen, twenty sides of paper would have been an astonishing achievement on the basis of a single quill pen (re-cut multiple times).[18] Michael Finlay has used eighteenth-century trade cards to ascertain that 'quill-dressers' made a lively trade and has concluded that both the activities of dressing raw quills and the making of finished pens were carried out by these tradesmen.[19] Therefore, the consumers could choose to buy quills that they could shape themselves or purchase ready-made ones depending on their own skill and budget.

Whilst the individual could avoid some of the more onerous aspects of producing ink and dressing their pen, all letter-writers had to engage with the process of folding and sealing their correspondence. This prevented their lines of ink from becoming public property. As Finlay points out, 'an essential accessory in the business of sealing was a convenient means of melting the sealing-wax'.[20] During this period, a small candlestick – a 'taperstick'[21] – was usually employed to hold a taper that could be used to gently melt the sealing wax and drop it onto the paper join. Sometimes this piece of writing paraphernalia was incorporated into the design of the Standish (the combined set of ink well and sander) which would sit on a well-dressed writing desk (Fig. 2.6). However, at the other end of the spectrum, no doubt the candle by which the writer's work was lit also provided the most convenient means of melting sealing wax.

Having considered the materials of letter-writing, the discussion will now focus on an example of the letters of a prolific seventeenth-century correspondent,

Figure 2.6   A French-made, ivory portable writing set, or 'penner', dating from the late eighteenth century – consisting of a quill and an ink well. These small writing kits were useful when individuals were away from home and could not secure a desk with full writing paraphernalia. From the Museum of Writing Collection at the Institute of English Studies, School of Advanced Study, University of London.

Mary Evelyn (c. 1635–1709), in order to trace the material within the textual. As a child, she had been the fortunate beneficiary of an extensive humanist education, unusual for girls and young women of this period. She was fluent in French and English, proficient in Italian and trained in mathematics, among other subjects.[22] At the age of thirteen, in June 1647, Mary Browne married the famous diarist and thinker, John Evelyn.[23] The Evelyn Papers represent a vast family archive including John Evelyn's famous diary,[24] account books, estate inventories and an expansive collection of family correspondence. Within this collection there are ten volumes of Mary Evelyn's collected correspondence, including her letter books composed of copies of selected letters that she had sent. Further examples of Evelyn's letters can be found in the collections of some of her more diligent correspondents.[25] Together, this collection provides a cross-section of one woman's varied correspondences, and the material evidence contained amongst these pages is revealing of her relationships with others.

Mary Evelyn was a prolific letter-writer and maintained intimate correspondences not only with her nearest relations but also with a range of friends outside of her immediate family circle. In particular, her son's tutor Ralph Bohun conducted an intellectual exchange with Evelyn in the 1660s and 1670s but he did not escape censure for his careless approach to the epistolary craft. Evelyn instructed Bohun:

> pray be advised to date y[r] letters, which hitherto I am in doubt if writtin in the old or new yeare; not to lay so much wax on them [meaning the letters] as to temper the fidelity of the post, who may Imagine all you write to be secrets, and that once in my life I may make a seasonable present, if you can but secure me of a safe conveyance, I will send you a seale to save y[r] fingers from burning. ... by those wee received, I guessed they had ben worne in the pocket some time or throwne about negligently, for I could hardly make the paper hold reading.[26]

These comments acknowledged that, by contemporary standards, signs of the author's intention were implicit in the material presentation of letters. This evidence was read alongside the written message and communicated important information about the letter-writer's state of mind and circumstances at the time of writing.

The material presentation of Evelyn's own letters is also instructive as to her intentions and relationship with the addressee. For example, the collection of correspondence from her son, Jack, was predominantly presented on large, fine paper and care was clearly taken over layout and handwriting. Letters to Jack also feature prominently in her letter books, where she copied out choice correspondence for her own records. In contrast, the substantial number of letters from Evelyn's daughter, Susanna, were far more modest offerings, exclusively on small sheets of paper (some bordering on tiny) and with the perfunctory appearance of regular, inconsequential correspondence. Moreover, letters that Mary Evelyn wrote to her daughters did not apparently warrant reproduction in her letter book. These physical differences point to the social distinctions made between Evelyn's epistolary relationships with her children. Letters to her son were more formally presented and deemed worthy of record, whilst letters to her daughters were relaxed, quotidian and ephemeral.

As an exiled royalist, Mary Evelyn's father, Richard Browne, remained in permanent residence in France and hence established a regular correspondence with his absent daughter. Despite displaying a consistently neat and functional Italian hand in her other correspondence, Evelyn took a far more calligraphic approach in some letters to her father. A plausible reason for the more elaborate presentation was Evelyn's concern to prove to her father that the lavish humanist education she had received as a child was not, in adulthood, being wasted. In general, this attention to form seemed simply to represent a desire to impress her father, but the most carefully presented letter of the collection was also significant for its serious subject matter. In September 1653 Evelyn wrote in the weeks prior to the birth of her second child, and the subject matter focused on finances and property. The letter had an official character and suggested that Evelyn was setting her affairs in order in case she should die during childbirth. It revealed the contemporary recognition that letters' diverse purposes could (and possibly should) be reflected in their material presentation.

Of the surviving examples of Richard Browne's letters to Mary Evelyn,[27] none of them showed signs of having been sealed with sealing wax and they did not include a written address, suggesting that they were sent as part of a larger parcel. There was, of course, a possibility that the complete lack of sealing wax indicated an alternative method of fastening. For example, string, crossed and knotted, may have been sufficient if the letter were sent by a trusted courier. However, the former theory is corroborated by Evelyn's frequent requests in letters to her father for specified consumables that he could obtain from a mutual acquaintance (and tradesman) in France. The list included 'shamois stockings for Jack', 'a pound of pouder for the haire'[28] and quantities of cloth. The commonplace nature of the requests for such items suggests an established traffic in goods at this time and supports the conclusion that many letters were sent, unaddressed and unsealed, as part of larger packages.

Thinking about the materiality of letter-writing forces us to consider and appreciate the technical processes behind the letter's construction – the procurement and use of the raw materials of ink, paper and wax as well as of the letter itself. Material evidence can also illuminate the movement of other objects that were packaged up with letters and which circulated through the postal system in this period. Thinking about these physical processes brings to mind the gestures and actions that shape human relationships with people and things. The act of sealing a letter, for example (as Mary Evelyn pointed out), necessitated physical actions that could singe the letter-writer's fingers in the absence of certain equipment. Acts of sealing with wax, tying with string and their opposite actions of untying and breaking the seal, all employed the senses. And this tactile, gestural and sensory engagement with a written medium must have informed individuals' relationships with writing, communication and exchange. All of these actions left their mark and this evidence was readily understood by contemporaries as they turned a letter over in their hands.

Correspondence as a Material Process

Whilst reliant on either the postal system or dependable carriers for their letters, women correspondents were highly knowledgeable about the times of the post and the likelihood of their addressees receiving a letter and having time to reply by the next post. The system of carriage that moved letters and goods from place to place was the most important communications technology of the time and factors such as location played a large part in a correspondent's likelihood of receiving post promptly. In 1737, Frances Robinson, who hailed from an important gentry family, based at Hovingham Hall near York, complained of just this problem in a letter to her husband:

> You will think me a strange creature for not writeing to you all this time but now that I am with my sister I cant get your letters tell the post after thay come to Hovingham wich is one reason that I wish myself att home.[29]

A good understanding of the postal system provided useful information about the likelihood of receiving a letter from an absent friend, but it also offered plausible excuses for the letter-writer. In particular, references to the cost or efficiency of the post infiltrated letter-writing language. On 3 March 1774, Frances Taylor wrote to her daughter and revealed the embarrassing (and costly) consequences of a poorly written, and then poorly posted, letter:

> before I proceed any farther, I must tell you that your last letter was charged dou-ble, oweing I believe to droping in seal wax at the ends, it's a foolish way & I would wish you would not do it again, we had 4 pence returned but little pusses scribble must be exposed at the post office, this is the only frank & indeed we diden know of this till lately, so your Brot[her] has taken the opportunity of writing to you both on one piece of paper, for he could not furnish subject enough for two Letters.[30]

For Taylor, the material construction of her daughter's letter was so inadequate it was the source of social anxiety and the correction of these epistolary habits would form an important part of young Frances' education.

One of the most alarming possibilities for the avid letter-writer was the pros-pect of letters being lost in the post.[31] Elizabeth Elstob, an early bluestocking and Anglo-Saxon scholar,[32] wrote to George Ballard, an antiquary and author,[33] on 8 January 1738/9, dwelling on the possible sources of anxiety for not hear-ing from a friend:

> I cannot forbear writing any longer, being apprehensive your want of health has prevented my hearing from you, or that a Letter I sent you near two months ago never came to your hands. I beg you will let me hear if possible by the next cross Post how you do.[34]

Similarly, an Oxfordshire gentlewoman, Anne Dormer, wrote to her sister in 1687:

> the fear of my letters not coming to you makes me not write of my affaires so freely as I would and has kept me from writing many times when it would be an ease to my heart to taulk to thee.[35]

Despite the recognised likelihood of losing letters in the post, and the anxiety that surrounded this, eighteenth-century correspondents still had high expecta-tions of maintaining regular epistolary contact with friends and relatives. Reliable carriage and delivery of letters ensured largely secure and regular exchange, a crucial prerequisite for satisfyingly sustained intellectual engagement.

Correspondence most commonly acted as a bridge across geographical dis-tance and a means of contact when personal visits were out of the question. But some correspondents deployed their letters differently, using the medium to enhance their existing social contact with a friend. For instance, when London-based gentlewoman Sarah Cowper[36] was first forming a close friend-ship with Anna Maria Mordaunt[37] in 1721, short letters were sent in the brief gaps between seeing one another. In a letter marked 'Thurs: night 45 mints past eleven' Cowper wrote to Mordaunt having just seen her earlier the same evening:

> I was very angry that I was forc'd to part with yo so soon y[esterday] even[ing]: I have now vented all my Rage on a piece of cold mutton. I have drunk your

Health, & in short my supper has compos'd me, & made me fit for sleep. I wish
to dream of being with you because I suppose what makes my Happiness awake,
will be so asleep.[38]

Cowper and Mordaunt were able to propel their new friendship forward
through an obsessive level of contact both in person and via their correspondence. Examples such as this show the flexibility with which women used letter-writing as a means of communication, adapting the practice to their own
needs. Nevertheless, a more common experience of corresponding would have
included the inevitable, and sometimes lengthy, pauses in epistolary contact
imposed by the system, and a much less frenetic pattern of issue and response.
Correspondences with loved ones abroad proved even less reliable as facts of
geography interacted with the particulars of postal transit and determined the
pace and security of exchange. It was this rhythm of communication and silence,
sending and receiving, which shaped women's experience of friendship, influence, intimacy and self-expression.

This relationship between system and person was the cause of an ever-present
tension in correspondence culture, a tension felt very deeply by dedicated letter-writers and one that shaped correspondents' relationships with each other.
Letters were an important tool for the deepening of personal relationships and,
in turn, intimacy was an important facet of intellectual friendship. These connections, between the material realities of epistolary contact and the emotional
conditions of engaging in intimate exchange at a physical distances, had ramifications for female intellectual lives in the eighteenth century.

The Letter as an Object

Correspondence acted as a means of bridging distance between people and,
as a material object, a letter's physical journey from writer to recipient gave
expression both to the geographical journey undertaken and to the mental
proximity of the correspondents, enjoined in mutual consideration. But whilst
correspondence carried these broad social associations, the symbolic meaning of the single letter was no less potent. After all, the letter could be seen
as a material token of its author and, as such, a uniquely prevalent gift, daily
exchanged in society. Letter-writers thus used the physical artefact of the letter to dwell on the question of physical separation and, conversely, on their
emotional proximity. Responses to physical separation could slalom between
anxiety-filled missives, obsessing about the unbridgeable distance, and letters
that revelled in the new-found intimacy of a regular correspondence. One
wife of a landed gentleman, Elizabeth, Lady Poley, wrote to her sister Anne,
Lady D'Ewes:

I could wish we mi[gh]t always in joy each other which is one of the greattist
comforts I take in this life espessially whare I find so much noblenes with many
realitis as distance or place or length of time doth rather unite our harts then
ackuse them of any neglects.[39]

Poley later told her sister: 'I take much comfort in your lines which want not often reading',[40] suggesting that the letter, as a physical memento, also played a part in the intimacy of their relationship.

The practice (common in this period) of an individual keeping old letters or even copying out her own correspondence resulted in the peculiar phenomenon of collated and preserved exchanges, recorded more accurately for posterity than any conversation that took place in a parlour or dining room. Today, this habit is mainly remarked upon in relation to the wealth of primary source material that it has secured for modern researchers. However, it is worth stressing that the practice of keeping (and perhaps re-reading) old correspondence naturally altered its meaning. For example, when Ann Worsley, a gentlewoman living in Yorkshire, wrote to her brother in 1737, she described her use of kept letters:

> his Letters to me are charming, I sometimes lock my self up to read some, ... but Alas when shall I be able to read em without Crying & tendering me too much.[41]

For Ann Worsley, at least, a collection of old letters provided emotional reading and an activity she would conduct in the privacy of a locked room.

Even within the lifetimes of the correspondents themselves, letters could take on alternative meanings: starting life with the immediacy of a recently posted message and, later, becoming part of a lifetime's collected memorabilia, steeped in sentimental meaning. Reviewing old letters (written or received) offered the possibility of tracking the development of an exchange of ideas over time or re-connecting with views held in the past, since evolved. Worsley's habit of re-reading old correspondence converted her relationship with letter-writing from the immediate to the historical, a critical factor for women who chose to deepen their thinking lives. Here the discussion will shift from the letter itself to the location of its writing, by considering the importance of place and space in female epistolary culture.

Writing Places and Spaces

Letters were written from quiet corners in busy households, on tables, desks, portable slopes or laps. The luxury of a lockable bureau or box gave some letter-writers the privacy they needed to pursue expansive correspondences with distant friends without the hindrance of familial surveillance. These places and spaces were frequently referenced in women's letters of this period.

The closet – a small antechamber often located adjacent to a bedroom – was a space particularly identified with female privacy, reading and writing.[42] For example, commemorative literature, accompanying the funeral of an important woman in the seventeenth century, often included material on how the deceased used her home and routinely referenced the closet as a space 'in which women read, prayed, meditated and conducted their devotions in private'.[43] Some closets were furnished, but others were 'little more than spaces through which there was no household traffic'.[44]

The letters of three young women writing in the 1740s confirms the closet as a key space for scholarly pursuits. When Jemima Grey (1722–1797)[45] moved back into her childhood home, Wrest Park, as a married woman, she wrote a letter to her two closest female friends. Grey's first comments on her change of residence related to the closet:

> I am writing in the prettiest Closet in the World, ornamented so elegantly, looking so neat & cheerful, – so, – in short that I am fonder of it than I ever was of my old Friend on t'other side of the House:[46] not to mention my Dressing room, which though the Closet is my greatest Attraction has its Merits too, & while your Two Pictures are there you can't doubt but I love it.[47]

This comparison of closets revealed that as a child, Jemima Grey was given her own closet, indicative of her aristocratic upbringing. In this period, country house design routinely incorporated the use of smaller rooms, away from the noise of larger social spaces, specifically aimed at women who wished to retire to quieter or more private spaces.[48] In a house the size of Wrest Park, it would therefore have been likely that even younger female members of the house would have had access to a closet or personal dressing room for reading or writing. Two years earlier, on a trip to London, Jemima Grey had detailed her reaction to the closet above other rooms in the residence in a letter to her friend, the diarist Catherine Talbot.[49] In this case she had been faced with sharing the workspace with her friend:

> I have taken Possession of the Lady's Closet, (which I may now again call Mine) & all her Papers & Books which strew the Floor, cover the Tea-Table & fill every other Table & Chair in the Room. So that after having committed great Devestations, displacing Drawers & laying out of the way many Curious Miscellanies, I have with some Difficulty found the Corner of a Table (which is at present cover'd with no less a Book than D[r] Middleton) to write upon.[50]

Grey's description reinforced the concept of the closet as a functional space for intellectual activities. Far from being just a femininely decorated little room, the closet was packed with 'Books', 'Papers' and 'Miscellanies' partially housed in 'Drawers' or on the 'Table', indicative of a room being daily used for reading, writing and thinking.

Whilst Jemima Grey revelled in her new found space on a large country estate, her friends, Mary Grey and Catherine Talbot, continued to share accommodation at their residence in Cuddesdon, Oxfordshire.[51] At times their proximity caused irritation, upon which Mary Grey provided a running commentary. In a letter dated 29 September 1740, she complained of Talbot's carelessness:

> Indeed I am very angry at Kate for she is rode out with the key of Her Bureau & so I cannot possibly get at a letter I began to my Dear Jem Yesterday & I have saunter'd away this morning in expectation of Her return rather than begin a new one w[ch] however I find my self reduced to after One OClock or else dissapoint you

on Wednesday, in this poor imprison'd letter I gave you an account of a journey my Ld Mrs Secker Mrs Talbot & my self took on Friday to Oxford.[52]

Grey concluded her letter more abruptly than usual, with the excuse: 'I am so out of humour at having lost my first letter that I cannot make this a long one.'[53] The letter ended with a note from Talbot to say:

> After a ride of three hours & a half I am returned Dear Lady Grey just time enough to beg your pardon for having hinder'd You of a Longer letter, tho' I assure You that that is locked up in my Bureau is not above half a page & You see I am making You what amends I can by adding this Postscript which at least will save You the disappointment on Opening Your letter of finding one Side blank paper.[54]

This anecdote shows that where a private closet was not available, writing-desks were shared between women within the household, but that the contents could be kept under lock and key. Mary Grey and Catherine Talbot operated a jovial communality in regard to their correspondence with their absent friend Jemima Grey – their lives constituting a concert of shared experiences. However, the accident reported in this letter revealed that, whilst they read and wrote together, there was room for personal privacy in the drawers of a locked bureau. Although Mary Grey and Catherine Talbot enjoyed intellectual proximity through the exchange of ideas, privacy was still important for activities requiring deeper thought and concentration.[55]

Conclusion

Ultimately, letter-writing was a technology that proved exceptionally important to women in this period. Women rarely gained access to many of the key institutional and social spaces of intellectual exchange that men occupied as a matter of course. Correspondence was a vital instrument for communication and one which was, very often, domestically situated. But by looking at the materials behind this practice, we find that the home becomes a different kind of space, one that could produce the tools of intellectual work – quill, ink and pounce; a space which interacted with an expanding economy of writing (paper merchants, stationers, ink sellers); and an industry that sought its ingredients across the globe. Women letter-writers had an intimate relationship with their writing materials, one of both production and consumption, and it is this messy material experience of writing that provides a new perspective on what the world of ideas (in ink on page) meant for them.

Elite writing materials were sometimes manufactured with female or male audiences in mind, their decorative scheme adapted accordingly.[56] However, it is not solely in this sphere of consumer culture that gender was materialised. Instead, it was in the many connections between writing materials and other domestic practices that their material resonance can be seen – the symbiotic relationship between female home production of goods (such as inks, salves, soaps or preserves) and writing; between women's domestic consumption of material things (paper, textiles or furniture) and letter-writing (as both the tool of the consumer and the product of consumption). The material and spatial experience of letter-writing helped shape the meaning of correspondence and, by the same token, influenced personal relationships. By attending to the material when we study eighteenth-century women's letters, we can move beyond the disembodied textual artefact and towards a vibrant network of meanings signified by the letter as an object and exemplified by the complex culture of exchange that was correspondence.

Notes

1. For example, the eighteenth century witnessed the flourishing of coffee shop culture, where public lectures were regularly presented on educational topics, see M. Ellis (ed.), *Eighteenth-Century Coffee-House Culture* (London: Pickering & Chatto, 2008). Men also had greater access to clubs, societies, and institutions which were dedicated to the pursuit of knowledge. Whilst the home was an important site of intellectual sociability in this period, letter-writing provided a crucial tool that allowed women to reach people outside of this space.
2. Figures for 1720 from D. Cressy, *Literacy and the Social Order: Reading and Writing in Tudor and Stuart England* (Cambridge: Cambridge University Press, 1980), pp. 129, 176. Elsewhere in the country as a whole only about a quarter of women were classed as literate.
3. L. Stone, 'Literacy and Education in England, 1640–1900', *Past and Present*, 42 (1969), pp. 69–139.
4. J. Eales, 'Female Literacy and the Social Identity of the Clergy Family in the Seventeenth Century', *Archaeologia Cantiana*, 133 (2013), pp. 67–81.
5. See S. Whyman, *The Pen and the People: English Letter-Writers from 1660–1800* (Oxford: Oxford University Press, 2009); and S. Whyman, 'Letter Writing and the Rise of the Novel: The Epistolary Literacy of Jane Johnson and Samuel Richardson', *Huntington Library Quarterly*, 70 (2007), pp. 577–606.
6. c. 1660–1750.
7. See, for example, D. Barton and N. Hall (eds), *Letter Writing as a Social Practice* (Philadelphia, PA: John Benjamins Publishing, 1999); S. Dalton, *Engendering the Republic of Letters: Reconnecting Public and Private Spheres in Eighteenth-Century Europe* (London: McGill-Queen's University Press, 2003); R. Earle (ed.), *Epistolary Selves: Letters and Letter Writers, 1600–1945* (Aldershot: Ashgate, 1999); and B. Redford, *The Converse of the Pen: Acts of Intimacy in the Eighteenth-Century Familiar Letter* (London: University of Chicago Press, 1986).
8. M. Finlay, *Western Writing Implements in the Age of the Quill Pen* (Carlisle: Plain Books, 1990).
9. Whilst there are several references to the post, postal processes and the Post Office, Brant's text is based on printed letters, rather than manuscript sources, and, as such, deals rather less with the material facets of letter-writing than with the wider literary and cultural meanings of epistolary culture.
10. See in particular the pioneering work of scholars such as Peter Stallybrass and Dena Goodman, and other recent publications such as K. Dierks, 'Letter Writing, Stationery Supplies, and Consumer Modernity in the Eighteenth-Century Atlantic World', *Early American Literature*, 41:3 (2006), pp. 473–494; and J. Daybell and P. Hinds (eds), *Material Readings of Early Modern Culture: Texts and Social Practices, 1580–1730* (Basingstoke: Palgrave Macmillan, 2010).
11. See K. Harvey, *The Little Republic: Masculinity and Domestic Authority in Eighteenth-Century Britain* (Oxford: Oxford University Press, 2012).

12. Sandarach is a gum that is derived from a tree akin to the Cypress, known as *Tetraclinis articulate*, which grows in north-west Africa and, in particular, in the Atlas Mountains. To the eye it is not unlike other forms of resin, such as gum Arabic. In early modern Europe it was used to make both varnish and pounce; for the latter it would have been ground up finely and used as a powder both to treat inadequate paper before writing and to help dry and fix the ink after the writing was complete.

13. Sanders were made in a variety of materials from inexpensive turned wood to silver, but ivory, bone, pewter, pottery and porcelain were all used besides. The sander sat in a pair with the ink well. For more information, see Finlay, *Writing Implements*, p. 34.

14. Alan Cole, collector of the historical writing materials that now compose the Museum of Writing (see http://www.ies.sas.ac.uk/library/ies-collections/museum-writing), explained this effect to me during a research visit to the collection store.

15. See, for example, E. Cocker, *The Pens Transcendency: Or, fair writings store-house* (1668), which gives a recipe for ink and advises on the ideal consistency.

16. Finlay, *Writing Implements*, pp. 59–60.

17. Ibid., p. 8.

18. See ibid., p. 10 – the book Holland claimed had been written with just one pen was a translation of Camden's *Britannia*. The collector of writing materials Alan Cole has managed to write a maximum of 18 sides of fine-lined script with one quill pen, which he had to re-cut frequently to keep it in use – as such, he doubts the veracity of Holland's claim.

19. Finlay, *Writing Implements*, p. 8.

20. Ibid., p. 61.

21. These are also referred to as 'wax-jacks', see ibid.

22. See J. K. Perkins, 'Evelyn, Mary (*c.* 1635–1709)', *Oxford Dictionary of National Biography* (hereafter *ODNB*) (Oxford: Oxford University Press, 2004; online edn, Jan. 2008).

23. See G. Darley, *John Evelyn: Living for Ingenuity* (London: Yale University Press, 2006); and D. D. C. Chambers, 'Evelyn, John (1620–1706)', *ODNB*.

24. E. S. de Beer (ed.), *The Diary of John Evelyn* (London: Oxford University Press, 1959), complete text of the six-volume edition published in 1955.

25. British Library (BL), Evelyn Papers (EP), Add. MS 78221, 78300, 78539.

26. BL, EP, Add. MS 78539, Mary Evelyn to Ralph Bohun, 13 March 1668/9.

27. Eleven in BL, EP, Add. MS 78431.

28. BL, EP, Add. MS 78221, Mary Evelyn to Richard Browne, 23 November 1665.

29. West Yorkshire Archive Service (WYAS), Newby Hall Papers (NH), 2822/16, Frances Robinson to Thomas Robinson, 21 June 1737.

30. Bodleian Library, Coleridge Papers, MS Eng letter c 142, f. 26, Frances Taylor to Frances Taylor (jnr), 3 March 1774.

31. Although fears were probably exaggerated, letters were certainly tampered with by Post Office officials – see H. Robinson, *Britain's Post Office: A History of Development from the Beginnings to the Present Day* (Oxford: Oxford University Press, 1953), p. 47 – and the loss of letters travelling long distances was a common occurrence.

32. See N. Clarke, 'Elizabeth Elstob (1674–1752): England's First Professional Woman Historian?' *Gender and History*, 17 (2005), pp. 210–220.

33. See R. Sweet, *Antiquaries: The Discovery of the Past in Eighteenth-Century Britain* (Hambledon and London: Bloomsbury, 2004), pp. 60–61, 70.

34. Bodleian Library, Ballard 43, f. 61, Elizabeth Elstob to George Ballard, 8 January 1738/9.

35. BL, Trumbull Papers, Add. MS 72516, f. 162, Anne Dormer to Elizabeth Trumbull, 30 May c. 1687.

36. Sarah Cowper was the daughter of the politician and Lord Chancellor, William Cowper, first Earl Cowper (1665–1723), and his wife Mary Cowper (née Clavering).

37. Anna Maria Mordaunt, one time Maid of Honour to Queen Caroline, married Stephen Poyntz in 1733 and then lived on her husband's estate at Thatcham in Berkshire.

38. BL, Althorp Papers, Add. MS 75460: Sarah Cowper to Anna Maria Mordaunt, 'Thurs: night', 1721.

39. BL, Harley Papers, Add. MS 382, f. 173, Elizabeth Poley to Anne D'Ewes, 1639/40.

40. Ibid., f. 177, Anne D'Ewes to Elizabeth Poley, c. 1639/40.

41. WYAS, NH, 2822/17, Ann Worsley to Thomas Robinson, c. June 1737.

42. K. Lipsedge, '"Enter into thy Closet": Women, Closet Culture, and the Eighteenth-Century English Novel', in J. Styles and A. Vickery (eds), *Gender, Taste, and Material Culture in Britain and North America, 1700–1830* (London: The Paul Mellon Centre for Studies in British Art, 2006), pp. 107–22.

43. A. Laurence, 'Women Using Building in Seventeenth-Century England: A Question of Sources?' *Transactions of the Royal Historical Society*, 13 (2003), p. 299.

44. Ibid.

45. J. Collett-White, 'Yorke, Jemima, *suo jure* Marchioness Grey (1722–1797)', *ODNB*.

46. Wrest Park was a grand Bedfordshire manor house situated amongst early eighteenth-century style formal wooded walks, canals and gardens, and from Grey's description, it is clear that it afforded extensive domestic space with more than one closet at its inhabitants' disposal.

47. Bedfordshire and Luton Archives and Records Service (BLA), Lucas Papers (LP), L 30/9a/1, f. 6, Jemima Grey to Mary Grey, 12 May 1743.

48. See C. Christie, *The British Country House in the Eighteenth Century* (Manchester: Manchester University Press, 2000), pp. 71–73.

49. R. Zuk, 'Talbot, Catherine (1721–1770)', *ODNB*.

50. BLA, LP, L 30/9a/3, f. 64, Jemima Grey to Catherine Talbot, 6 June 1741.

51. The two women were living with Thomas Secker, Bishop of Oxford, who in earlier years had taken in Catherine Talbot and her mother – who had lost her husband several months before Catherine's birth. From 1737 onwards, Thomas Secker spent summers at the Palace in Cuddesdon and during the winter he resided at the deanery of St Paul's; the Talbots remained members of his household during this period.

52. BLA, LP, L 30/9/53/9, Mary Grey to Jemima Grey, 29 September 1740.

53. Ibid.

54. Ibid.

55. On this theme more generally, consult P. Meyer Spacks, *Privacy: Concealing the Eighteenth-Century Self* (London: University of Chicago Press, 2003).

56. Dena Goodman has argued that letter-writing – and the consumption of the material culture of writing – was a sphere in which women could exercise agency and discernment, see *Becoming a Woman in the Age of Letters* (London: Cornell University Press, 2009).

3

Men's Hair: Managing Appearances in the Long Eighteenth Century

Susan Vincent

On 17 September 1666, Samuel Pepys recorded what seems to have been relief at being able to get rid of his stubble: 'Up betimes, and shaved myself after a week's growth; but Lord how ugly I was yesterday and how fine today.'[1] Pepys's simple diary mention reminds us of the significance of ordinary activities, both as single occurrences that make a particular difference to an individual, and also in their cumulative importance, whereby they shape the normative understandings of how, in this case, a gentleman ought to look and behave.

This chapter examines the engagement of men with the practices and paraphernalia of hair care in the long eighteenth century. It does so to help further our understanding of the complex and mutually constitutive relationship between the material world of things and the amorphous realm of abstract ideas. In other words, by looking at the detail of hair care – how it was undertaken, by whom, how often, with what tools and where – we can learn a lot about how contemporaries understood gender and, more specifically, about what it meant to be a man. As we will see, 'doing' hair did not necessarily come easily. Not only did men in the long eighteenth century have to learn specific skills, but physical circumstances – for example, a blunt razor or sensitive skin – might become impediments to the successful presentation of a masculine and civil persona. Likewise, researching men's management of their hair is not without challenges for the historian. Although ubiquitous, everyday practices tend to leave little trace in the historical record: they are too private for public documentation and usually too mundane for personal recollection. As Victoria Kelley has noted, the 'everyday, routine and repetitive … often lies beneath the historical radar'.[2] The following relies heavily, therefore, on infrequent asides found in the personal writings of three particular men who documented aspects of their lives in unusual detail: Samuel Pepys (1633–1703), a naval administrator who became Chief Secretary to the Admiralty; Jonathan Swift (1667–1745), the writer and cleric; and James Woodforde (1740–1803), a Norfolk country parson.

As professional men who were not members of a titled aristocracy, Pepys, Swift and Woodforde could all be regarded as part of the broad and varied 'middling sorts'. However, their experiences of managing hair were not necessarily specific to their social position. To some extent hair was a great leveller. Men placed in social strata both above and below had to deal with a similar bundle of physiological and fashionable demands, and came up with similar answers, as the ubiquity of wigs and barbering services attests. Perhaps most crucially, the personal accounts of Pepys, Swift and Woodforde enable us to glimpse an experiential side to what would otherwise be a mere sequence of actions. But there are limitations to this kind of source. Much – perhaps most – remains unsaid, and so to retrieve a practice that only occasionally surfaces in the written record it is necessary to engage with pictorial sources and, of course, the evidence of the objects themselves. We also need to use our imagination.

In the discussion that follows, we will look first at hair removal, or 'manscaping' as we might choose to think of it. Although coined in the early twenty-first century to describe the 'waxing, shaving, lasering, or simply shaping [of] any hairy region of the male body',[3] applying the term in a historical context to describe the activity of male depilation can bring this grooming into focus in two ways. First, 'manscaping', as the play on 'landscaping' suggests, makes evident that grooming is cultural work applied to a 'natural' body; second, it also suggests that there is labour involved, that the shaved and smoothed skin is achieved with effort and deliberation. After considering who undertook this manscaping, how often, and where – and in the process uncovering evidence for a female presence in barber shops, as both clients and practitioners – the chapter leads on to a discussion of wigs, that iconic accessory of the eighteenth century. It closes by looking at how this investigation into the material practices of hair care fits into a broader theoretical framework within dress history.

Hair removal

As we have seen, in the September of 1666 Samuel Pepys had been eager to shave off his heavy growth of stubble, thinking himself ugly with it and 'fine' without. In contrast to the sixteenth and earlier seventeenth century, when beards were the accepted sign of manhood,[4] by the 1660s to be cleanly shaven was the manly norm.[5] Dene October has observed the significance of shaving in modernity, but his comment that the 'repetition of the shaving ritual makes it an important site for the cultural production of masculinity' applies equally to the experiences of the seventeenth- and eighteenth-century men considered here.[6] Historian Alun Withey has speculated about the reasons for this early modern change in facial hair fashions, considering as potential influences the decline of humoral medicine, the rise of a more 'open' and youthful aesthetic as compared with the model of rugged and bearded masculinity, and technological advances in steel-making that meant that razors were sharper and easier to use.[7] In addition, we need to remember that fashion is articulated by departures from a previously established norm, and also that in this period beardlessness developed in tandem with wig-wearing, with contemporary aesthetics (and possibly issues of comfort) opposing, rather than combining, wigs and beards.

For Pepys and his contemporaries, rather than masculinity being declared and constructed by facial hair, it was therefore embodied by the need for, and the practice of, its removal. However, material conditions dictated that this presented an ongoing and never fully resolvable problem. Pepys occasionally made mention of the difficulties he found in dealing with his stubble, or, to put it another way, in performing this part of his gendered identity. Initially he used the services of a barber, but then in May 1662 began to use a pumice stone to scour off his whiskers. This he found 'very easy, speedy and cleanly', an assessment that suggests he was making a comparative judgement and that his experiences of barbering were at times difficult, slow and messy. He resolved to continue to pumice.[8] This method of depilation by abrasion is an ancient one, so although the following description comes from a nineteenth-century manual on hair removal, it is likely that Pepys used a similar technique. The manual's author advises oiling the skin first to soften it, then, using small pieces of pumice, stretching the skin slightly and with 'a light hand' working in a to-and-fro movement against the direction of the hairs' growth. He warns, though, that care should be taken to stop as soon as the hairs have been ground short enough, and that on the delicate skin around the mouth, pumice 'is apt to cause rawness'.[9]

Pepys did not have a manual from which to learn; instead, he was taught to use pumice on his facial hair by an older acquaintance Mr Marsh, Storekeeper of the Ordnance, with whom he was in contact in a professional capacity. Pepys was in Portsmouth on naval business when Marsh showed him what to do: it seems likely that Pepys was looking for a barber, or they were chatting about the difficulties of getting a good shave. That Pepys was impressed with the pumice method is clear, and he must have resolved to try it himself. He was so struck with the ease and speed of self-pumicing that on impulse he cut off his moustache, 'only that I may with my pumice-stone do my whole face, as I now do my chin, and so save time – which I find a very easy way and gentile'.[10] Despite such good beginnings, the pumice turned out not to be the answer after all. Perhaps he used the stone too heavily, or found that it did indeed aggravate the sensitive skin around his mouth as the nineteenth-century manual warned it might. For whatever reason, after four months Pepys was again getting himself shaved, though he seems to have been happy to pumice 'where I cannot conveniently have a barber'.[11]

Sixteen months later, however, in January 1664, Pepys experimented again. This time he stopped using a barber and instead began to shave himself. 'This morning I begun a practice which I find, by the ease I do it with, that I shall continue, it saving me money and time – that is, to Trimme myself with a Razer – which pleases me mightily.'[12] Pepys described the advantages of his new method of depilation with the same ideas of ease, convenience and time, and with the added consideration of cost. However, the drawbacks quickly became apparent, and within days he wrote that he had twice cut himself, which he blamed on the bluntness of the razor.[13] This reminds us that shaving required a set of additional skills and further equipment. First the razor needed to be kept sharp, both by regularly using a strop (a strip of leather against which the razor was smoothed to sharpen its edge) and occasionally having its edge honed or reground.[14] It also needed soap, a shaving brush, linen (that in turn needed to be regularly laundered), a mirror, and hot water. Hot water meant not only that, summer and winter, the water had to be fetched, but that it was necessary to build, light and tend a fire to heat it. Shaving was a practice, then, in which equipment needed to be actively maintained and the supporting material resources replenished. Less than two years later Pepys was back to regularly using a barber.

Like Pepys, James Woodforde, a country parson whose diaries were written during the second half of the eighteenth century, both shaved himself and used the services of a professional. He noted buying new razors and the purchase of items like soap, shaving brushes and shaving powder, and a hone (a whetstone used for sharpening). Although from time to time he recorded having his old razors sharpened and reset by a razor grinder or cutler, in between he used a strop. In a memorandum diary entry of March 1769 – a note to self – he wrote: 'as I was going to shave myself this morning as usual on Sundays, my Razor broke in my Hand as I was setting it on the Strap without any violence'. He added, and this is the point of the memorandum, 'May it be always a warning to me not to shave on the Lord's Day or do any other work to profane it pro futuro.'[15] Here Woodforde was referring to the enduring prohibition on Sunday shaving, subject of repeated civic, guild and parish regulations, though probably more honoured in the breach than the observance.[16] As a clergyman, it is not surprising that he felt he ought to be dutiful in this regard. For our purposes, the significant aspect of the prohibition and Woodforde's uneasy conscience is that shaving was indeed considered work: it required time and effort. Grooming the male body was labour.

The sense that we get of Pepys and Woodforde making the best of an inconvenient chore is echoed in comments made by Jonathan Swift in the 1710s. On what he called his 'shaving days', Swift repeatedly made reference to how much time this activity demanded and that he had to consciously build it into his morning schedule or risk missing later appointments.[17] Also like Pepys, he was familiar with the problem of a poor cutting edge. 'The Razors will be a great Treasure to me', he wrote in acknowledgement to his friend Charles Ford. He added that, 'for want of good ones I pass one hour in eight and fourty very miserably'.[18] This simple comment suggests a number of things. First, it shows his shaving days to have been alternate (he shaves once in forty-eight hours); second, it indicates the sort of time the task consumed (one hour); third, it reinforces the point that male grooming could be incorporated into the pattern of friendships, with the exchange of objects, advice and anecdote. Similarly, James Woodforde also participated in an informal exchange economy with his peers when a student at Oxford University. On one occasion he swapped the lace from his hat for 'a very neat Razor'.[19]

At this point it is helpful to consider the razor as a specifically gendered object (Fig. 3.1). Alun Withey has proposed that in the second half of the eighteenth century razors were explicitly linked to masculinity through discourses of technological advance, and that newly crafted blades became aesthetically desirable as personal belongings. I want to look at this gendering in a slightly

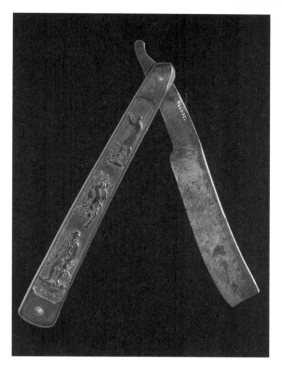

Figure 3.1 Razor, steel, 1780–1805. Wellcome Library, London. Library reference no. Science Museum A650921. Razor belonging to Lord Horatio Nelson. The handle is decorated with scenes of hunting game, and on this side bears the words 'Shooting' and 'Evening'.

different way by bringing into the frame evidence from the household receipt (recipe) tradition, a genre that appeared in the sixteenth century and lasted through to the nineteenth. These manuscript texts, most of which were compiled by women, often feature recipes for hair-care products, including depilatories, which were clearly considered suitable for, although not confined to, female use. Some printed manuals make this explicit. In puffing the virtues of a depilatory recipe, one author claimed that 'some women that have haire growing on their lips, (an unseemly sight to see) would give any thing for this Secret'.[20] Such evidence suggests that it was not depilation *per se* that was so resoundingly masculine, or even depilation of facial hair. Rather, it was cutting it off with a razor, combined with the sort of growth against which such an implement was effective, that was located squarely within the gender performance of a man. As a contributor to *The Englishman's Magazine* later put it, 'A razor is surely the emblem of manhood.'[21]

As well as being masculine, shaving was situated as a polite practice: it 'was socially, culturally and fashionably imperative'.[22] It is clear that for all three of our diary writers, being groomed was a significant part of their self-presentation, a pre-condition for social readiness. To take Woodforde's case first, although he made only infrequent mentions of actually shaving himself, it is telling that he specifically noted doing so before the bishop's visitations and when preaching in Oxford before the Vice-Chancellor. Reading these entries, one has the feeling that he was consciously preparing and putting his best ecclesiastical foot forward. Likewise, he noted shaving before a day's outing to see the royal family.[23] Conversely, if unshaven in the company of visitors Woodforde felt ill-kempt and ill at ease. If these visitors included the Squire's wife, Woodforde refused the social interaction altogether: 'M[rs.] Custance with 3. of her children and M[rs.] Collier called here this morning & stayed some time – The Captain [Woodforde's nephew] and self purposely took a walk out of the way, not being shaved or properly dressed.'[24]

If obliged by circumstances to miss being shaved, Pepys and Swift felt similarly uncomfortable and inadequate. 'Mr. secretary St. John sent for me this morning so early that I was forced to go without shaving,' complained Swift, 'which put me quite out of method: I called at Mr. Ford's, and desired him to lend me a shaving, and so made shift to get into order again.'[25] For Pepys, a morning spent working from home was an opportunity to avoid the bother of shaving and instead settle straight to business. However, he found that without being properly groomed he felt unfocused and unprepared; his professional persona eluded him. In his words:

> Up betimes, and down to chamber, without trimming [shaving] myself or putting on clean linen, thinking only to keep to my chamber to do business today; but when I came there, I find that without being shaved I am not fully awake nor ready to settle to business, and so was fain to go up again and dress myself; which I did, and so down to my chamber and fell roundly to business.[26]

Despite the social significance of being groomed, however, daily shaving was rare. As we have seen, it was a bodily discipline that required an investment of time and resources, and also fortitude in the face of discomfort and wounds. Pepys, Swift and Woodforde all shaved two to three times per week, and despite the ample eighteenth-century portrait evidence depicting full wigs and smooth chins, in reality stubble must have been a common sight. This is a clear instance of the power of material conditions to shape social practice, leading subjects towards particular, congruent behaviours – in this case, militating the desire to be closely shaved. Such a reality does not undermine the normative reading of clean-shaven, polite masculinity, but nuances it with an appreciation of contemporary physical experience, material reality tempering the theoretical ideal.

Barbers

The alternative to self-shaving was to use the services of a professional barber, the most common option for men in the eighteenth century (Fig. 3.2). Domestic and professional shaving were not mutually exclusive, however, and a man in the middle orders might combine these grooming practices as Pepys did. For James Woodforde the decision of whether to shave himself or use a barber seems to have been based on geography. When living in Oxford, or in

Figure 3.2 'A Barber's Shop', coloured etching with aquatint by T. Rowlandson after W. H. Bunbury (n.d.; c. 1785). Wellcome Library, London. Library reference no. ICV No 20082. The central figure swathed in linen is having his hair dressed by a barber, helped by an assistant who is using curling tongs. Other customers are at various stages of being shaved, and the print depicts many of the accoutrements of barbering. The man waiting his turn reads a newspaper, a typical barbershop entertainment.

his Somerset home of Ansford, Woodforde was tended by a barber. When he moved to his Norfolk parish of Weston Longville he took up the razor himself, although he continued to use a barber when away from home, particularly on his regular overnight visits to nearby Norwich. It seems likely therefore that Weston was too small to sport a resident barber. If a gentleman could pay for it he could buy the convenience of a home visit. If this were the case, it is probable that the client supplied the shaving equipment, including the razor, taking responsibility also for keeping the edge honed. Throughout the years during which Woodforde was being visited by a barber, his diaries record purchases of a full range of shaving equipment.

Barbering could be performed at any point in the day. Whether in a shop or at the home of a client, barbers were on call virtually all hours: Pepys called for a barber one evening after supper, who then stayed so late 'that he was locked into the house', the servants having made all secure for the night and retired to bed.[27] As with self-shaving though, professional barbering was not a daily experience. Woodforde entered into contracts with his barbers to visit him at first twice, and then three times a week. Regular clients like Woodforde were usually billed in arrears, quarterly; recurring entries in his Ansford diaries repeatedly note the paying of his barber's 'quarterage', usually a sum of five shillings.

This practice of quarterly billing meant that customers and barbers could build longstanding relationships, particularly in rural areas with small, stable populations and little professional competition. Casual, single shaves could of course also be bought, and it was common to find barbers attached to inns for the convenience of an increasingly mobile population served by a growing coaching network and better roads. Although portable cases of grooming equipment were available – indeed, in remaining fundamentally unchanged from at least the seventeenth to the nineteenth century they reflected a long continuity in shaving practices[28] – it is easy to envisage that a man needing linen, hot water, mirror, razor, soap and shaving brush, might well prefer the convenience of a resident barber.

Historians describe the barber's shop as being a site of homo-social pleasures. A convivial all-male space that supplied its clients with the opportunities to socialise, listen to or play music, catch up on the news, perhaps purchase tobacco, and of course receive the attentions of a razor and other grooming tools.[29] Such a locus is indeed glimpsed through certain of Pepys's experiences. Where he recorded drinking ale with his barber, being entertained by the barber's boy playing the violin, and listening to a literary discussion that took place amongst the barbershop clientele, Pepys's diaries do indeed open a window on just such a world as historians have pictured.[30] I want not so much to problematise, as to round out this account in two ways.

First, the material conditions that could make domestic shaving so uncomfortable could also render the services of a professional deeply unenjoyable, especially if that practitioner was only indifferently skilled (Fig. 3.3). Woodforde, for instance, dismissed a barber three weeks into a new contract 'because he hurt me very much in shaving and not punctual in coming to me'.[31] Alexander Hamilton (1712–1756), a Scottish doctor who emigrated to America, contrasted being shaved by a barber who 'did his job lightly and to a hair', and one 'whose hand was so heavy that he had almost flead [flayed] my chin and head'.[32] In assessing the material realities of barbering we need also to appreciate the intimacy of the act and the proximity it enforced on both parties. The barber needed to get up close, he stretched and pulled at the skin to make a taut surface, he grasped the client's nose to get at his upper lip. Trapped in a chair and keeping still beneath the razor's edge, a man might easily find such intimacy unpleasant. 'In the morning my barber came to shave me', complained Alexander Hamilton, 'and almost made me sick with his Irish brogue and stinking breath.'[33] For Benjamin Franklin (1706–1790), this was reason enough for a young man to learn to shave himself, so that he could be saved 'the dirty fingers or bad Breath of a slovenly Barber'.[34] Thus, while it is undeniable that the barbershop did offer pleasures, they were not necessarily unalloyed.

Second, it appears that the barbershop was not an exclusively male province (Fig. 3.3). Certainly most barbers were men, but not all. Seventeenth-century guild records show there to have been a small but significant number of widows who carried on their husband's business and also that some women and girls were apprenticed in their own right.[35] A recent history of London barbers, citing the example of Maria Cohen, the daughter of a merchant, who was

Figure 3.3 'Sketches in a Shaving Shop', coloured etching by Richard Newton, 1794. Wellcome Library, London. Library reference no. ICV No 41273. A series of comic vignettes playing with different customer–barber interactions. Several of these depict unpleasant experiences. However, three scenes feature a female barber and decidedly contented-looking clients.

apprenticed in 1702, suggests that barbering became an increasingly respectable occupation for women, stating that 'There are many examples of girls from well-to-do families entering the trade.'[36] Female barbering continued at least into the early nineteenth century; in 1815, draughtsman and antiquary John Thomas Smith described the experience of visiting just such a barbershop. Although something of a curiosity to him (and, one suspects, not without a certain frisson), in Smith's description the female barber is neither bizarre nor scandalous:

> On one occasion, that I might indulge the humour of being shaved by a woman, I repaired to Seven Dials, where, in Great St. Andrew's-street, a slender female performed the operation, whilst her husband, a strapping soldier in the Horse-Guards, sat smoking his pipe. There was a famous woman in Swallow-street, who shaved; and I recollect a black woman in Butcher-row, who is said to have shaved with ease and dexterity.[37]

In addition, there is evidence to suggest that the barbershop clientele might have been more mixed than has otherwise been assumed. James Woodforde, a conventional country parson for whom flouting social convention would have been inconceivable, visited a barber and took with him his twenty-nine-year-old niece, Nancy.

> Nancy walked with me to one Smiths in Surry Street, Strand, a Barber, and there had her Hair full dressed – Smith was Sam Woodfordes Hair dresser [the Royal Academy painter and Woodforde's nephew] – I was shaved and had my Wig Dressed there. I gave him for shaving and dressing 0.1.6 [one shilling and sixpence].[38]

While the barbershop was predominantly male, therefore, it was not exclusively so; and while many visits were relaxing and sociable, some were merely to be endured.

Wigs

On 30 March 1765, Woodforde paid a barber called Hitchcock six shillings and sixpence to shave his scalp as well as whiskers because, like the majority of eighteenth-century Englishmen, Woodforde wore a wig.[39] Kept on a block or stand overnight (perhaps akin to the 'turned stand' Woodforde bought 'to hold 4 Wiggs having four branches'[40]), like razors, wigs were masculine. Indeed, in referring to his wig within the pages of his diary, Woodforde sometimes even used the masculine pronoun 'he'.[41] While false hair was a common item on the dressing table of female fashion, full wigs were only used by women when illness or age had thinned a woman's hair to the point where such prosthesis was necessary. Conversely, a wig was used by men of all ages (regardless of the quality of their own hair) and was presumed to enhance masculinity. Indeed, the wig was so important to ideals of manliness that both natural hair and wigs were styled to look artificial and as wig-like as possible. In a period in which intellect, manners and taste were held to be improved by training, where self-control and bodily comportment attained new levels of desirability, the aim was to look styled and the end product of skilled intervention. If dressed hair was thus 'polite' and controlled hair, wigs could be held to materialise even greater levels of gentility. In cutting hair off, crafting it into a garment and placing it on another's head, base nature had been elevated to the level of art(ifice).

Being masculine garments worn on the head – the seat of reason – it is easy to see how wigs came to connote propriety, dignity, wisdom and control. Additionally, the wig's material properties – its size, weight, and perhaps insecure fit – inclined the wearer to measured movements made with deliberation. The sense of authority that the eighteenth century invested in the wig is (half) humorously summed up by a comment from *The Spectator* of 1711: 'I have indeed my self observed that my Banker ever bows lowest to me when I wear my full-bottom'd Wig.'[42] Such significance was mutually reinforced by the wig becoming associated with the legal, medical and ecclesiastical professions. The law retains its association with wigs even today, and in the horsehair worn in courts we can see the last remnants of a three-hundred-year-old masculine fashion.

However, as Mr Spectator's comment suggests, this reading of wigs was simultaneously endorsed and refused. It was accepted both that wigs signalled dignity and status and that for any individual this might be an empty signal. This dual awareness underlies the contemporaneous satire of certain wig-wearers, for instance the caricatures of the 'macaroni', a figure of extreme fashion and enormous hair pieces.[43] The precarious foundations to the wig's ascendancy are revealed also in the mildly contemptuous term 'bigwig' (first used, according to the *Oxford English Dictionary*, from 1703). Furthermore, as much as the level of gravitas that could be accorded to a wig-wearer, such was the potential for loss of face to occur through an unskilled performance: if, for example, a wig was bedraggled by the rain or worn askew, or plucked off to reveal a bald vulnerable head on public show. This is quite painfully illustrated by an anecdote told by writer and journalist John Taylor (1752–1822), concerning the once-successful actor-manager Samuel Reddish. Reddish, Taylor explained, had been acting the part of Hamlet at Covent Garden when in the fencing scene the man playing Laertes had 'made so clumsy a lunge, that he struck off the bagwig of Hamlet, and exposed his bald pate to the laughter of the audience'. The mortification, according to Taylor, turned Reddish's mind, and he eventually ended his days in York Asylum.[44] Although we would ascribe a different aetiology to such a breakdown, that contemporaries found the link credible tells us much about how they constructed the notion of propriety and public fitness, and the contribution made by bodily and sartorial control in general, and the wig in particular. In a less dramatic but equally informative account, the diarist James Boswell (1740–1795) reported having his wig stolen while sharing a room at an inn. He described himself as 'an object of laughter', and without a wig felt himself barred from polite society.[45] It was for similar reasons that Jonathan Swift – swimming to cool off in the hot June weather that he found so extremely trying – covered his shaven head, even in the water. He borrowed a napkin from his landlady for the purpose, though unfortunately as he ducked down to get wet 'the napkin fell off and is lost, and I have that to pay for'. The next day Swift went in again, but this time 'I dived to dip my head, and held my cap on with both my hands'.[46]

Although generating widespread cultural agreement as to their gendering, their social importance, and the consequences if ineptly managed, wigs were not a monolithic item of dress (Fig. 3.4). Fashions changed over time, and different styles were inflected with different meanings and varied greatly in cost. According to hairdresser James Stewart, 'All conditions of men were distinguished by the cut of the wig.'[47] Allowing for a certain degree of professional enthusiasm on Stewart's part, his summation of the wig as a carrier of social information is accurate. Woodforde, for instance, bought a variety of styles – 'a brown Six bob Wigg', a 'feather-top Wigg', an 'Elastic Wigg' that pleased him so much he immediately ordered another, and a new wig which 'is a more fashionable one than my old ones, a curled one'.[48] He makes mention, too, of giving his brother a grey wig that had belonged to their father, but he did look droll in it, says Woodforde.[49] These sorts of comments reveal that tastes changed, and that styles that might be considered appropriate at one point or for one individual might be peculiar or unfitting when transposed to a different time or head.

Figure 3.4 'Wigs', coloured etching published by Matthew Darly, 1773. Wellcome Library, London. Library reference no. ICV No 20220. Print caricaturing different types of wigs and wearers.

Both Woodforde and Swift also made distinction between everyday wigs and those they kept for best. The latter perpetually changed in and out of his company clothes as the occasion merited, for this purpose keeping 'my best gown and periwig' with a friend in the city, so as to save them from getting soiled on his walk to and from his Chelsea lodgings.[50] Wigs, then, marked out a broad category of manliness, though within these boundaries there were many variations on the type of bewigged masculinity enacted. Along with beginning to shave, wearing a first wig must therefore have constituted a significant achievement in a youth's passage to a gendered maturity. It is noteworthy that when James Woodforde first left home for Oxford as an undergraduate, he took with him two wigs and also a pair of curling tongs for styling them.[51]

These curling tongs show that the physical condition of wigs was subject to change. Far from its being merely bought, worn and discarded, the purchase of a wig instead involved its owner in a cycle of maintenance.[52] A wig required regular combing, re-curling and styling either by the wearer, a servant, or a barber/wigmaker – Pepys called it keeping his wigs 'spruce'.[53] A wig might also need to be mended or adapted to accommodate changing fashions and owner requirements; Woodforde several times recorded sums of money disbursed for this purpose. Like other garments, wigs participated in male economies of reuse, either materialising the differential status of relationships and the reciprocity of gift and obligation (as in Woodforde's habit of giving away his old wigs to various men further down the social ranks, from his impecunious brother to an

Oxford oysterman), or fracturing such relationships when wigs were stolen (as James Boswell found when his wig was taken by a fellow traveller with whom he shared his inn room). Such reuse, of course, shows wigs to have been financially, as well as socially valuable; Marica Pointon has identified them as perhaps the most expensive item of clothing a gentleman owned.[54]

Despite these many demands, there were various practical advantages to wig-wearing. While money and time did need to be spent on their maintenance, it was easier for a wearer to do this than to sit for long periods to have his own hair similarly cleansed, combed and dressed. Furthermore, wigs were warm, which for much of the year in eighteenth-century Europe might be counted as a definite benefit. Wigs also interestingly levelled the playing field of physiological inequality, ironing out differences in age and the disadvantages of thinning hair and male pattern baldness. And ironic though it might seem when wigs were commonly powdered, the man who wore one need feel neither concern at his own greying locks, nor that he was disadvantaged by hair of any other undesirable shade, such as red.[55]

The final point about wigs is that their status is unclear. Owned by the wearer yet usually made from hair belonging to another, they are neither quite garment nor body part – subject or object – existing instead in some ontological no-man's land. Although scholars have fruitfully canvassed this for what it can tell us about early modern understandings and anxieties,[56] such concerns did not necessarily trouble individual eighteenth-century wig-wearers. Perhaps in a society in which service and slavery were commonplace, and in which authority dealt leniently with body snatching (tacitly supporting the supply of corpses for anatomising regardless of public horror at the practice), concerns about objectification and the sale of body parts were less acute. Moreover, it has to be said that when it comes to hair, such ideas do not unduly trouble the modern world, real hair extensions being considered superior, and costing more, than synthetic alternatives. Likewise, in the eighteenth century the best wigs were made from human hair, the poorer ones from animal, and for the former, there was a trajectory of desirability of different qualities and grades. Regardless of the provenance of the hair however, as far as the wearer was concerned, once a wig was purchased it became his property, and I have found no evidence to suggest that individuals were troubled by its origins. Moreover, given that there was generally no way for a wearer to trace the source of his wig's hair, and that it was in all probability crafted from the products of many different heads, such a concern was all but meaningless. As R. Campbell in *The London Tradesman* (1747) explained:

The Hair-Merchant is the principal Tradesman the Wig-Maker deals with; he is furnished by him with Hair, ready picked, dressed, and curled, for weaving. The Hair-Merchant buys Hair of those who go up and down the Country of *England* to procure it, and imports some from abroad; then sorts it into Parcels, according to its Colour and Fineness; employs Pickers, to pick the Black from the White, and the Dead from Live Hair, and Hands to mix it into proper Shades of Colour, and curl it, which is done by rolling it up on Pipes and baking it in the Oven. They have a Method of dying Hair black, and bleaching other Hair white, of putting off Horse and Goat Hair for Human Hair, and many other Tricks peculiar to their Trade.[57]

According to Campbell's account, therefore, by the time the hair was sewn into the foundation of the wig, any ghostly subjectivity it may once have possessed had been exorcised by the processes of manufacture. The only exception of which I am aware is found in Pepys's diary, in a well-known passage where he worries that his new wig might be a carrier of the plague. 'And it is a wonder', he muses, 'what will be the fashion after the plague is done as to periwigs, for nobody will dare to buy any haire for fear of the infection – that it had been cut off of the heads of people dead of the plague'.[58] Although in the eighteenth century imported hair was quarantined for this reason,[59] it must be remembered that in this respect wigs were no different from other items of apparel, which had long been feared as carriers of contagion and in outbreaks of plague were the target of medical advice and government directive regarding fumigation or incineration.[60]

However, although for all three of our diarists the purchase of false hair conferred ownership and Pepys's interest in its provenance was motivated only by health concerns, the objectified nature of the wig did, in a subtle way, have an impact on the identity of its wearer. This becomes clearer by looking at Woodforde's account of meeting with an old acquaintance whom he had not seen for some time. The encounter happened in 1789, when wigs were falling from favour and increasingly worn only by the professions, the conservative and the unfashionable – by just such a person as was by this stage the aging James Woodforde. Seeing his former acquaintance, Mr Dalton, Woodforde notes that Dalton no longer wears a wig, and because of this Woodforde did not recognise him: 'I did not know Old Mr. Dalton at first as he now wears *his* Hair.'[61] The situation in which a man looks less like 'himself' when he wears his own, rather than someone else's hair, surely complicates our notion of an authentic self.

After the day's social demands – which, as we have seen, in Swift's case meant changing in and out of his best wig as he judged an occasion merited – the off-duty nature of the evening domestic space meant that for relaxation and comfort a gentleman would remove his wig. Having returned it to the wig stand, in its place he would then, for warmth and propriety, put on a cap. A fashion grounded entirely in the material and social consequences of the shaven scalp, a cap kept a bald or close-cropped head covered from the cold and society's view. On retiring for the night, this substantial cap, perhaps made from velvet or fur-trimmed like two that belonged to Swift,[62] was replaced by a linen variety for sleeping. And as Samuel Pepys so often wrote at the close of his diary entries, 'and so to bed'.

Conclusion

We have seen the importance of hair removal to the performance of eighteenth-century masculinity, but have also found that as a material practice it could not be achieved casually. On the contrary, it required time, resources and bodily discipline, and if badly or inadequately done, left a man physically and socially discomforted. Although advice and grooming tools were exchanged within male friendship circles, the realm of barbering was not as exclusively masculine as might be expected. Like depilation, the wearing of a wig – or for some, hair styled to look like a wig – was a social necessity. This garment of hair offered the wearer styling choices, the connotations of which were readily appreciated by contemporaries, and as with shaving, a gauche performance undermined a wearer's social acceptability.

My approach to this investigation of hair care has been informed by certain theoretical assumptions that underlie my work as a dress historian.[63] Within dress history it is presumed that clothing has meaning. For both wearers and viewers, dress prompts emotional and aesthetic responses and communicates information and ideas. But while meaning can be 'read' from different garments and their juxtapositions, it is not inherent. On the contrary, how a garment is perceived varies according to who is wearing it, how it is worn, in what context it appears, and also in which historical moment. So while the meaning of dress is potent, it is also fleeting and unstable. What is inherent to clothes, however – and this is the second point that I wish to highlight – is their material properties. Garments have weight, colour, texture, volume and sound. These qualities impact on wearers and viewers, and contribute to the interpretation of a garment's meaning, although the interpretations can, of course, be multiple and contradictory.

The next point that follows is that garments have agency. Their materiality helps configure our lives, both predisposing individuals towards certain congruent movements and behaviours, and patterning social interactions. Their temporal demands (the effort and labour required to acquire clothing, wear it, launder and look after it) can be a significant part of lived experience, and the effect of dress on the realms of thought and feeling comes quickly into focus if we consider, for example, the profound feelings of discomfort caused by wearing the 'wrong' thing. We have seen this very powerfully evidenced in the demands depilation made on Pepys, Swift and Woodforde: they had to invest time, money and effort in the performance of shaving; their desire for a smooth facial appearance was modified by the difficulties that this involved; and all three described the emotional discomfort caused by an overgrowth of stubble.

The fourth point is that identities are performed. Our multiple aspects of self, whether age, ethnicity, gender or anything else, are understood by others and ourselves through the practices of everyday life – that is, through engaging with material culture. Such performances do not just disclose identities, they also help construct them. We are, then, simultaneously articulated and constituted through engagements with the materiality of the surrounding world. I am not suggesting that there is nothing beyond this performance. Rather, in the debate between the either/or of essentialist and relativist understandings, I adopt not so much a middle position as a mutual one, heeding the call of archaeologist Nicole Boivin, who urges that the humanities take the intellectual, material and biological into account. As she cogently writes, 'mind and matter, and form and substance continually bring each other into being'.[64] For Pepys, Swift and Woodforde, therefore, shaving every two or three days was part of their identity – it was an important contribution to creating a masculine and genteel persona. Similarly, their choice of a wig and the way they wore it played a part in who they felt themselves to be and in how others perceived them. This is revealed by something Pepys wrote in his diary after a shopping expedition to a wig-makers: 'there bought me two periwigs, might fine; endeed, too fine I thought for me; but he persuaded me'.[65]

The last thing I want to note is that owing to its intimate relationship with its wearers, dress is an especially privileged site for exploring this performance of identity. Perhaps more than any other aspect of material culture, clothes configure our physical and social personae, and, in becoming imbued with traces of their wearers, stand as proxy for the self. Finally, and more specifically to this chapter, hair stands in an even more potent position.[66] Like other forms of body modification it challenges the distinction between body and dress; in the case of wigs and extensions made from other people's hair, it also undermines the dichotomy between subject and object, and self and other. As Woodforde reflected to himself, 'I did not know Old Mr. Dalton at first as he now wears his Hair.'

Notes

1. R. Latham and W. Matthews (eds), *The Diary of Samuel Pepys*, 11 vols (London: Bell, 1970–1983) [hereafter *Diary*], VII, p. 288.
2. V. Kelley, 'Time, Wear and Maintenance: the Afterlife of Things', in Anne Gerritsen and Giorgio Riello (eds), *Writing Material Culture* (London: Bloomsbury, 2015), pp. 191–197, at p. 196.
3. M. Immergut, 'Manscaping: the Tangle of Nature, Culture, and Male Body Hair', in L. J. Moore and M. Kosut (eds), *The Body Reader* (New York: New York University Press, 2010), p. 287.
4. W. Fisher, *Materializing Gender in Early Modern English Literature and Culture* (Cambridge: Cambridge University Press, 2006), ch. 3.
5. Note though that some men wore thin, narrow moustaches, such as pictured in the portraits of Charles II in this period.
6. D. October, 'The Big Shave: Modernity and Fashions in Men's Facial Hair', in G. Biddle-Perry and S. Cheang (eds), *Hair: Styling, Culture and Fashion* (Oxford: Berg, 2008), p. 67.
7. A. Withey, 'Shaving and Masculinity in Eighteenth-Century Britain', *Journal for Eighteenth-Century Studies*, 36 (2013), pp. 225–243. Though it has to be said that the technological developments of which Withey writes post-date the demise of beards by nearly a century, and so while pertinent to the rise in self-shaving, their relevance as an explanatory model for fashionable change is in this respect compromised.
8. *Diary*, III, p. 91.
9. B. Squire, *Superfluous Hair and the Means of Removing It* (London: Churchill, 1893), pp. 49–50.
10. *Diary*, III, pp. 96–97.
11. *Diary*, III, p. 196.
12. *Diary*, V, p. 6.
13. *Diary*, V, p. 29.
14. For further information about the technical equipment required for shaving, see J. Stevens Cox, *An Illustrated Dictionary of Hairdressing and Wigmaking*, rev. edn (London: Batsford, 1989), *s.v.* hone, strap, strop, and related entries.

15. Unless otherwise stated, notes refer to the editions of the diaries published by the Parson Woodforde Society (with no place of publication), edited by R. L. Winstanley or P. Jameson. Those cited are:
The Ansford Diary of James Woodforde, Volume 2: *1764–1765* (1979) [hereafter Vol. 2];
The Ansford Diary of James Woodforde, Volume 3: *1766–1771* (1985) [hereafter Vol. 3];
The Ansford Diary of James Woodforde, Volume 4: *1769–1771* (1986) [hereafter Vol. 4];
The Ansford Diary of James Woodforde, Volume 5: *1772–1773* (1988) [hereafter Vol. 5];
The Oxford and Somerset Diary of James Woodforde, *1774–1775* (1989) [hereafter Vol. 6];
James Woodforde: Diary of the First Six Norfolk Years 1776–1781, Volume 1: *1776–1777* (1981) [hereafter Vol. 7]; *James Woodforde: Diary of the First Six Norfolk Years 1776–1781*, Volume 2: *1778–1779* (1983) [hereafter Vol. 8]; *The Diary of James Woodforde*, Volume 11: *1785–1787* (1999) [hereafter Vol. 11]; *The Diary of James Woodforde*, Volume 12: *1788–1790* (2001) [hereafter Vol. 12]; *The Diary of James Woodforde*, Volume 13: *1791–1793* (2003) [hereafter Vol. 13]; *The Diary of James Woodforde*, Volume 14: *1794–1795* (2004) [hereafter Vol. 14]. The quote is taken from Vol. 4, p. 21.

16. E.g., W. Andrews, *At the Sign of the Barber's Pole: Studies in Hirsute History* (1904; repr. Gloucester: Dodo Press), pp. 15–17; R. W. Proctor, *The Barber's Shop* (Manchester: Thomas Dinham, 1856), pp. 22–23, 83–85; Theologos, *Shaving: A Breach of the Sabbath* (London, 1860).

17. H. Williams (ed.), *Journal to Stella*, 2 vols (Oxford: Blackwell, 1974), I, pp. 13, 144, 223, 326, 355.

18. H. Williams (ed.), *The Correspondence of Jonathan Swift*, 5 vols (Oxford: Clarendon Press, 1963), III, p. 89.

19. W. N. Hargreaves-Mawdsley (ed.), *Woodforde at Oxford 1759–1776*, Oxford Historical Society, n.s. 21 (1969), p. 87.

20. La Fountaine, *A brief collection of many rare secrets ... very necessary for all sorts of people* (1650), sig. Br.

21. 'A Discourse on Barbers', *The Englishman's Magazine*, 1 (1852), p. 48.

22. Withey, 'Shaving and Masculinity', p. 233.

23. Vol. 13, p. 35; Vol. 6, p. 186; Vol. 14, p. 172.

24. Vol. 11, p. 83.

25. Williams, *Journal to Stella*, I, p. 155. Note that this was the same Charles Ford who later sent Swift some razors.

26. *Diary*, VIII, p. 247.

27. *Diary*, I, p. 298.

28. For example, see from the V&A Museum: Gentleman's toilet set, 1640–1650, museum no. 7201:1 to 20-1877 (available at: http://collections.vam.ac.uk/item/O10974/gentlemans-toilet-set-unknown/) compared with Dressing case, c. 1850, museum no. AP.621:1 to 21 (available at: http://collections.vam.ac.uk/item/O77824/napoleon-napoleon-dressing-case-wilson-walker-co/), both accessed 17 January 2014.

29. Most importantly, M. Pelling, 'Appearance and Reality: Barber-surgeons, the Body and Disease', in A. L. Beier and R. Finlay (eds), *London 1500–1700: The Making of a Metropolis* (London: Longman, 1986), pp. 82–110; and M. Pelling, *The Common Lot: Sickness, Medical Occupations and the Urban Poor in Early Modern England* (London: Longman, 1998), pp. 203–229.

30. *Diary*, I, p. 90; IV, p. 237; V, p. 352.

31. Hargreaves-Mawdsley, *Woodforde at Oxford*, p. 105.

32. C. Bridenbaugh (ed.), *Gentleman's Progress: The Itinerarium of Dr. Alexander Hamilton* (Chapel Hill: University of North Carolina Press, 1948), pp. 18, 196.

33. Ibid., p. 192.
34. J. A. Leo Lemay and P. M. Zall (eds), *Benjamin Franklin's Autobiography* (New York: W. W. Norton, 1986), p. 108, n. 9.
35. D. Evenden, 'Gender Difference in the Licensing and Practice of Female and Male Surgeons in Early Modern England', *Medical History*, 42 (1998), pp. 194–216, at pp. 196–197, 201; D. Willen, 'Guildswomen in the City of York, 1560–1700', *The Historian*, 43 (1984), pp. 204–228, at p. 217. In addition, S. Cavallo has suggested that in early modern Italy the involvement of women in those trades that dealt with the care of the body, including barber-surgeons, was much greater than has been recognized: *Artisans of the Body in Early Modern Italy: Identities, Families and Masculinities* (Manchester: Manchester University Press, 2007), pp. 160–180.
36. I. Murray, 'The London Barbers', in Ian Burn (ed.), *The Company of Barbers and Surgeons* (London: Ferrand Press, 2000), p. 77.
37. J. T. Smith, *Ancient Topography of London* (London, 1815), p. 38. Also Andrews, *At the Sign of the Barber's Pole*, pp. 11–12.
38. Vol. 11, p. 145. Note that there was also a fluidity in naming in this period, as the emergent profession of 'hairdresser' overlapped with the traditio
39. Vol. 2, p. 105.
40. Vol. 3, p. 116.
41. Hargreaves-Mawdsley, *Woodforde at Oxford*, pp. 35 (wig as 'him')
42. D. Bond (ed.), *The Spectator*, 5 vols (Oxford: Clarendon pp. 91–92.
43. On the macaroni, see A. Rauser, 'Hair, Authenticity, and the Self *Eighteenth-Century Studies*, 38 (2004), pp. 101–117; P. M Masculinities', *Fashion Theory*, 4 (2000), pp. 373–403.
44. J. Taylor, *Records of My Life*, 2 vols (London, 1832), I, p. 49.
45. Quoted in M. Pointon, *Hanging the Head: Portraiture and So Eighteenth-Century England* (New Haven, CT, and London: Yale University Press, 1993), p. 120.
46. Williams, *Journal to Stella*, I, pp. 285–286, 287.
47. J. Stewart, *Plocacosmos: or, the Whole Art of Hair Dressing* (London, 1782), p. 204.
48. Vol. 3, p. 83; Hargreaves-Mawdsley, *Woodforde at Oxford*, pp. 111, 112; Vol. 7, pp. 81, 89; Vol. 6, p. 8.
49. Vol. 5, p. 171.
50. Williams, *Journal to Stella*, I, pp. 252, 256, 256–257, 274, 283.
51. J. Beresford (ed.), *The Diary of a Country Parson: The Reverend James Woodforde 1758–1781* (London: Oxford University Press, 1924), p. 11.
52. M. K. Gayne, 'Illicit Wigmaking in Eighteenth-Century Paris', *Eighteenth-Century Studies*, 38 (2004), pp. 119–137.
53. *Diary*, IX, 217.
54. Pointon, *Hanging the Head*, p. 120.
55. The enduring unpopularity of grey and red hair is evidenced by newspaper advertising for commercial products specifically to alter these colours: for example, the 'celebrated hair dye' invented by perfumer James Wittman, 'for changing red or grey hair to a fine brown, black, or other shades' (*Star*, 11 May 1795); or a liquid sold by another perfumer called Sangwine who had a shop in the Strand, which 'in one hour, will, without injury, dye red or grey hair of a glossy brown or black' (*Gazetteer and New Daily Advertiser*, 19 September 1772).
56. Pointon, *Hanging the Head*, pp. 107–137; L. Festa, 'Personal Effects: Wigs and Possessive Individualism in the Long Eighteenth Century', *Eighteenth-Century Life*, 29 (2005), pp. 47–90.

57. R. Campbell, *The London Tradesman* (London, 1747), pp. 205–206.

58. *Diary*, VI, p. 210. Pointon also looks at the wig as carrier of infection, *Hanging the Head*, p. 121.

59. According to Stewart, *Plocacosmos*, p. 302.

60. See *Orders, thought meete by her Maiestie, and her priuie Councell, to be executed throughout the counties of this realme ... infected with the plague* (London, 1578).

61. Vol. 12, p. 160. Emphasis mine.

62. Williams, *Journal to Stella*, I, p. 85.

63. For overviews and an introduction to the whole field of fashion studies and fashion history, see: L. Welters and A. Lillethun (eds), *The Fashion Reader*, 2nd edn (Oxford: Berg, 2011); and G. Riello and P. McNeil (eds), *The Fashion History Reader: Global Perspectives* (London and New York: Routledge, 2010).

64. N. Boivin, *Material Cultures, Material Minds: The Impact of Things on Human Thought, Society, and Evolution* (Cambridge: Cambridge University Press, 2008), p. 23.

65. *Diary*, VIII, p. 136.

66. There is a wide and multi-disciplinary literature on hair. A good starting point is Biddle-Perry and Cheang (eds), *Hair*, esp. pp. 3–12, 243–254.

4

Craftsmen in Common: Objects, Skills and Masculinity in the Eighteenth and Nineteenth Centuries[1]

Karen Harvey

What was the nature of British men's engagements with material culture during the late eighteenth century? This seems an appropriate way to begin an exploration of men and objects, and one in a book about gender and material culture. Important scholarly work in this area has given comparatively little attention to men.[2] Within the history of consumption, for example, masculinity was sometimes hidden by the 'historical and scholarly feminisation of consumer culture, shopping, and fashion'.[3] In the case of the early modern period, one reason for this is the importance of the household in processes of consumption and the apparent agency of women in domestic space.[4] Only recently have historians begun to look more carefully at men's important roles in the household, including their interest in and control of certain forms of consumption and their more general investment in the material culture of the house.[5] As a result, historians now look beneath the truism that 'Western society links shopping and women as natural practice', examining the decision-making process at the point of purchase or the accounting practices (and marital relationships) that underpinned the act of commercial consumption.[6] As the introduction to this volume, and the contributions by Houlbrook, Smith and Vincent, make clear, historical work now charts men's frequent and regular consumption of all manner of things. For the period covered by this chapter, as important as the finding that men consumed and owned a great range of things, is the fact that material culture and the role of consumer and owner was an important component of masculine identities.[7] As property owners, as overall managers of the household but also as individuals who took visceral pleasure in things of value, memory and beauty, men engaged with material culture throughout their lives.

These findings about men and material culture need to be integrated more fully into our general understanding of masculinity in this period, and particularly with regards to the clear changes in masculine identity that many historians have located from the second half of the eighteenth century. These changes involved a shift away from traditional codes of civility, politeness and Civic Republicanism based on moderation and restraint that were closely linked to Britain's development as a commercialising nation. In contrast, rougher, tougher and more taciturn styles of manhood became more important. This seems to have taken place at the same time as late seventeenth-century models of politeness were joined by a discourse of sensibility and feeling from the 1760s.[8] Self-control and independence were forever important to men, but military defeats and political crises in mid-century Britain provided the context for a newly invigorated emphasis on moral and physical strength and, in art and culture, a model of 'heroic masculinity'.[9] While the emphasis on cultural styles or codes (such as 'politeness' or 'sensibility') might suggest that this general shift affected only the educated and elite, it does accord with what we know about changes to masculinity caused by other widespread transformations. Socio-economic changes during this period affected men of any social status. A closer association between masculinity and work or occupational identity was embedded in the increasingly important idea of the 'breadwinner'; the growing coherence and visibility of a working-class identity were part of this same process. As Matthew McCormack points out, 'Occupation became more important to male identities, as economic activity became increasingly identified with the political and civil public domain.'[10] I am interested in a question that arises from this brief survey of these two bodies of work on men and material culture and on changing masculinities: how did a shift away from dominant codes of masculinity that were linked to a commercial elite and a growing focus on men as workers relate to men's ongoing engagement with material culture as consumers? Did this increasingly close identification of men as workers and *producers*, limit men's engagement with material culture as *consumers*?

A collection of ceramics held by Museums Sheffield provides one example of the kind of material object associated with and owned by men in the late eighteenth and early nineteenth centuries. They are a group of ceramic vessels, inscribed with the owners' names, and decorated in distinctive ways, dating from 1781 to 1803. All of the objects are now held by Museums Sheffield in their decorative art collection. They were all made in or near to Sheffield and several – possibly all – were donated to the museum in the early to mid-twentieth century by a descendant of the original owner. Although these vessels are not associated with famous individuals (either owners, makers or designers) they enable considerable insight into male consumption and masculine identity. In this chapter I will use these objects – ceramic vessels with personalised decoration, belonging to men – as a distinctive entry point to the historical debates discussed above and in particular as a way to explore men's identities as both consumers and producers.

Happily, students of material culture have at their disposal well-tried methods that enable precisely this examination of both production and consumption. On the one hand, the method of examining the life-cycle of the object looks at the generic narrative of an object. On the other hand, an object-biography approach focuses on a specific and individual object and its particular trajectory.[11] The sources for the objects discussed do not easily allow for the latter approach, but because I wish to focus on particular objects – and in this case on objects that are unique and attach to identifiable people – I will combine the two approaches, however imperfectly.[12] Objects can provide unique answers to historical questions and in this case I hope to show that objects articulate information about material culture, masculine identity and work. On the one hand, I am using the material record to help address an apparent tension between different bodies of historiography about masculinity. On the other hand, using objects in the contexts of these historical debates generates new interpretations of those objects. In focusing on objects as both a source and a topic, my analysis will take the form of an object-centred (rather than an object-driven) approach. In other words, while I begin with the material culture, a rounded analysis must situate these objects alongside other sources if it is going to chart the biography of these objects and reconstruct a general historical context for them.[13] In this way the chapter centres on objects in a museum collection but draws upon documents such as parish registers (for biographical information on owners), depictions of work in newspapers and other written sources, and select documentary and commemorative visual representations of workers in portraits and townscapes.

With regards to material culture, writes Glenn Adamson, 'disappearance is the norm, and preservation is the exception'.[14] Preservation is more likely for objects that are particularly fine examples of style or technique or that belonged to the wealthy. The survival of these objects is extraordinary because they fit into neither category. These objects are rare and unusual today, but they were widely available, everyday items in the eighteenth and nineteenth centuries. Biographical evidence discussed below, and their survival in some numbers, suggests that they were rather common objects. Moreover, their individuality (each one has a slightly different design) offers the historian the unrivalled opportunity to situate them in the specific context of owner, time and place. They were donated to Sheffield's city collections not because of their artistic quality but because of their historic connection to the city of Sheffield. In focusing on five of these objects, I will consider the elements of form, decoration and materials; I will also supplement this analysis of the objects with supporting written documents (some directly linked to the objects and some more contextual). Combining these sources allows us to consider men's engagements with objects as both producers and consumers. In contrast to the subject of decorative objects, domestic space and women that dominates histories of material culture, and which Frank Trentmann mischievously characterises as 'soft', this chapter deals with the 'hard' stuff of objects, politics, production and masculinity.[15]

Hard Objects

Let us begin with the objects. The first (Fig. 4.1) is a large blue and white painted jug decorated with 'Joseph Gallemore 1781'.[16] The central medallion beneath the lip is bordered with a simple pattern, but either side there are two

Figure 4.1   'Joseph Gallemore 1781' jug, glazed earthenware, probably Leeds pottery.
Museums Sheffield: K.1931.1.

Chinoiserie landscape scenes each containing a simple building and delicately painted trees. Clear information on 'Gallemore' is difficult to find, partly because the spelling of names was often inconsistent in the records. A Joseph Gallimore, son of the case maker Samuel, was apprenticed to Revitt William in 1809 for seven years (aged twenty-seven).[17] The 1841 Census lists this Gallimore as a silversmith living to the north of Sheffield, aged fifty-seven.[18] The museum catalogue information, however, says he was a whitesmith (a polisher or finisher of metal goods) and son of John Gallimore, whitesmith and tool-maker. It also states that the jug was given as a prize at a berry show, 'Joseph Gallimore having exhibited the largest gooseberries'. The jug was presented by a descendant of Gallimore and this information may be correct. However, the catalogue also records the indenture for Joseph Gallimore – the contract that would have bound him as an apprentice to a trade – dated 15 September 1798 (now missing).[19] An indenture of this date would be very late for someone who exhibited winning gooseberries in 1781.

The second object is a two-handled cup (or 'loving cup') inscribed 'Hugh Gosling 1795' (Fig. 4.2).[20] The object was made locally in a south Yorkshire pottery (possibly the Don or Rawmarsh, according to the curators). Brown circles around the base and rim, coordinated details on the handles and a burnished red pattern inside the lip of the cup unify the object. A complementary colour scheme has been used on the two sides: the green, red and pink foliage that frames 'Hugh Gosling' and a stylised oriental figure standing in a simple landscape framed with over-sized foliage (Fig. 4.3). Presented by a descendant, the cup has a museum catalogue description that includes a newspaper announcement of Gosling's death, aged eighty-eight, in 1861 or 1862, in which

Figure 4.2 Front of 'Hugh Gosling 1795' loving cup, glazed earthenware, probably Don pottery. Museums Sheffield: K.1929-113.

he is described as 'the oldest and last workman of the late Joshua Walker, Esq. Rotherham forge'.[21] A forge was the place where metal was heated and then shaped with a hammer or mould. Another paper reported that he died on 7 November 1861, aged eighty-seven, in Attercliffe near central Sheffield.[22] Indeed, the same notice was included in the next day's issue of that newspaper.[23] Again, the written documents verify the provenance information in the museum catalogue and help substantiate the biography of the owner. In the 1851 Census the seventy-seven-year-old forge-man Gosling was living in a household headed by his daughter Martha and also including his granddaughter Martha (aged eight). By 1861, just months before his death, Gosling was living alone, now listed as 'Retired Forgeman'. This loving cup was to mark the twenty-first birthday of this young man and future forge worker.

Figure 4.3 Rear of 'Hugh Gosling 1795' loving cup, glazed earthenware, probably Don pottery. Museums Sheffield: K.1929-113.

Figure 4.4 Front of 'William and Jane White, Eckington. 1801' loving cup, glazed earthenware, Yorkshire pottery. Museums Sheffield: K.1951.7.

The designs on the third object, also a loving cup, are a set of builder's tools, painted in a muddy brown, symmetrically arranged and including mallets, pointed trowels, small axes, right-angle rulers and a claw hammer.[24] The rest of the decoration is colourful, dominated by green, blue and bright mustard. The painter has misjudged the placement of some of this decoration, though (Fig. 4.4). On the front, the lettering is clear, 'William and Jane White, Eckington. 1801', but 1801 is not centred. On the back, the downward strokes of the green and blue border crowd in on the tools below; it looks as if the tools were painted first, centrally placed on the vertical axis, and the border was squeezed in afterwards (Fig. 4.5). Eckington is a village twelve kilometres

Figure 4.5 Rear of 'William and Jane White, Eckington. 1801' loving cup, glazed earthenware, Yorkshire pottery. Museums Sheffield: K.1951.7.

Figure 4.6   'Benjamin Allott. Grenaside, Spindle-Maker. 1802' jug, glazed earthenware, probably Leeds Pottery. Museums Sheffield: K.1930.9.

south-east of Sheffield. We know that many rural farming households were shared enterprises and this may be why both William's and Jane's names are included.[25] Or the object may have been a wedding gift.

The fourth object is a large jug painted with the name 'Benjamin Allott', identifying Allott as a spindle-maker from 'Grenaside' and dated 1802 (Fig. 4.6).[26] A lease of 18 December 1793 shows that Allott paid a yearly rent of ten shillings for a piece of land in the village of Grenoside, north of Sheffield, and upon which he 'hath lately erected several Messauges or Tenements and Buildings'.[27] Allott's jug shows the wooden and metal tools used to make spindles, the parts that take up the thread in hand or machine spinning. These pictorial elements and the lettering are painted in a drab brown; the objects are painted simply and flatly. The border around the neck of the jug is colourful and the flowers on either side of the jug are particularly ornate and detailed. This juxtaposition in colour and style is present on another, very similar, object.

Benjamin Wadsworth's creamware jug, the final object, was manufactured in the local Don pottery and dated 1803 (Fig. 4.7).[28] Wadsworth was a farmer and a woodman and the two tools illustrated on the jug are a bill-hook (used for pruning) and an axe (for chopping). The donor of the object, the granddaughter of Wadsworth, reported in the early twentieth century that Wadsworth was born around 1782 and had lived in a village twelve kilometres north of Sheffield (close to Barnsley) called Stainborough.[29] Census records for 1841 and 1851 show a Benjamin Wadsworth, farmer, living first in Silkstone, near to Stainborough, and then in Ecclesfield, with a birth date of c. 1787, thus substantiating the provenance given by the object's donor. Though the top

Figure 4.7   'Benjamin Wadsworth. 1803' jug, glazed earthenware, probably Don pottery.
Museums Sheffield: K.1931.39.

rim and some of the painted decoration of the jug is now chipped, the quality of the floral decoration is still evident. The top of the jug is decorated
with a plum and grey repeating pattern, while the body of the jug is a riot of
colour with the central motif of a mid-pink rose or peony flanked by daisies
and cornflowers.

Each of these objects is unique. The decorative schemes are distinctive. The
shapes and sizes also differ. They were made at different dates and for men in
a range of trades: two farmers, a man who made objects in wood and another
in metal, and finally a man who worked in the heavy metal trades. Yet we can
treat these objects as a group that represents a particular object type: there are
many other objects surviving which have names and symbols of workers on their
sides and we can speculate that a great many more have not survived. They are
white-bodied and glazed ceramic objects rather than highly fashionable and
more expensive porcelain. They take the traditional forms of round-bodied vessels. Their decoration is confidently and well applied though it is not particularly
fine or high end. The documentary sources for each object are very limited and
treating them as a group is arguably the most promising way to write a rich history of them.

Men's Skills

The first feature I wish to focus on is the depiction of workers' tools. This
is a striking – and, in the context of the historiographical separation of production and consumption, surprising – feature of these nicely painted ceramic
objects. Tools were highly articulate objects themselves. One newspaper report

from 1793 gives a glimpse of how important they were in public performances of labouring identity. When a new navigation canal was first laid out near Wakefield, the procession of Gentlemen, Proprietors and the Town's Constable were accompanied by 'a great number of workmen, each carrying some implement of his profession'. The spectacle concluded with a rousing rendition of 'Rule Britannia' and 'three times three cheers'.[30] This display of national identity suggests not just the public but the political significance of these decorative working-men's tools.

When historians have examined masculinity, class identity and the politics of material culture, they have done so mainly with a focus on consumption. For example, middling-sort urban men in the mid-eighteenth century used particular drinks and associated material culture to forge powerful fraternal identities; later, a bourgeoisie used more sombre dress to fortify their formal political power.[31] Indeed, landed political reformers during this period used the design of domestic objects to articulate their arguments about nationhood and the franchise.[32] Historians have begun to discuss the politics of the design and technology of production, underlining how these stages were part of a process of identity building, particularly with regards to national identity.[33] Social historians have long been aware that the making stage of production has also been culturally and politically freighted. E. P. Thompson's analysis of artisans' standards of living and wages, in *The Making of the English Working Class* (1980), considered how the fine gradations within these communities were shaped by the specificities of trade and the cultural value of related skills and workmanship.[34] Informed by an anthropological approach, Thompson developed this focus on culture in *Customs in Common* (1991), touching on how objects worked as symbols in public discourse.[35] Workers began to organise themselves according to 'their economic interests *as producers*, craftsmen and workers' and used objects iconographically as they performed and asserted their communal power as a trade group.[36] The ceramic objects discussed above clearly and eloquently articulate the workmanship of craftsmen. They do so, however, on the body of a fashionably decorated ceramic jug, rather than on a broadsheet, a banner or an object produced by the individual craftsman in question. Reading the iconography of the worker's tools in this material and decorative context complicates its symbolic content: these objects speak of a man's consumer as well as producer identity.

Another common feature of these objects, of course, is that they originate from the city of Sheffield and its environs. This specific local context is important in understanding the material culture and what it can tell us about male workers and identity. For Engels writing in 1845, after textiles, metalwares were the most important products of English industry; alongside Birmingham, Sheffield was a centre of metalware production and innovation. Crucible steel was invented by Huntsman, and Old Sheffield Plate by Boulsover in 1742. Rapidly, Sheffield became a major centre for both the heavy steel and the light plated and silver trades. Well known around the globe for fashionable tableware and decorative objects, Sheffield was nonetheless often described as an impolite and grimy city, remarkable for its smoky skies, noisy forges and brawny male workers. Divisions between the skills of design and the process of making were unsustainable given the physical realities of metalware production in the small workshops of eighteenth-century Sheffield where design, craft and industry merged. Sheffield was not a special case in this regard: handwork was not replaced by machines until the late nineteenth century; instead, the significant change in production during the eighteenth and early nineteenth centuries was subdivision, not the introduction of machinery.[37] Rather than an anomaly, then, Sheffield was 'a classic example' of British industrialisation and its workshop structure was not a mark of enduring traditionalism but a key feature of its modernising process.[38] These workplace practices were nevertheless linked to 'the continuity of political and cultural traditions in the making of working-class communities' that Thompson observed.[39] In the highly differentiated metal trades in eighteenth- and early nineteenth-century Sheffield it was easy to observe the complicated gradations amongst artisans and labourers that Thompson identified as characteristic of the working class until 1830.[40]

The degree to which Sheffield metal workers experienced a making of the English working class in this period has been the topic of much debate. They are thought by many historians to have experienced 'a far greater degree of independence' than labourers in factory systems.[41] And given the significance of independence to masculine identity and civic identity,[42] we might conjecture that Sheffield workers were the most manly of men. Yet the 'little mesters' or small master manufacturers were increasingly exploited by small merchants (or 'factors').[43] The economic and social consequences of this took decades to come to fruition and a clear cultural and political distinction between artisans and proletarians was probably not clearly established in Sheffield until the early twentieth century.[44] Nevertheless, Clive Behagg shows that by the second quarter of the nineteenth century power relations in small workshop trades were inequitable. Moreover, accounts of workers in different trades were being brought together in the form of a generalised language of labour – if not yet 'the working class'. This language straddled occupational boundaries while also accommodating difference: 'Thus the work experience was being universalized in terms that went beyond occupational barriers while still reinforcing specific workplace practices in individual trades.'[45]

These objects thus date precisely from this period of an emerging collective language of craftsmen's economic interests (for Thompson) and labour (for Behagg). According to John Rule 'an historically specific labour consciousness' developed that was centred specifically on skill.[46] While this property of skill had always been assumed and 'hidden', threats to the position of the artisan caused artisans to publicly articulate their skill more clearly. The 1814 repeal of the Act that had required apprenticeships (the Statute of Artificers Act of 1564) appeared to downgrade artisans' skills.[47] In Sheffield and cities like it this period of intense industrialisation took the form of a shift from the artisan-master to the small producer. In response, artisans publicly declared their value to the commonwealth, underscoring the relationship between their skills and honour and defining artisanal skill as a collective property not an individual one.[48] This was achieved partly through unionisation. In Sheffield specifically, each branch of the metal trades had its own union (not just grinders, for example, but axe grinders and saw grinders and so on).[49] The objects discussed above are fascinating in this context. They show the distinctiveness of workers' tools operating

in an increasingly industrialized society, masculinity is proven by craft as shorthand for specific artisanal skills; their varied designs and individuality focus on distinctive occupational identities, with the vessels decorated to reflect the trade of a forge-man, woodman or spindle-maker. However, while the tools are specific, they employ a similar lexicon or format that suggests a more generalised collective identity of craftsman. And this lexicon of tools was a distinctively male language, just as the articulation of the artisan's skills emphasised 'a male "property"'.[50] The universalising of work that took place in this period was therefore thoroughly gendered. While the economic and political independence of the artisan – the little master or 'mester' – may have been increasingly tenuous, there was a defensive consolidation of the myth of the independent male artisan during the early nineteenth century, and one that would have a detrimental effect on women's work opportunities.[51]

Hard Men

The third common feature of these objects that I wish to discuss is the decorative floral design. These are softly and loosely painted flowers rather than careful botanical designs, and in that sense are typical of English ceramics from the second half of the eighteenth century.[52] It might be presumed that floral themes are particularly 'feminine', but flowers had long been a standard decorative feature on ceramics and notably on objects that might be associated with both men and women: including mugs, jugs, snuff boxes, vases, tea and coffee pots, cups and saucers and tankards.[53] This underlines the point that Houlbrook makes in Chapter 7 of this volume, that ideas of sexual difference and gender – and their intersection with material culture – are historically specific.[54] A gendered reading of the flowers on these objects is not sustainable and other interpretations are therefore necessary. It is notable that other representations of Sheffield workers were often situated in landscapes and gardens. This is perhaps a surprising view of the city renowned for light and heavy metal industries. Sheffield was certainly renowned as a 'smoky workshop' in the bowl created by the hills and several adjoining rivers.[55] Yet while the air may have been 'almost continually thickened with the sooty exhalations', the city was also recommended as 'a modern well-built town' with clear and spacious streets.[56] A tourist of 1787 noted that while the city was 'naturally dirty from its abundant manufactures', it was 'wonderfully improved within a few years'.[57] Travellers came to marvel at the manufactories and Sheffielders were proud of this; as a report in one local newspaper commented on the visit of Prince Poniatowski of Poland in 1790, 'He is making a tour of England, to see whatever is rare or curious and of course our manufactories arrested a share of his notice.'[58] The Sheffield cutler working in these central grimy workshops was even presented as a model of healthy living. The several editions of William Buchan's *Domestic Medicine* (first published in 1769) reported that in Sheffield, 'where the great iron manufacture is carried on, there is hardly a journeyman cutler who does not possess a piece of ground, which he cultivates as a garden'. While it may, Buchan, said, 'seem romantic to recommend gardening to manufacturers in great towns', the cutlers in Sheffield showed that it could be done, and that the benefits of working outdoors and eating freshly grown produce were available to all.[59] For Buchan,

Sheffield mechanics were a great example of why these workers should live in the country; put simply, they 'are far more happy'.[60] Archaeological evidence suggests that while domestic housing was located very close to workplaces (or in fact shared the same space), in some areas occupancy rates compared very favourably with those of other large cities.[61]

The earliest images of workers display not the small central workshops or the workers' gardens, but a more natural landscape. These are picturesque scenes, even 'romantic' (using Buchan's word). They naturalise the industrial landscape, subsumed within the natural world around it. The sketch of the Thorncliffe Iron Works (Fig. 4.8), for example, blends the manufactory with the trees and other foliage in the valley. The sketch of the Silkstone pottery (Fig. 4.9), which was located further out of the city, shows brawny workmen in a rural industrial setting. During the eighteenth century this manufactory produced a variety of objects, specialising in press-moulded objects with mottled decoration (a streaked glaze in varying shades of honey and brown), and probably producing the sorts of objects discussed earlier in this chapter.[62] Several artists were painting industrial landscape scenes at this time, including Paul Sandby and John Ingleby. Fox argues that these works reduced the power of human toil in relation to the natural environment.[63] The sketches of Sheffield workers – and the objects themselves – seem instead to allude to the coexistence of nature and industry, and man's manipulation of natural resources – wood, coal, water – in the process of manufacture.[64] This coexistence of nature and industry is vividly reflected in the combination of floral decoration and images of tools on the ceramic vessels.

Figure 4.8 Thorncliffe Iron Works, c. 1800–1850. Sheffield Archives: s00458 (Courtesy of Sheffield Archives, Sheffield City Council).

Figure 4.9   Silkstone Pottery c. 1807–1809, drawing by J. C. Nattes. Cannon Hall Museum (Courtesy of Barnsley Metropolitan Borough Council, Arts, Museums and Archives Service).

Representations of Sheffield workers were affected by other traditions, including documentary industrial scenes and Dutch genre scenes of workshops.[65] Godfrey Sykes, himself an engraver in the metal trades before becoming a painter, created several workshop scenes in the city (Fig. 4.10).[66] As in his others paintings, the worker in *The Two Grinders* (c. 1858) is attentive to the task; his hands, tools and materials are all engaged; the open door casts light on the work and reveals the rich foliage outside. It is instructive to compare these Sheffield scenes with those of Pittsburgh, another great 'steel city'. Pittsburgh was depicted through the two recurring tropes of 'the Smoky City and the Great Workshop', in which the body of the brawny male worker represented manliness and innovation but also a sense of tradition.[67] Similarly in Sheffield, 'robust artisans' operated as mythic figures.[68] Indeed, it was at this point that male labour was firmly established in the iconography of the city in the coat of arms granted to Sheffield Borough Council in 1875, which depicted Thor and Vulcan – the smiths of the Scandinavian and Greek and Roman Gods respectively – and the tools of their trade: a hammer, anvil and pincers.[69]

There are some significant differences in the way the male worker is represented in images of the two cities, however. The worker's body in Pittsburgh was invariably topless, in both image and reality, communicating simplicity, timelessness and innocence.[70] In contrast, the worker's body in Sheffield was always clothed, indicating the less established class differences in the city and the claims of Sheffield workers to artisanal status. The viewer in the picture plane

Figure 4.10   Godfrey Sykes, *The Two Grinders*, c. 1858, oil on canvas. Museums Sheffield: K.1921.28.

underlines the proud display of these noble workers. Another important difference is that while Pittsburgh workshops are stifling interior industrial scenes, the workshops of Sheffield are porous places, located in a natural landscape with verdant foliage crowding in through open doors and windows. These distinctive qualities of the Sheffield workshop scenes are significant because, while they might register the increasing influence of the Sublime and its 'brutal and primal forms of heroism' uncoupled from luxury and consumption,[71] these physically powerful but controlled workers do not conform to the excesses of heroic male bodies but offer a counterpoint to high art. These natural elements in the Sheffield scenes also provide another context for the naturalistic elements on the five objects discussed above, and further suggest how such motifs were particularly meaningful to Sheffield trades.

Conclusion

The analysis of this group of decorated ceramic vessels first examined all the available information from the material object and other sources on the makers and owners, before considering three common features of their decoration: tools, location and the natural world. I then analysed these features in the context of other written and visual sources and historical writing on masculinity, class and work. I have argued that these objects expressed men's individual and distinctive occupational identities but as part of a broader language of craftsmen in common, one rooted firmly in the specific location of Sheffield and its environs. This took place at the same time that other artisans were establishing a shared collective language as workers. In this way, I have tried to show how these consumed objects connect to men's working identities more broadly. Central to the preceding discussion is the theme of skill, and in this conclusion I want to build on my arguments about eighteenth- and nineteenth-century Sheffield to engage with the historiography and methodology on this topic.

Let us return to Godfrey Sykes' painting, *The Two Grinders* (c. 1858). One of the notable features of Sykes' paintings is his disguise of or failure to represent the actual process of making: the viewer cannot quite see the task of grinding the blade being performed in *The Two Grinders*, for example. Sykes' paintings might suggest that there is something secret about this industrial process. This disrupts the chronology given in Glenn Adamson's *The Invention of Craft* (2013), that, after 1750, mystery was explained out of craft, and writers and illustrators sought to reveal the regularity and generic nature of the skills and techniques behind made objects.[72] This was itself a way to control workers, to depersonalise them and devalue their skills.[73] Images of Sheffield workshops resist this discourse in portraying making as a process that cannot be instructed or represented but only felt or enacted. Because 'history leaves no more than the traces of skill', the tools that are wielded by the worker as an extension of his body represent artisanal skills both visually and materially.[74]

These images – and the objects displaying tools – thus reflect the endurance of what Pamela Smith terms 'embodied cognition' and 'artisanal epistemology', and that Richard Sennett calls 'material consciousness'.[75] In the eighteenth century, this concerned the mechanical arts and practical knowledge, as opposed to the liberal arts and philosophical or scientific knowledge. For some contemporaries this was an artificial distinction and historians have sought to overcome this with the concept of 'the mindful hand'.[76] The author of *Valuable Secrets concerning Arts and Trades* (1778) celebrated 'professed Mechanics' and their 'evident and real' occupations as amongst first rank 'British Artists'.[77] As Pamela Long has pointed out, 'For every craft there is a significant body of knowledge that can be "known" only by actually practising the craft with one's own hands.'[78] While these historians, like Adamson, see an increasing openness about the mechanical arts from the Renaissance onwards, this is not what descriptions of Sheffield trades suggest. For visitors, the quality of Sheffield's consumer goods was palpable. Cutlery was 'most highly finished'.[79] The newer plate work (used for candlesticks, for example) was 'of the highest perfection, and scarce inferior in pattern or polish to real silver'.[80] Observers knew that accretion of skill around an object occurred during many processes: as John Housman pointed out, 'the meanest knife passes through the hands of five cutlers, in different branches of cutlery, before it is finished'.[81] Smaller metal objects 'pass, within a short time, through some hundred hands, before they arrive to their perfection. No less than forty different hands are busied about the metal which produces a needle.'[82] But the skills of these workers proved more difficult to describe. Grinders in Sheffield were paid highly not just because the job was dangerous, but also 'owing partly to their skill, and the nicety requisite in finishing edge-tools'.[83] The word 'nicety' is a striking one to use in a section in which the author explains how fast-moving chunks of the grinder's stone could fly off and kill him (the danger has been lessened, he says, by the fixing of 'a very thick strong chain' around the stone). Nicety meant precision, but also fineness and delicacy; the word could also mean something dainty for consumption.[84] How skill became nicety was unclear, though it concerned touch as well as sight. Commenting on the different velocities of the grindstones used for different stages of grinding, the same traveller noted 'that of the finisher is such that the eye scarce sees that it moves'.[85]

These descriptions fail to convey very much at all of the experience, skill and feeling of the process of making. Authors of general books on trades and mechanics could provide little more detail on what the worker actually did in making metal or metal products. *Valuable Secrets concerning Arts and Trades* mentions the worker not once in the chapter on metal.[86] The only mention in *The Mechanic: or, A Compendium of Practical Inventions* (1825) is that the successful operation of machinery in the dry-grinding of needles required workers to give attention that 'should be constant in its action, and inseparable from the use of the machinery'.[87] Again we see the continuum between a worker's body and his tools. Indeed, watching a skilled craftsman at work reveals to the viewer the sympathetic relationship between object, tool and maker.[88] Drawing on our own material experiences is a legitimate method for historical research, particularly powerful when combined with documentary evidence.[89] Yet because skill is difficult to describe in words, written documents are not always forthcoming. The study of material culture is an intrinsically interdisciplinary endeavour and the topic of skill is certainly one area where insights from other disciplines such as psychology and social anthropology can be very helpful to the historian. Scholars in these disciplines have sought to develop approaches that avoid the division between the body on the one hand and society/culture on the other and which can therefore attend to processes of place-specific embodied learning or making. For Edward Reed, for example, embodiment and culture are interdependent: 'meaning is embodied in the *experience* of animate, sentient beings'.[90] Skills are body and place-specific: they are 'relationships among objects in special places, with highly organized understanding of the causal or dependency relationships constituting the steps of the task'.[91] Place and the environment are critical to the acquisition and execution of skill. The social anthropologist Tim Ingold also looks to avoid the apparent dichotomy of the 'biophysical and sociocultural'.[92] He describes skill in this way: 'skill is not an attribute of the individual body in isolation but of the whole system of relations constituted by the presence of the artisan in his or her environment'.[93] An important insight of this work, then, is that the process of making and its social and political meanings must be examined in the context of the environment.

This work also underscores the finding of historians that skills are not conceptual. Instead, they are 'learned *perceptually*'.[94] They depend on haptic or auditory information: the feel or sound of a file on a grindstone, for example. Reed's example is of making a bow: 'the transformation of substances often requires learning specialized exploratory strategies: the only way to know whether the shaved stick is supple enough to be used as a bow is to bend it in a specific way and feel its resilience'.[95] Crucially, the maker uses perceptual skills and information based partly on his understanding of the requirements of the finished object. To put this simply, the maker is both a producer and a consumer. This disrupts an essentially Marxist approach to objects, one which has been significant to an understanding of how people's relationships with things have changed over time. In general terms, such an approach will high-light the social and economic changes that caused the devaluing of the makers (or labour) involved in production, and a changing conception of the outputs of that production as industrial objects rather than craft objects that bear the traces of their human makers. Matthew Johnson, for example, offered a prehistory to the argument that modern capitalist society relates to objects through consumption, by showing how during the late medieval and early modern period the meanings of objects were transformed through a process of 'commodification'.[96] Instead, Ingold's insistence on the 'entanglements' between makers and things presents material culture as 'grown' rather than 'made'.[97] This invites us to recognise the worker's skill as embedded in things, and is a vision of labour and of things that resists traditional theories of alienation in economic, political and historical writing.[98]

Micro-analyses of objects are perhaps uniquely placed to rediscover everyday lost practices and to ensure that our engagement with 'big' questions and 'big' narratives remains grounded in everyday experience.[99] In this chapter I have used a particular type of object, along with other sorts of historical source, to explore men's relationships with material culture and developing forms of masculine identity in the late eighteenth and early nineteenth centuries. The common features of this group of objects provide new – clearer – evidence for established arguments but also suggest revisions to the history of gender and material culture. Certain types of occupational or breadwinner identities, becoming ever more important politically, were built upon men's claims to arti-sanal skills. I have explored how these skills were represented – how they were gendered – in the design and materials of objects. These skills were profoundly embodied and masculinised. If consumption was a gendered practice, so pro-duction too constituted a profoundly gendered relationship with certain forms of material culture.[100] Yet these objects palpably and firmly resist this gendered distinction between consumption and production and proclaim men as both producers and consumers.

Notes

1. I thank Museums Sheffield and in particular the Curator of Decorative Art, Clare Starkie. I am also grateful for the helpful comments of the other contributors to and editors of this volume.
2. M. Daly Goggin and B. Fowkes Tobin, *Material Women: Consuming Desires and Collecting Practices* (Farnham: Ashgate, 2009).
3. L. Brekke, '"To Make a Figure": Clothing and the Politics of Male Identity in Eighteenth-Century America', in J. Styles and A. Vickery (eds), *Gender, Taste and Material Culture in Britain and North America 1700–1830* (New Haven, CT, and London: Yale University Press, 2006), p. 228.
4. J. de Vries, *The Industrious Revolution: Consumer Behaviour and the Household Economy, 1650 to the present* (Cambridge: Cambridge University Press, 2008).

5. H. French and M. Rothery, *Man's Estate: Masculinity and the English Landed Elite, c. 1680–1900* (Oxford: Oxford University Press, 2012); K. Harvey, *The Little Republic: Masculinity and Domestic Authority in Eighteenth-Century Britain* (Oxford: Oxford University Press, 2012); and J. Bailey, *Parenting in England, 1760–1830: Emotion, Identity, and Generation* (Oxford: Oxford University Press, 2012).

6. A. Smart Martin, 'Ribbons of Desire: Gendered Stories in the World of Goods', in Styles and Vickery (eds), *Gender, Taste and Material Culture*, pp. 179–200; A. Vickery, 'His and Hers: Gender, Consumption and Household Accounting in Eighteenth-Century England', *Past and Present* (2006, Supplement 1), pp. 12–38. Quote from Smart Martin, 'Ribbons of Desire', p. 180.

7. M. Donald, '"The Greatest necessity for every rank of men": Gender, Clocks and Watches', in M. Donald and L. Hurcombe (eds), *Gender and Material Culture in Historical Perspective* (London: Macmillan, 2000), pp. 54–75; D. Hussey, 'Guns, Horses and Stylish Waistcoats? Male Consumer Activity and Domestic Shopping in Late-Eighteenth and Early-Nineteenth-Century England', in D. Hussey and M. Ponsonby (eds), *Buying for the Home: Shopping for the Domestic from the Seventeenth Century to the Present* (Aldershot: Ashgate, 2008), pp. 47–69; and M. Finn, 'Men's Things: Masculine Possession in the Consumer Revolution', *Social History*, 25 (2000), pp. 133–154; Harvey, *Little Republic*, pp. 99–133.

8. K. Harvey and A. Shepard, 'What Have Historians Done with Masculinity? Reflections on Five Centuries of British History, circa 1500–1950', introduction to a Special Feature on Masculinities in *The Journal of British Studies*, 44 (2005), pp. 274–80; K. Harvey, 'The History of Masculinity, circa 1650–1800', article in a Special Feature on Masculinities in *The Journal of British Studies*, 44 (2005), pp. 296–311.

9. M. Myrone, *Bodybuilding. Reforming Masculinities in British Art 1750–1810* (New Haven, CT, and London: Yale University Press, 2005), p. 10.

10. There are several works on this, including S. Horrell and J. Humphries, 'Women's Labour Force Participation and the Transition to the Male-Breadwinner Family, 1790–1865', *Economic History Review*, 2nd ser., 48 (1995), pp. 89–117. See also M. McCormack, *The Independent Man: Citizenship and Gender Politics in Georgian England* (Manchester and New York: Manchester University Press, 2005), p. 17.

11. A. Appadurai, 'Introduction: Commodities and the Politics of Value', in A. Appadurai (ed.), *The Social Life of Things: Commodities in Cultural Perspective* (Cambridge: Cambridge University Press, 1986), pp. 3–63; I. Kopytoff, 'The Cultural Biography of Things: Commoditization as Process', in Appadurai (ed.), *Social Life of Things*, pp. 64–94.

12. On this method, see K. Dannehl, 'Object Biographies: from Production to Consumption', in K. Harvey (ed.), *History and Material Culture: A Student's Guide to Approaching Alternative Sources* (London: Routledge, 2009), pp. 123–138.

13. See also Chapters 2 and 5 in this volume, by Leonie Hannan and Vivienne Richmond, which – in different ways – combine close analyses of the material artefact with other (textual and visual) sources.

14. G. Adamson, 'The Case of the Missing Footstool', in Harvey (ed.), *History and Material Culture*, p. 192.

15. F. Trentmann, 'Materiality in the Future of History: Things, Practices and Politics', *Journal of British Studies*, 48 (2009), p. 287.

16. Museums Sheffield: K.1931.1.

17. 'Appendix XVII. List of Apprentices and Freemen', in R. Eadon Leader, *The History of the Company of Cutlers in Hallamshire, in the County of York* (Sheffield: Company of Cutlers, 1906), Vol. 2, p. 11.

18. 1841 Census of England, Yorkshire, Sheffield, Sheffield North, District 31, Joseph Gallimore household (Mill Lane). Accessed via Ancestry.com, accessed 29 September 2013.

19. Index card for object, Museums Sheffield: K.1931.1.

20. Museums Sheffield: K.1929-113.

21. Index card for object, Museums Sheffield: K.1929-113.

22. *The Sheffield & Rotherham Independent* [*SRI*], Friday 8 November 1861. Accessed via *19th Century British Library Newspapers*, http://find.galegroup.com/bncn/, accessed October 2013.

23. *SRI*, Saturday 9 November 1861. Accessed via *19th Century British Library Newspapers*, http://find.galegroup.com/bncn/, accessed October 2013.

24. Museums Sheffield: K.1951.7.

25. On family as a shared enterprise at different periods, see M. Hunt, *The Middling Sort: Commerce, Gender and the Family in England, 1680–1780* (Berkeley: University of California Press, 1996); and L. Davidoff and C. Hall, *Family Fortunes: Men and Women of the English Middle Class, 1780–1850* (London: Routledge, 1992). On rural farming families, see N. Verdon, '"... Subjects Deserving of the Highest Praise": Farmers' Wives and the Farm Economy in England, c. 1700–1850', *Agricultural History Review*, 51 (2003), pp. 23–39.

26. Museums Sheffield: K.1930.9.

27. Lease for Benjamin Allott, Grenoside, Sheffield Archives Arundel Castle: MS.SD. 868-193.

28. Museums Sheffield: K.1931.39.

29. Index card for the object, Museums Sheffield: K.1931.39.

30. *The Sun*, Saturday 5 October 1793. Accessed via 17th–18th Century Burney Collection of Newspapers, http://find.galegroup.com/bncn/start. do?prodId=BBCN&userGroupName=su_uk, accessed October 2013.

31. K. Harvey, 'Ritual Encounters: Punch Parties and Masculinity in the Eighteenth Century', *Past and Present*, 214 (2012), pp. 165–203; D. Kuchta, 'The Making of the Self-Made Man: Class, Clothing and English Masculinity, 1688–1832', in V. de Grazia and E. Furlough, *The Sex of Things: Gender and Consumption in Historical Perspective* (Berkeley and London: University of California Press, 1996), pp. 54–78; and D. Kuchta, *The Three-Piece Suit and Modern Masculinity: England, 1550–1850* (Berkeley: University of California Press, 2002). See also T. H. Breen, '"Baubles of Britain": the American and Consumer Revolutions of the Eighteenth Century', *Past and Present*, 119 (1988), pp. 73–104; and T. H. Breen, *The Marketplace of Revolution: How Consumer Politics Shaped American Independence* (Oxford: Oxford University Press, 2004).

32. K. Harvey, 'Politics by Design: Consumption, Identity and Allegiance', in S. Schmid and B. Schmidt-Haberkamp (eds), *Drink in the Eighteenth and Nineteenth Centuries: Perspectives in Economic and Social History* (London: Pickering & Chatto, 2014), pp. 11–22.

33. M. Berg, 'The British Product Revolution of the Eighteenth Century', in J. Horn, L. N. Rosenband and M. Roe Smith, *Reconceptualizing the Industrial Revolution* (Cambridge, MA: MIT Press, 2010), pp. 47–64. M. Berg, 'From Imitation to Invention: Creating Commodities in Eighteenth-Century Britain', *Economic History Review*, 55 (2002), pp. 1–30; J. Styles, 'Manufacturing, Consumption and Design in Eighteenth-Century England', in J. Brewer and R. Porter (eds), *Consumption and the World of Goods* (London: Routledge, 1993), pp. 527–554; J. Styles, 'Design for Large-Scale Production in Eighteenth-Century Britain', *Oxford Art Journal*, 11 (1988), pp. 10–16.

34. E. P. Thompson, *The Making of the English Working Class* (London: Victor Gollancz, 1980), pp. 259–296.
35. E. P. Thompson, 'Introduction; Custom and Culture', in E. P. Thompson, *Customs in Common* (London: Merlin Press, 1991), pp. 1–15.
36. Thompson, *Customs in Common*, pp. 58, 60–61. Italics original. On the material culture of earlier guilds as the product both of individual embodied labour and of corporate artisanal identity, see Helen Smith, 'Gender and Material Culture in the Early Modern London Guilds', Chapter 1 in this volume.
37. G. Adamson, *The Invention of Craft* (London: Bloomsbury, 2013), pp. xvi, 147.
38. R. Grayson, 'Who Was Master? Class Relationships in Nineteenth-Century Sheffield', in A. Kidd and D. Nicholls (eds), *The Making of the British Middle Class? Studies of Regional and Cultural Diversity since the Eighteenth Century* (Stroud: Sutton Publishing, 1998), pp. 42–57. See also C. Behagg, *Politics and Production in the Early Nineteenth Century* (London and New York: Routledge, 1990), pp. 2–3.
39. Thompson, *Making of the English Working Class*, p. 211.
40. Ibid., pp. 259–260.
41. Grayson, 'Who Was Master?' p. 44.
42. McCormack, *Independent Man*, passim; R. Sweet, 'Freemen and Independence in English Borough Politics, c. 1770–1830', *Past and Present*, 161 (Nov. 1998), pp. 84–115.
43. Grayson, 'Who Was Master?' p. 51. See also, R. Grayson and A. White, '"More Myth than Reality": the Independent Artisan in Nineteenth Century Sheffield', *Journal of Historical Sociology*, 9:3 (September 1996), p. 346 and passim.
44. Massimiliano Mollono, *Made in Sheffield: An Ethnography of Industrial Work and Politics* (New York and Oxford: Berghahn Books, 2009), pp. 5–8.
45. Behagg, *Politics and Production*, p. 5.
46. J. Rule, 'The Property of Skill in the Period of Manufacture', in P. Joyce (ed.), *The Historical Meanings of Work* (Cambridge: Cambridge University Press, 1987), pp. 99–118. Quote at p. 118.
47. Rule, 'Property of Skill', p. 104.
48. Ibid., pp. 108–111.
49. Grayson, 'Who Was Master?' p. 53.
50. Rule, 'Property of Skill', p. 108.
51. Grayson and White, '"More Myth than Reality"', pp. 336–337.
52. W. Baer, 'Botanical Decors on Porcelain', in V. Woldbye (ed.), *Flowers Into Art: Floral Motifs in European Painting and Decorative Arts* (The Hague: SDU Publishers, 1991), p. 84.
53. See, for example, Woldbye (ed.), *Flowers Into Art*, pp. 164–176.
54. Matt Houlbrook, 'Queer Things: Men and Make-up Between the Wars', p. 124 in this volume.
55. 14 March 1811, Louis Simond, *An American in Regency England* (1815; London: Pergamon, 1968), p. 113.
56. J. Housman, *A Descriptive Tour and Guide to the Lakes, Caves, Mountains, and other Natural Curiosities in Cumberland, Westmorland, Lancashire and a part of the West Riding of Yorkshire* (Carlisle: F. Jollie, 1800), p. 4.
57. [S. Stebbing,] *A Tour, in 1787, from London, to the Western Highlands of Scotland* (London: L. Davis, [1788?]), p. 263.
58. *Sheffield Register*, 20 May 1791. Accessed via 17th–18th Century Burney Collection of Newspapers, available at: http://find.galegroup.com/bncn/start.do?prodId=BBCN&userGroupName=su_uk, accessed October 2013.

59. W. Buchan, *Domestic Medicine: or, A Treatise on the Prevention and Cure of Diseases*, 5th edn (London: W. Strahan, 1777), p. 56.

60. Ibid., p. 57.

61. T. Cooper, 'Historic Report for ARCUS London Rd Site 760, Sheffield, South Yorkshire', unpublished ARCUS archive report, quoted in J. Symonds, R. O'Neill and O. Jessop, 'What Can we Learn from the Excavation and Building Recording of Cutlery Sites in Sheffield?' *Post-Medieval Archaeology*, 40 (2006), p. 215.

62. D. Ashurst, C. Cumberpatch, D. Higgins and H. Willmott, 'Glass and Pottery Manufacture at Silkstone, Yorkshire', *Post-Medieval Archaeology*, 40 (2006), pp. 182–184. Unfortunately I have been unable to locate any complete items made at either Thorncliffe or Silkstone, and certainly none with names or extant biographical details.

63. C. Fox, *The Arts of Industry in the Age of Enlightenment* (New Haven, CT, and London: Paul Mellon Centre for Studies in British Art, and Yale University Press, 2009), pp. 394–401, 426.

64. This is also the case for the frontispiece (designed by W. M Craig) to *The Mechanic: or, A Compendium of Practical Inventions* (London: Caxton Press, 1825). This shows a workman in the woods surrounded by three mythical figures who present him with raw materials (including wood and fire). Holding a saw and wearing an apron, he is clearly a worker. But he sits on an ornately carved chair – made by him? – in a natural setting.

65. Fox, *Arts of Industry*, p. 365.

66. Sykes went on to design the ten-panelled frieze for the Workers' Institute, in which a range of Sheffield workers paraded with the tools of their trade.

67. E. Slavishak, *Bodies of Work: Civic Display and Labor in Industrial Pittsburgh* (Durham, NC, and London: Duke University Press, 2008), pp. 9, 148.

68. Grayson and White, '"More Myth than Reality"', p. 346.

69. See www.sheffield.gov.uk/out--about/tourist-information/town-hall/coat-of-arms.html, accessed October 2013.

70. 'The City of Pittsburgh', *Harper's New Monthly*, 62 (December 1880), p. 58. Quoted in Slavishak, *Bodies of Work*, p. 106.

71. Myrone, *Bodybuilding*, p. 11.

72. Adamson, *The Invention of Craft*, pp. 54–89.

73. Ibid., pp. 6–9.

74. L. Roberts, 'Introduction' (to part III, 'Geographies of Skill'), in L. Roberts, S. Schaffer and P. Dear (eds), *The Mindful Hand. Inquiry and Invention from the late Renaissance to Early Industrialisation* (Amsterdam: Koninklijke Nederlandse Akademie van Wetenschappen, 2007), p. 192.

75. P. H. Smith, 'What is a Secret? Secrets and Craft Knowledge in Early Modern Europe', in E. Leong and A. Rankin (eds), *Secrets and Knowledge in Medicine and Science, 1500–1800* (Farnham: Ashgate, 2011), p. 66; P. H. Smith, *The Body of the Artisan: Art and Experience in the Scientific Revolution* (Chicago, IL, and London: University of Chicago Press, 2004), p. 8; and R. Sennett, *The Craftsman* (London: Allen Lane, 2008), pp. 119–146.

76. Roberts, Schaffer and Dear (eds), *Mindful Hand*.

77. *Valuable Secrets concerning Arts and Trades: or, Approved Directions from the best Artists* (Dublin: James Williams, 1778), p. 1.

78. P. O. Long, *Openness, Secrecy, Authorship: Technical Arts and the Culture of Knowledge from Antiquity to the Renaissance* (Baltimore, MD, and London: Johns Hopkins University Press, 2001), p. 73.

79. [Stebbing], *A Tour, in 1787, from London*, p. 265.

80. Ibid., p. 264.
81. Housman, *Descriptive Tour*, p. 4.
82. F. A. Wendeborn, *A View of England Towards the Close of the Eighteenth Century* (London, 1791), p. 225.
83. *Sketch of a Tour into Derbyshire and Yorkshire* (London, 1778), p. 123.
84. *Oxford English Dictionary* definitions for 'nicety', numbers 5, 7, 8 and 9.
85. *Sketch of a Tour into Derbyshire and Yorkshire*, p. 123.
86. *Valuable Secrets concerning Arts and Trades*, pp. 10–22.
87. *The Mechanic: or, A Compendium of Practical Inventions* (London: Caxton Press, 1825), vol. 1, p. 281.
88. There are many opportunities to observe skilled artisans. Museums often include videos in displays and exhibitions, and small workshop-based manufacturers still exist.
89. Dannehl, 'Object Biographies', pp. 131–132.
90. E. S. Reed, *Encountering the World: Towards an Ecological Psychology* (New York and Oxford: Oxford University Press, 1996), p. 7.
91. Ibid., pp. 145–146.
92. T. Ingold, *The Perception of the Environment: Essays in Livelihood, Dwelling and Skill* (2000; London and New York: Routledge, 2002), p. 3.
93. Ibid., p. 291.
94. Reed, *Encountering the World*, p. 124.
95. Ibid., p. 124.
96. M. Johnson, *An Archaeology of Capitalism* (Oxford: Blackwell, 1996), p. 190.
97. Ingold, *Perception of the Environment*, pp. 290–291, 339–348. See also T. Ingold, 'Bindings against Boundaries: Entanglements of Life in an Open World', *Environment and Planning*, vol. 40 (2008), pp. 1796–1810.
98. For a discussion of how this traditional view has left out domestic service, see C. Steedman, *Master and Servant: Love and Labour in the English Industrial Age* (Cambridge: Cambridge University Press, 2007), pp. 72–75, 219–230.
99. S. Pennell, 'Mundane Materiality, or, Should Small Things be Forgotten? Material Culture, Micro Histories and the Problem of Scale', in Harvey (ed.), *History and Material Culture*, p. 179; Adamson, 'Case of the Missing Footstool', p. 205.
100. M. Daly Goggin and B. Fowkes Tobin, 'Introduction: Consumption as a Gendered Practice', in Goggin and Tobin (eds), *Material Women*, pp. 3–4.

5

Stitching Women: Unpicking Histories of Victorian Clothes

Vivienne Richmond

It might be supposed that, as an historian of English nineteenth-century working-class dress, my research would begin with extant garments in costume collections. But most labouring people owned very few clothes, wore them till they fell to pieces, then salvaged any remnants for patches, rugs, or sale as rags, and so very few have survived. In fact many material culture historians do not work with actual artefacts since their concerns about what objects mean – their social and cultural value, rather than their practical application – can often, and sometimes must, be addressed through other sources such as written documents, images and oral histories. Indeed, among dress historians there has been a longstanding debate about the relative merits of object- and document-based research methods.[1] More widely, the proliferation of written material resulting from the industrialisation of the eighteenth and nineteenth centuries, and concomitant spread of literacy, has led many modern historians to prioritise textual sources. They often feel more comfortable with words than objects, as if the former's specific intention to convey information through a familiar, shared language makes that information more accessible, more transparent. But all sources require interpretation, comparison with and contextualisation among others, and just as we must learn how to read written sources to tease out both their intentional and unwitting testimony and decipher how they were understood at the time, so we can learn to 'read' objects to uncover the evidence they contain. This is not to suggest that where object-based research is possible it should be automatically privileged over other methodologies. Rather, we should embrace the different possibilities offered by different approaches, adopting those best fitted to answer the historical questions in hand. But here I wish to highlight the special sensory excitement of working with objects, feeling their weight and texture, looking inside and out, seeing the materials they are made of, the way they are constructed, the colour (albeit often faded), the marks of use and wear.

Working with objects also offers the possibility of accessing elusive historical subjects who wrote little or nothing, but expressed themselves through things they made. In this chapter I am going to discuss how the unexpected discovery of a pair of late nineteenth-century calico drawers (an item of women's underwear) and a plain-sewing sampler, with only scant accompanying information, acted as the catalyst for historical enquiry. Like Karen Harvey's similarly object-based study in the preceding chapter, I drew on a range of written primary sources, as well as secondary material and my existing knowledge, to help uncover the evidence my objects contained and answer some of the questions they prompted.[2] By doing so I was able to shed a little light on the personal lives of young working-class women, which is important because working-class women have been historically marginalised, since they neither belonged to the male ruling elite, nor lived in a way that encouraged the production of the historians' favoured textual sources. Yet they formed a large proportion of the population and played a key role in many of the processes of industrialisation. They worked, for example, in the metal, mining and textile trades and comprised the majority of the expanding number of domestic servants. They were also the lynchpins of their homes and families, on the comfort and moral order of which, it was widely believed, rested national peace and efficiency.[3] Even when working-class women have come under the historical lens it has tended to be collectively. I aim to demonstrate how material culture, in the form of hand-crafted objects, can help to uncover specific individual gendered histories which in some respects are unique to the people who made the objects, but in other ways are representative of more widely-shared gendered experience. The historical objects that interest you, the questions they raise and the people who made them, may well be very different from the young Victorian women and their needlework I will be discussing here. But my methods, approaches and mistakes have a wider relevance which I hope will provide food for thought, as well as practical assistance, to students starting out on their own material culture research projects or trying to evaluate the work of other historians.[4]

In most academic history books the authors present their results – the findings of months, often years, of research, (hopefully) organised into a coherent, structured argument, the evidence selected and deployed to support that argument and interwoven with the existing historiography to demonstrate how the work furthers our knowledge and deviates from or agrees with the theories of previous scholars. It is through consideration of the selected sources and the way the author has used them that historians assess the credibility of each other's theories, and an experienced historian reading my work would look at the footnotes and bibliography to ascertain how I constructed my argument. But the novice can find this much more challenging and in this chapter, rather than focusing on the end product of my labours, I am going to trace the process through which, after finding the drawers and sampler, I tried to answer the questions they raised and, eventually, write up my findings. This was my first attempt at using artefacts – artefacts, furthermore, with little information about their provenance – as the starting point for my research. You will see that, far from the straightforward linear research process implied by the finished chapter, I spent hours online and in the physical archive sifting through much irrelevant or tangential – albeit often tantalising and intriguing – material before lighting on a crucial nugget, and expended considerable time and energy

following treasured theories up blind alleys. This was accompanied by the gradual widening of my historiographical net as I came to realise the range of issues
I needed to understand to contextualise my work, the utility of lateral thinking,
the potential unreliability of the (official, written) evidence, and the dangers of
making assumptions.

Serendipity in the Archive

I found the drawers and sampler by chance when, in order to create an online
exhibition, I began to research the Girls' Friendly Society (GFS) archive held
at the Women's Library.[5] I had come across the GFS, as a provider of sewing
classes, during my doctoral research on the dress of the poor some years earlier,
but knew little more about it, and I started by browsing the 227-page archive
catalogue. From this I learned that the GFS was a popular Anglican organisation, established in 1875 to befriend and protect young, rural, working-class
women moving to the city to take up employment, mainly as domestic servants.
It was managed centrally from its London headquarters and provided hostels,
employment bureaux, holiday and convalescent homes for its members, with
whom it communicated via a range of magazines. It operated locally through
a network of branches, established on a parish basis and run by middle- and
upper-class women, which offered regular meetings with a variety of social and
educational activities.[6]

I also discovered that the archive comprised 260 boxes of material (plus 24
unboxed banners), containing 'minutes, reports, organisational files, memo-
randa books, recipe book, personal papers of members, photographs, journals/
magazines, books and artefacts such as badges'.[7] They amounted to thousands
and thousands of documents (printed, typescript and manuscript), images and
objects, with many of the boxes containing bundles of papers, photographs or
illustrations not individually catalogued. Everything was stored in the Library's
strong room and had to be requested item by item and I felt overwhelmed by
this mass of material with only the brief catalogue entries to guide me. Given
my interest in needlework and dress, I decided to start with boxes 244 and
246 when I saw that the catalogue listed their respective contents as 'GFS
St. Andrews Branch: various hand-sewn items, possibly for a doll. Emily Kenniff
aged 12', and 'Pantaloons and gloves – hand-stitched 2 objects'.[8]

I requested the boxes and they duly arrived at the issue desk. The 'Pantaloons
and gloves – hand-stitched' turned out to be a pair of voluminous cream-
coloured calico drawers, the main, straight seams machine-sewn but the garment hand finished, and a rather odd pair of large calico gloves.[9] The drawers
are of the 'open' variety, meaning that they have no crotch seam, but are left
open between the legs. They are gathered onto a waistband which fastens with
a button, measure seventy centimetres around the waist (sixty-five centimetres
when buttoned) and seventy-four centimetres long (measured along the side
from the top of the waistband). The bottom of each leg is decorated with
five horizontal tucks above a machine-made *broderie anglaise* insert, a further
three tucks and a final *broderie anglaise* border.[10] Attached to one leg are
two small labels: one, handwritten and fastened on with a pin, states,

Figure 5.1 The drawers.

'E Kenniff / 1 Prize / Pr Drs / Lady Mayoress', the other a pretty printed card attached by a thread, on which is handwritten, '1ˢᵗ Prize'. As winner of the Lady Mayoress's first prize, they had evidently been entered into a competition, and they are very well made. (See Fig. 5.1.)

The 'various hand-sewn items' are eleven small pieces of needlework, mostly made of unbleached calico, mounted on a piece of deep-pink glazed fabric (possibly cotton), approximately 45 cm square, to form a sampler of plain-sewing techniques.[11] They include examples of patching, darning, inserting a gusset, gathers, tucks, buttonholes and a button. In the centre a square worked in blue, red and gold cross-stitch proclaims, 'GFS / S Andrew's / Branch / E Kenniff / Age 12', and at the bottom is a small handwritten card with a printed decorative border which repeats the cross-stitched information, adding 'Employment at school' and revealing that the 'E' of E. Kenniff stood for Emily. In contrast with the beautifully-crafted drawers, the standard of sewing on the sampler is competent for a twelve-year-old girl, but nothing more. Yet the arrangement of the items on the mounting fabric together with the card at its base indicates that it too had been a competition entry. (See Fig. 5.2.)

'Reading' the Artefacts

So what could I learn from these pieces of needlework? The catalogue, which mistakenly suggested the sampler items were 'possibly for a doll', also dated them as '1980s', but they were clearly much older than this. Furthermore, I had previously made an extensive study of school sewing manuals and the nineteenth- and early twentieth-century government Education Codes which

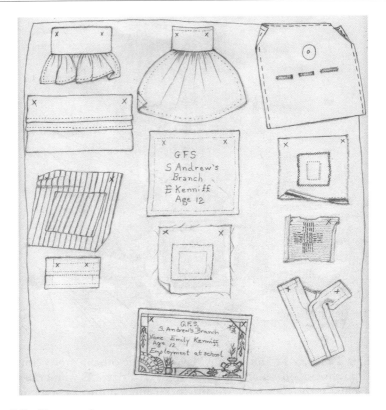

Figure 5.2   The sampler.

set out the curricula for state-funded elementary schools. These required all female pupils to devote a great proportion of their school hours to learning the utilitarian plain sewing which would enable them to make and maintain basic garments. The items on Emily Kenniff's sampler were not dolls' clothes but examples of the plain-sewing exercises set out in the school curricula and sewing manuals, and many of the techniques had been used in the manufacture of the drawers. Emily's sampler, then, demonstrated that the official theory was actually put into active practice.

Also in accordance with the instruction manuals, the sampler items were mostly made of cheap cotton calico. Again, I already knew that one of the distinctive features of nineteenth-century working-class dress was the replacement of linen and wool, which continued to be worn by the elite, with cheap cotton. Calico became the virtually ubiquitous fabric for working-class underwear such as shirts, shifts and petticoats, and the drawers in the GFS archive were also made of calico, firmly identifying them as a garment for a working-class woman. In the closing chapter of this volume, Stella Moss similarly highlights the scarcity of surviving plebeian artefacts as well as the elusiveness of substantive information about working-class culture. It is difficult to exaggerate my (admittedly rather singular) excitement at finding these drawers, because if extant Victorian working-class clothing *per se* is scarce, underwear is even more rare. I had long been trying to ascertain when working-class women began to wear drawers, which seemed to be not until at least the 1870s, and the catalogue date of '1900s' for this pair therefore seemed plausible. But there was nothing to indicate how it had been determined. So, in addition to the drawers' intrinsic value as a rare example of late Victorian or Edwardian working-class under clothing, there was the possibility that if I could find out when they were made they would go a little way toward solving the mystery of when drawers came into general use. And if I could find out more about their maker, I might also be able to find out more about the creation of a female working-class gendered identity and the role of needlework within it.

I was intrigued by these items as they raised far more questions than they answered: Who was Emily Kenniff? Why – and when – did she enter a pair of drawers in a competition? What was that competition? How could I account for the difference in the quality of the sewing between the two items. Why were they in the archive? This last question was particularly puzzling on two counts: first, I knew that the archive contained almost exclusively the records of the central administrative offices, such branch records as exist being lodged in local repositories. Yet among all the archive's papers, images and official souvenirs were these few items of branch-member craftwork. The only other needlework in the archive was a collection of small samples of knitting and sewing submitted by 'invalid' members applying to join the Society's employment scheme for disabled women (run from the London headquarters). These were quite distinct from the drawers and sampler, as well as being separately boxed and catalogued. Second, why had Emily not wanted to keep the drawers herself? This puzzled me not only because it might be assumed that, as a prize-winning garment, she would want it for its own sake, but also because I knew that poverty meant most late nineteenth- and early twentieth-century working-class people possessed very few clothes. Surely Emily (or perhaps her mother – they are adult-size) would have wanted the drawers back to wear.

I thought the different standards of needlework evident in the two items might be explained by the drawers having been made some while after the sampler, when Emily's expertise had improved. But this only confused matters further, because if I could not explain why, seemingly, she alone of all the hundreds of thousands of GFS members had, aged twelve, sent her sampler to the London headquarters, I was at an even greater loss to explain why she followed up with a pair of drawers a few years later.

Finding Emily

I thought finding out more about Emily might help to answer some of my other questions, so I made that my first task. But where to start? The only information I had was that attached to the items themselves, and the catalogue entries, many of which simply repeated what was on the drawers and sampler or were wrong. And the archive itself seemed to offer little prospect of assistance given its size and my lack of familiarity with it. In fact, my work on the online exhibition meant I did not have time to immediately pursue the answers to my questions.

While this was initially frustrating, when I returned to them after completing the exhibition I was much more familiar with both the GFS and its archive and, therefore, more optimistic about the possibility of finding answers.[12]

The archive contained the Annual Reports of the GFS from its inception in 1875 and I knew that these listed all the branches as their number increased from year to year. Working on the basis that the drawers were made around 1900 and the sampler some years earlier, I thought a skim through the early Annual Reports would be a quick way to locate the St Andrew's branch and that, with luck, this knowledge might lead me to a local repository containing the branch records and further information about Emily. But here I encountered my first setback: the Annual Reports up to 1900 returned at least seven St Andrew's branches spread across the country.[13] So, I turned to the Census.

The Census of England and Wales has been conducted every ten years since 1801, collecting increasingly detailed information about the inhabitants of every dwelling. The aggregate information – such as demographic and occupational statistics – is published soon after it has been collated, but the detailed information about individuals – such as name, age, occupation, place of birth – is restricted for a hundred years. At the time of my enquiry, the latest detailed information available was for the 1901 Census, and given the plausibility of the 1900s date for the drawers, this seemed a good place to start. I registered with ancestry.co.uk, the National Archives' partner agency for access to pre-1921 census records, and searched for Emily Kenniff.[14] This time luck was on my side because Emily Kenniff turned out to be an extremely unusual name. Had it not been, my investigation might have ended there, but the 1901 Census listed just two Emily Kenniffs, both aged 23 and both registered in London. 'Emily One' was living in the Holborn Union Workhouse and was born in Clerkenwell. 'Emily Two' had been born in Holborn where she still lived in 1901 – in the civil parish of St Andrew where, the GFS Annual Reports revealed, there had also been a branch of the GFS. This much I had ascertained from open-access information but by paying to view images of the original census record I discovered that on census day 1901 Emily Two was a book-sewer, living with her father Daniel, a printer's warehouseman, her mother Eliza, her thirty-five-year-old sister, also Eliza and, like Emily, a book sewer, and her brother William, 14, the family occupying three rooms at no. 1 Greville Street.[15]

I had, it seemed, found Emily. I could not be absolutely certain that the one I was seeking was Emily Two and not Emily One (and sadly there turned out to be no branch records in the local archives to help me) but a number of factors significantly increased the probability. Members joined the GFS branch in the parish of, or nearest to, their residence. It is possible that Emily One had been living in the parish of St Andrew, Holborn, at the age of twelve, between her birth in the parish of Clerkenwell and her admission to the Holborn Union Workhouse (in the parish of Shoreditch). But this would have been around 1890, and I could find nothing to suggest such residence in either the 1881 or 1891 censuses. I did, though, find an Emily Keniff, aged thirteen, living in the parish of St James, Clerkenwell, in the 1891 Census. Although her birthplace was given as Shoreditch, and despite the small variation in the spelling of her surname, its rarity, however spelled, together with the vagaries of the census records, mean this is probably Emily One.[16]

In contrast, Emily Two (hereafter just Emily) is shown living in Greville Street in 1881, and in 1891 her family were still there – although she and her sister were in-patients at the Homerton Fever Hospital on census day – and her father had been living there in 1871 (at which point his wife was in hospital).[17] The seeming facility with which I make that statement, however, belies the work required to gather the information, because when I searched for one of the Kenniff family in the pre-1901 census records they appeared only in 1871. Yet since the 1901 Census recorded that all three of the Kenniff siblings then living in Greville Street had been born in London between around 1866 and 1887, they had to be in there somewhere. It transpired that in the summary lists of census entries 'Kenniff' had been variously transcribed as 'Kanniff', 'Kerriff' and 'Kennitt', and looking at images of the original entries it is easy to see how these mistakes occurred, but that is to put the cart before the horse. To find those original entries I had to think of different ways to look for members of the family other than just entering their correct names. Alternative spellings of Kenniff, such as Kennif or Keniff, got me so far, but eventually (there being no simple way to search by address) I had to resort to much more generalised searches – such as anyone called Daniel, born in Holborn around 1840, living in the parish of St Andrew and with a wife named Eliza – and whittling down the results. Thus, tracing the family in all the relevant census records proved an extremely time-consuming process.

It also presented an anomaly – since Emily's age was given as twenty-three in the 1901 Census, it should have been, respectively, three and thirteen in the 1881 and 1891 Censuses, and her birth year either 1877 or 1878 depending whether her birthday fell before or after the census night of 31 March/1 April 1901. But in the 1881 Census her age was given as five, and as fifteen in 1891. Since one of the few pieces of information I had about Emily was that she made the sampler when she was twelve, it was important to know her correct year of birth to be able to accurately date the sampler. So, I turned to the birth indexes for England, where a search for Emily Kenniff born in 1877 plus or minus two years returned just one exact match – Emily Lilian Kenniff, whose birth was registered in Holborn in January 1876.[18] To ensure this was the right Emily and get her precise birth date meant buying a copy of her birth certificate, but this proved a worthwhile investment when I received a document confirming her as the daughter of Daniel and Eliza, born at Greville Street on 19 December 1875 (the birth being registered on 28 January 1876).[19] Her birth date had been wrongly recorded in the 1901 Census.

It had taken a long while, but I could now date the sampler to either the very tail end of 1887, after Emily's twelfth birthday in December, or, more probably, 1888. I still didn't know when the drawers were made, but slowly I was beginning to sketch out a picture of Emily and her family. The census records from 1871 to 1901 showed me that they had lived in the same street for at least forty years, and had moved from one room in number 3 Greville Street to three rooms in number 1, presumably as their prosperity increased. This was a notable stability, it being very common for working-class families to move frequently, and often surreptitiously, when unable to pay the rent. To find out something about the area they lived in I consulted the poverty maps of Charles Booth, a wealthy philanthropist who, between 1886 and 1903, conducted a mammoth survey of the living conditions of working-class Londoners. His results included a series of colour-coded maps indicating his perceived level of poverty in each street. The Greville Street neighbourhood is mostly pink, 'Fairly comfortable. Good ordinary earnings', and purple, 'Mixed. Some comfortable, others poor', placing it roughly equidistant from the black 'Lowest class. Vicious, semi-criminal' at the bottom of the scale, and the yellow 'Upper-middle and Upper classes. Wealthy', at the top.[20] Greville Street, therefore, was a respectable area.

There were also indications that the family was internally stable, since the 1891 Census shows Emily's older brother John still living in the parental home at the age of twenty-six, and the 1901 Census shows Eliza and Emily still there aged respectively thirty-five and twenty-five. The census gives Daniel's occupation as a printer's warehouseman and Eliza and Emily both became book-sewers – that is, they sewed together the sections of books to be bound into finished volumes. So the sisters and their father were all in the print trade, and the historiography told me that bookbinding was among the respectable trades for women, not least because their parents were usually also employed in it and therefore able to ensure their daughters were not mistreated.[21] I was, of course, also struck by the correlation between Emily's GFS needlework and her subsequent occupation – needlework was not only something she did at school or in her leisure time, but also the means by which she came to earn her living. The growing picture of family respectability and stability was further emphasised by Emily's membership of, and evident active participation in, the GFS, with its stated aim of preserving chastity among working-class girls, provision of wholesome entertainment and useful instruction, and its Anglican affiliation.

What's in a Pair of Drawers?

But what of the drawers? Previous research, among both primary and secondary sources, had confirmed needlework as a cornerstone of nineteenth-century femininity.[22] It was, then, no surprise that the GFS organised, and its members entered, needlework competitions. But while notions of excessive Victorian prudery have long been contested, and although I did not yet know how many people would see the competition entries, the drawers nevertheless seemed a peculiarly intimate item to put on display.[23] And why *open* drawers? Turning to the historiography I found that changing ideas about propriety, coupled with the medical opinion that wearing drawers promoted good health, resulted in their common use among elite women by mid-century. I knew that they were rarely, if at all, worn by working-class women at that time, and it emerged that the adoption of drawers signalled conformity with the values and standards of the middle- and upper-class women who ran the GFS and who deemed it their duty to educate the members. And whereas today closed drawers are associated with respectability while open drawers conjure images of sexual adventure, the reverse was true in the Victorian period. Bifurcated garments with a crotch seam were too similar to male garments and threatened to blur the boundaries between male and female.[24]

Entering a pair of open-crotch drawers in the GFS competition was, then, a demonstration of the entrant's respectability. But given the possibility they offered of access to or exposure of the genitals I did still wonder if they really were as sexually neutral as the historiography suggested. A little more reading confirmed that there was indeed a section of the prolific Victorian pornography industry that focused on their erotic potential.[25] This meant that the drawers, when entered for the competition, risked becoming the site of sexual fantasy, even if the maker had no intention, nor even awareness, of such an interpretation.

I also knew that in the school sewing curricula for working-class girls, decorative needlework was strictly forbidden as suggestive of idleness and inappropriate class aspiration, embroidery being the preserve of elite females. Yet there was decorative cross-stitch work on the sampler, and the tucks and *broderie anglaise* of the drawers. In neither case was the decoration excessive but it suggested that while Emily demonstrated her respectability through her needlework skills, she also revealed an independent mind and a sense of self-worth.

Noticing Eliza

I began to write up my findings, arguing that my evidence showed Emily to be a member of a stable, industrious family and that her needlework, combined with her membership of the GFS, demonstrated her conformity with contemporary notions of female respectability; but also that the embroidery on her sampler and decoration on the drawers – at odds with the directives to pursue only plain sewing – indicated a degree of independence, autonomy and self-esteem. I was frustrated by my inability to answer all the questions the items had prompted, but with my submission deadline looming I tried to resign myself to the fact that this was the historian's lot, given the often erratic survival of the relevant evidence. But my failure to adequately account for the difference in the quality of the needlework on the drawers and the sampler, or to explain why they were in the archive, really vexed me. Lying awake puzzling it over yet another night, it suddenly struck me – I had simply assumed that the E. Kenniff who made the drawers and the Emily Kenniff who made the sampler were the same person, completely overlooking the fact that Emily's sister Eliza, ten years her senior, was also E. Kenniff. Was it not possible – probable, even – that she had made the drawers at the same time that Emily had made the sampler and that both had entered their work in the same competition?[26] This would also account for the adult size of the drawers.

The next day I raced back to the archive to search for evidence that Eliza was also a member of the GFS. Although I knew I would not find the branch records, I did know that the Society's magazine, *Friendly Leaves*, contained reports of various branch events and that these sometimes mentioned individuals. Might a prize-winning pair of drawers be worthy of such a commendation? Alas not, but I did find out that in 1888 the St Andrew, Holborn, branch organised an 'Exhibition of Trades and Needlework Competition'.[27] I also discovered that some GFS needlework competitions had a special category for pairs of drawers, suggesting a determined attempt to encourage their use, and that, in

1892, at the GFS Grand Triennial Exhibition Eliza Kenniff won first prize in the competition for 'One Pint Lemonade or other Temperance Drink'.[28] Eliza was, then, a member of the GFS, entered its competitions – and won them. It was not incontrovertible proof, but it was convincing evidence that the drawers were made by Eliza and entered in the 1888 needlework competition, rather than by Emily some years later.

My continued attempts to understand why the articles were in the archive further added to my conviction that Eliza had made the drawers. In my search for her I had also found, in an 1888 edition of *Friendly Leaves*, an article on the items a young working-class woman should amass for her trousseau. The list included two pairs of plain, and two pairs of 'best' drawers, and the article emphasised that these should be home-made, unused – not even washed – before marriage and that young women should not wait until their marriage was imminent, but begin to assemble the numerous recommended items as soon as they had any thought of marriage.[29] The archive drawers have clearly never been worn or washed and it is not, I think, coincidental that the trousseau list appeared in the same year as the St Andrew's needlework competition. Eliza would then have been twenty-two or twenty-three – an age at which she might well have been thinking of marriage, even if she had no immediate expectation of it. But the 1901 census showed that, at thirty-five, Eliza was still single (and not widowed), and nor does she appear subsequently in the marriage indexes. It is therefore possible that, as recommended in the GFS magazine, Eliza made the drawers as a trousseau item, then entered them in the competition. Perhaps when the exhibition ended something happened to prevent the sisters collecting their needlework and, since Eliza never married and so had no pressing need to reclaim the trousseau drawers, she never did. This is, of course, speculation, and it does not explain why the GFS Central Office rather than the St Andrew's branch kept the needlework. But the Central Office most probably had better storage facilities and, being also based in London, was very possibly involved with the 1888 Exhibition, which was quite a sizeable event attracting over 600 visitors.[30]

Searching to see if Eliza had married piqued my interest in Emily's subsequent history, which, it transpired, was very sad. Through further searches of the birth, marriage and death indexes and the purchase of more certificates, I discovered that in 1903 Emily married a clerk, Thomas Farnham, two years her junior.[31] She moved to his Brentford home where she gave birth to two sons, Ronald George in 1904 and Leslie William in 1905, but Ronald died before Leslie was born, and was followed by Emily herself in 1906 and Leslie in 1907.[32] In just three-and-a-half years, Thomas Farnham had married his wife, fathered two sons and buried them all.

Gender and Material Culture

The prize-winning status of Eliza's drawers marks them out as an exceptional piece of needlework at the time they were made, and by their rarity they remain exceptional today. Examples of plain sewing exercises are a little more common, though the fact of Emily's being gathered together, arranged and entered for competition and exhibition makes her sampler distinctive and suggests she took a pride and pleasure in her work that was by no means universal among Victorian schoolgirls. But the sampler is, nevertheless, a tangible, physical representation of the shared experience of millions of nineteenth-century working-class girls, who spent a large proportion of their school days stitching away at the compulsory, humdrum exercises dictated by the Education Codes. My research had begun with the discovery of two intriguing pieces of needlework, and to unravel the makers' histories and unlock the deeper meaning of their sewing I had to call upon parliamentary papers, sewing manuals, the census records, birth, marriage and death certificates, Booth's poverty maps, the annual reports and magazines of the Girls' Friendly Society, the historiography of needlework, the print trade, underwear and pornography, as well as my own existing knowledge as an historian and needlewoman. Through this I was able to trace the lives of the sisters from birth to death, taking in their occupations, their homes and aspects of their home life, leisure activities and, in Emily's case, marriage and motherhood. I could see how Emily followed in her older sister's footsteps, until their paths diverged, Emily meeting a husband and early death, and Eliza continuing life as a spinster. I learned comparatively little of this directly from the drawers and sampler alone, but without them I would have learned nothing.

I was quite an experienced researcher when I began investigating the Kenniff sisters' needlework, but I had never worked in quite the same way before and it was both exciting and instructive. It emphasised the importance of remaining curious and open to the serendipitous possibilities of an archive; that finding-aids are extremely useful, especially for getting to grips with the scope and structure of the archive, but may not be entirely accurate or complete; that I should not be deterred by a lack of information about an interesting object, but focus on the questions it raises and try to think creatively about how I might answer them; and that I must not make assumptions – especially unwittingly. But above all I learned that there is a particular thrill in making a physical connection with the people you are researching, knowing that their hands have held – sometimes made – what you touch with your own.[33]

Notes

1. For the best explication of this debate, and the uses and limitations of different approaches, see L. Taylor, *The Study of Dress History* (Manchester: Manchester University Press, 2002).
2. That research was published as, V. Richmond, 'Stitching the Self: Eliza Kenniff's Drawers and the Materialization of Identity in Late Nineteenth-Century London', in M. Daly Goggin and B. Fowkes Tobin (eds), *Women and Things: Gendered Material Practices, 1750–1950* (Farnham: Ashgate, 2009), pp. 43–54. While I hope that you will also wish to read that chapter, it is not requisite in order to understand what follows here.
3. Defining 'working class' is problematic, and it is therefore not possible to determine the precise size of the female working-class population. Here I have used the simple, and simplistic, definition of 'working class' as those engaged in, or dependent upon others engaged in, skilled, semi-skilled or unskilled manual work. This was the status of about 80 per cent of adult males in the second half of the nineteenth century,

see E. J. Evans, *The Shaping of Modern Britain: Identity, Industry and Empire, 1780–1914* (Harlow: Pearson Education, 2011), p. 254. For an introduction to women's industrial work and domestic responsibilities, see M. Berg, 'What Difference Did Women's Work Make to the Industrial Revolution?' *History Workshop Journal*, 35 (1993), pp. 22–44; and S. Alexander, 'Women's Work in Nineteenth-Century London: a Study of the Years 1820–60s', in S. Alexander, *Becoming a Woman and Other Essays in 19th and 20th Century Feminist History* (New York: New York University Press, 1995), pp. 3–55.

4. I also recommend K. Harvey (ed.), *History and Material Culture: A Student's Guide to Approaching Alternative Sources* (Abingdon: Routledge, 2009), especially Harvey's 'Introduction: Practical Matters'; and L. Jordanova, *The Look of the Past: Visual and Material Evidence in Historical Practice* (Cambridge: Cambridge University Press, 2012).

5. The Women's Library, then at London Metropolitan University, moved to the LSE Library in 2013. My online exhibition, 'Bear Ye One Another's Burdens, The Girls' Friendly Society 1875–2005', did not survive the move.

6. The Women's Library, C. Ashcroft, '5/GFS Records of The Girls' Friendly Society (1800–2001)', unpublished catalogue (The Women's Library, 2004), pp. 2–6. The GFS still exists today, though in a very different and much smaller form, principally providing support for teenage mothers.

7. Ashcroft, '5/GFS Records', p. 12.

8. Ashcroft, '5/GFS Records', pp. 160–161.

9. TWL, GFS, 5GFS/12/1/16, pantaloons and gloves. The gloves were something of a mystery, which has subsequently increased with their disappearance and substitution with a pair of white modern gloves featuring a plastic popper, possibly of the sort worn by museum and gallery curators when handling objects. There are similarities with the size and colour of the original gloves and the only explanation I can offer (the Women's Library staff being equally mystified when I questioned the substitution) is that the originals were taken out of the box when the drawers were removed for exhibition display, and accidentally replaced by the modern pair. For the purposes of this chapter I will leave them to one side.

10. *Broderie anglaise*, 'English embroidery', was a form of decorative needlework popular in the nineteenth century.

11. TWL, GFS, 5GFS/12/1/11, various hand-sewn items.

12. Readers are unlikely to have the same opportunity to familiarise themselves with their archive, but taking time to thoroughly browse the catalogue to gain an overview of the collection's size, scope and content, should give you a good idea of promising items to consult to begin your search. Talking to the archivists is also invaluable – they know their collections better than anyone and can often highlight items not easily identifiable in the catalogue.

13. TWL, GFS, 5GFS/03/001-025, Associates Lists and Annual Reports 1875–1900/01.

14. ancestry.co.uk (http://home.ancestry.co.uk), accessed in February 2007.

15. The National Archives of the United Kingdom, 1901 Census of England and Wales, RG13/247.

16. TNA, 1891 Census of England and Wales, RG 12/225.

17. TNA, 1881 Census of England and Wales, RG 11/342; 1891 Census of England and Wales, RG 12/220, RG 12/203; 1871 Census of England and Wales, RG 10/375, RG 10/144.

18. ancestry.co.uk also provides open access to the registers of births, marriages and deaths.

19. General Register Office for England and Wales, BXCC 404248, birth certificate of Emily Lilian Kenniff. Copies of birth, death and marriage certificates priced at £9.25 each in 2014.

20. Booth Poverty Maps, available at: http://booth.lse.ac.uk/, accessed in March 2007.

21. Alexander, 'Women's Work', pp. 34–36.

22. See V. Richmond, *Clothing the Poor in Nineteenth-Century England* (Cambridge: Cambridge University Press, 2013), ch. 4.

23. For an influential discussion of Victorian attitudes to sex, see M. Foucault, *The History of Sexuality*, trans. R. Hurley, 3 vols (London: Allen Lane, 1979), vol. 1, *An Introduction*.

24. C. Saint-Laurent, *A History of Ladies Underwear* (London: Michael Joseph, 1968), pp. 123, 127; V. Steele, *Fashion and Eroticism: Ideals of Feminine Beauty from the Victorian Era to the Jazz Age* (New York: Oxford University Press, 1985), pp. 198–199; J. Nunn, *Fashion in Costume 1200–2000* (London: Herbert, 2000), p. 117; S. Tobin, *Inside Out: A Brief History of Underwear* (London: The National Trust, 2001), p. 12; J. Fields, 'Erotic Modesty: (Ad)dressing Female Sexuality and Propriety in Open and Closed Drawers, USA, 1800–1930', *Gender and History*, 14 (2002), pp. 492–515; C. Brush Kidwell and V. Steele, *Men and Women: Dressing the Part* (Washington, DC: Smithsonian Institution Press, 1989), pp. 14–15; A. Ribeiro, *Dress and Morality* (Oxford: Berg, 2003), pp. 120–121; A. Carter, *Underwear: The Fashion History* (London: Batsford, 1992), p. 46; and C. Willett and Phillis Cunnington, *The History of Underclothes* (London: Faber & Faber, 1981), p. 124.

25. J. Dines Johansen, 'Literature, Pornography, and Libertine Education', *Orbis Litterarum*, 59 (2004), pp. 39–65; F. Chenoune, *Hidden Femininity: 20th Century Lingerie* (London: Thames & Hudson, 1999), p. 22.

26. Although Emily's mother was also called Eliza, as a married woman she could not have entered the drawers in a GFS competition. The GFS viewed marriage as the natural and desirable destiny of all women and the GFS's aim was to help members preserve their virginity for marriage. Any member known to have lost her virginity was expelled from the GFS, and the presumed, though honourable, loss of virginity on marriage disqualified wives and widows from membership.

27. TWL, GFS, 5GFS/10/012, *Friendly Leaves*, 13:143 (July 1888).

28. TWL, GFS, 5GFS/10/015, *Friendly Leaves*, 17:191 (August 1892); *Friendly Leaves*, 18:197 (January 1893).

29. TWL, GFS, 5GFS/10/012, *Friendly Leaves*, 13:138 (February 1888).

30. Ibid., *Friendly Leaves*, 13:143 (July 1888).

31. GRO, XD 186880, marriage certificate of Thomas George Farnham and Emily Lillian [*sic*] Kenniff.

32. GRO, BXCC 883233, birth certificate of Ronald George Farnham; DYB 876877, death certificate of Ronald George Farnham; BXCC 883236, birth certificate of Leslie William Farnham; DYB 525674, death certificate of Emily Lilian Farnham; DYB 876790, death certificate of Leslie William Farnham. Because of the limited information in the registers of births, I had to purchase four birth certificates to ascertain how many children Emily had borne, two of them, it transpired, being the offspring of a different Mr and Mrs Farnham.

33. Of course, the same sensory experience can be derived from original written documents, but that is to focus on them as objects – material culture – rather than on their textual content.

6

Grooming Men: The Material World of the Nineteenth-Century Barbershop

Jessica P. Clark

In 1869, the trade quarterly *The Hairdressers' Chronicle* published an anonymous column lamenting the loss of 'real old genuine' barbershops, which had only recently served London's diverse metropolitan neighbourhoods. Despite his concerted efforts, the columnist was unable to explain how humble shops had been transformed into 'the more pretentious establishments which now represent the business of the "Coiffeur".' Deliberating upon a range of factors accelerating the demise of London's barbershops, the author ultimately impugned 'the vain aspirations of the members of the ancient art and mystery'. The columnist concluded that metropolitan barbers' desire 'to become "professors" of hairdressing establishments, promoters of new "systems" of polarisation, and in general "coiffeurs" led to the gradual abandonment of shaving, as a little known, if not a lost art'.[1] As we have seen in Chapter 3, shaving was an everyday practice that played an important role in constructing male identities. This chapter considers how this activity was transformed in the nineteenth century, and the new gendered spaces that it created.

Unashamedly sentimental, the editorial nonetheless reflected significant commercial and cultural shifts occurring in the late 1860s, shifts that altered London's hairdressing trades for both its tradesmen and clients. In the first half of the nineteenth century, London's barbershops had provided personal grooming services to different social classes of male clientele. As Susan Vincent argues earlier in this volume, eighteenth-century barbershops functioned as venues for homo-social networking, where patrons of mixed social standing procured simple shaves. This continued into the early nineteenth century, as patrons caught up on local news, debated the latest political developments, or placed bets on the day's races.[2] From the late 1860s, however, expanding opportunities for luxury consumption and a new emphasis on consumer pleasures contributed to the delineation of distinct categories of male grooming establishment: utilitarian penny barbershops concentrated in the East End, efficient middle-class shops located throughout the metropolis, and elite West End hairdressing saloons developed in conjunction with those catering to new female shoppers.

Looking to the organisation of these commercial spaces, this chapter analyses both material culture and space to understand customers' experiences in Victorian barbershops. It focuses on material transformations – changes in shop organisation, design, décor, and trade accoutrements – to highlight the barbershop's development from a site of quotidian grooming practices to one of increasingly elaborate male self-fashioning and consumption. Rather than focusing on surviving material objects, it relies upon a diverse range of print and visual sources to aid in the reconstruction of the Victorian barbershop as a commercial interior and lived space. In the absence of surviving interiors or objects, the best way for historians to find out about these spaces and what contemporaries thought of them is to sift through contemporary print culture. Accounts from the satirical and sporting press, along with reports from contemporary social researchers, emphasise the minimalist (and sometimes disorderly) nature of the working-class barbershop. Neighbourhood and trade reports supplement press coverage, detailing the sometimes-arduous living conditions of working-class barber assistants. Profiles of the trade's leading and less fortunate members in guild and trade journals underscore the material disparities separating elite and working-class shops. Leaseholds and architectural plans describe saloon interiors, while visual depictions of barbershop space reveals the diverse decorating schemes of upper- versus middle-class shops. Careful analysis allows us to understand gendered patterns of grooming and consumption in the urban metropolis. More importantly, it illuminates the role of men as consumers of beautifying and grooming services, thereby aligning with scholarship that asserts the importance of male as well as female fashionable consumption.[3] This chapter shows how analysing the way contemporaries created spatial and material worlds can shed light on gendered social practices in daily life.

While our sources tell us about material culture in the Victorian barbershop as well as the arrangement of shop space, they tell us little about the customers who walked through the front doors. Accounts from Victorian consumers of grooming products and services are rare, especially in the case of male shoppers. However, as Christopher Breward has noted of men's fashion in this period, it is possible to analyse how shops catered to circulating stereotypes of urban men: the elite gentleman, the white-collar bachelor, the working-class swell. Breward argues that consuming practices thus reinforced 'role models [and] types' that were available to men in the Victorian period; in other words, by soliciting certain shops men could align themselves with particular class and gender identities.[4] This argument extends to barbershops, where barbers used advertising to convey their desired class of customer. For example, advertisements for West End shops targeting an elite market intimated that Britain's leading men solicited the luxurious saloons: Westminster politicians, the peerage, even members of the royal family.[5] Meanwhile, in London's financial and publishing capital, City shops advertised the efficiency and speed of their services, thereby publicising their services for businessmen, married and unmarried. In working-class shops, barbers relied on word-of-mouth to attract local business, but also advertised the affordability of their penny shaves with lettered placards and signs.

The modesty of their displays was a sign for patrons, communicating the humble nature of their services.

As we will see, it was not only advertising that conveyed the class standing and desired clientele of barbershops; elements of material culture and the design of space also reinforced the class and gender standing of these businesses. This chapter subsequently reveals that, from the mid-nineteenth century, barbershops were designed to attract particular clientele, be it the upper-class gentleman or City businessman. Decorating schemes, the range of available proprietary goods, and the organisation of saloon space bolstered divides of class and sex, communicating who was welcome to solicit the shop. Like other contributions to this volume, this chapter takes as a starting point the significance of material culture as a means of understand new consuming practices amongst men. It also interrogates the ways that commercial space was increasingly organised along class and gender lines, in the wake of growing urban consumption from the 1860s.

The Victorian Hair Trades

Aside from a few notable exceptions, the hair trade and its practices have been ignored by historians of the nineteenth and early twentieth centuries, much as hairdressers and barbers were dismissed by their Victorian contemporaries.[6] Often represented in satirical and mainstream print as effete and indolent, London's hairdressers and barbers nonetheless played an important role as hosts of a particular form of urban masculine sociability.[7] This social function dated to the early modern period, when hairdressers enjoyed a much higher social standing than they did later, so that contemporary elites reportedly 'thought it no disgrace in that simple age to lodge in Fleet Street, or take rooms above some barber's shop'.[8] In the long eighteenth century, hairdressers' social influence as arbiters of taste became problematic, when they became associated with radical political discourses. Historian Don Herzog argues that in this moment, hairdressers were central to the 'reproduction of social status' by fashioning the elaborate and ostentatious hairstyles that marked England's elite.[9]

By the nineteenth century, London's 2,300 hairdressers and barbers experienced a steady decline not only in reputation, but also in professional and financial standing.[10] Barbers' wretched working conditions also made for a significant socio-economic disparity between tradesmen and their clients.[11] Despite the barbers' diminished status, the relatively universal demand for haircuts and shaves meant that London's barbers hosted an unprecedented level of cross-class social interaction in the mid-nineteenth century. This was amplified by hairdressers' and barbers' service of a diverse range of clientele. One barber, recalling his apprenticeship in the late 1840s, noted 'they were the days for barbers' shops, the customers being of "all classes and conditions of men"'. In the mornings, his master served elderly noblemen and gentry from the local region, followed by 'a sprinkling of well-to-do tradesmen, and on Saturday nights and Sunday mornings, a good number of mechanics, Irish labourers … and others'.[12] As another trader noted, a customer 'may be a nobleman, [and] the next perhaps a neighbouring shopkeeper, while a third may possibly be a lady of title or a milliner's apprentice'.[13]

Artistic renderings of barbershops from early in this period, including George Hunt's 1825 *Sunday Morning*, capture the disorderly, mixed-class nature of the barbershop (Fig. 6.1). While certainly exaggerated for comedic effect, the piece highlights some key features of an early nineteenth-century barbershop on a weekend morning, Sunday being the busiest day in a barber's week. Clients sit on rudimentary chairs placed haphazardly throughout the room. Two small mirrors hang on the walls for consultation after the cut or shave is complete. In the background, a woman climbs a flight of stairs in clear view of male patrons. Whether a female client on her way to the ladies' shop or the mistress of the house ascending to domestic space above the shop floor, there is no attempt to prevent the mixing of sexes. Moreover, there are no material or spatial divides separating customers from one another. Rather, the open arrangement makes for an informal communion of vendors, patrons, and passers-by, not to mention a local animal or two.[14]

Aligning with artistic renditions of barbershops, trade accounts suggested that, despite their decline, modest utilitarian barbershops functioned as important sites of masculine sociability in working-class neighbourhoods through the later nineteenth century. Aside from public houses and 'cookshops', the penny barbershop was one of the few commercial spaces in London's plebeian enclaves that remained open past the dinner hour. Through the summer, the shops functioned as venues for late night socialising, drinking, and gambling. Charles Booth, a nineteenth-century social investigator who mapped the class makeup

Figure 6.1 George Hunt, after Theodore Lane, *Sunday Morning* (c. 1820), LMA/ Bridgeman Art Library.

of London's diverse neighbourhoods, included these spaces in his citywide survey. One member of his investigatory team noted of a South London working neighbourhood that barbers' shops showed great activity throughout the night, 'matched only by a man staggering' along the road and some 'rather gay dancing on the side walk'.[15] Shops were so well trafficked that tradesmen complained of shaving and cutting through the weekend without break, and one small-class hairdresser estimated his working hours as between eighty-five and ninety-two hours a week.[16]

Gender and Space in Haircutting Establishments

This was to change from the mid-century, when new consumer developments transformed a haircut from a cross-class necessity into a high-end luxury. Grooming services grew in popularity amongst all classes of consumer, as new modes of urban consumption extended notions of luxurious self-grooming beyond the elite classes. This was due in large part to the introduction of elite and upper middle-class female customers to West End hairdressing saloons, which recalibrated the consumer experience of their extant male clients. New gendered divisions of high-end hairdressing shops not only accommodated polite feminine sensibilities, but also demarcated a space specifically for masculine grooming rituals, transforming hairdressing and barbering from an everyday routine into a commercialised, potentially elaborate grooming experience. Much as Stella Moss argues of the interwar public house, the mid-nineteenth-century barbershop functioned as a key site of performative masculinity, where male customers enacted gender via rituals and practices of grooming.[17] Specifically, new trends in West End establishments reconfigured the choices that London's men could make about grooming as a reflection of their class status and, subsequently, their relationship to masculinity. Elite and middle-class clients could now eschew utilitarian, mixed-class barbershops, or haircuts and shaves at home, to participate in new, amplified modes of beauty consumption at elite haircutting saloons.

A mid-century advertisement for Frederick 'Professor' Browne's Fenchurch Street hairdressing rooms depicts this transitional moment, in the move away from utilitarian barbershops to middle- to upper middle-class saloons (Fig. 6.2). As one of London's best-advertised barbers, Browne offered a number of amenities that were to become standard in the 1860s and 1870s. The haircutting room featured elaborate decorations, from luxurious light fixtures to visible wallpaper and ornate mouldings. Meanwhile, a number of mirrors adorned the walls for the shared use of clients, in addition to an array of brushes and ointments for sale. The room lacked clear spatial or material divisions between customers, and in this regard, more closely resembled a gentleman's club than a site of bodily services. Two men congregate beside the fire, one of them about to consult the newspaper in hand. Another draws his child's attention to the various goods on display and available for purchase. An exclusively masculine site of luxury and leisure, the space encouraged the open mingling of clients, all the while displaying many of the material items that, as we will see, would increasingly feature in male hairdressing saloons.

Figure 6.2 Professor Browne's Saloon (1850), John Johnson: Beauty Parlour 1(14a), Bodleian Library and ProQuest LLC.

Propelling the commercial shift that positioned hairdressing as both a service and a luxury was the accommodation of newly mobile female consumers by one of Bond Street's leading hairdressers, Robert Douglas (1821–1887). In 1867, Douglas became the first in the trade to offer special amenities for London's female shoppers when he introduced female hands to serve female customers.[18] Initially taking on four female employees to counter a strike amongst his male assistants, Douglas soon realised their pecuniary advantages. In 1870, he expanded their ranks by an additional seventeen lady hairdressers.[19] Soon after, his friend and Bond Street neighbour H. P. Truefitt (1824–1909) also 'tried the experiment' of employing women just down the street from Douglas's rooms.

Having introduced female labourers, both Douglas and Truefitt took the opportunity to make their businesses more hospitable to female clientele through the careful redesign of commercial space and the creation of rooms devoted explicitly to the 'feminine'. Previously, neither businessman provided private areas for female customers venturing outside the home to have their hair cut and dressed.[20] Following other commercial trends in the West End aimed at attending elite women, Douglas and Truefitt invited mobile, increasingly visible female consumers into refurbished spaces specifically organised to ensure gendered propriety and bodily privacy. West End masters used expanding media culture to explain the new gender and class configurations of their palaces of grooming, and their renovation projects gained extensive publicity in the periodical press in the form of interviews and self-produced advertisements. Truefitt marked the occasion with a series of large pictorial advertisements devoted to the 'extensive alterations' to his shop at 13 and 14 Old Bond Street, which 'obtain[ed] a splendid suite of rooms for carrying out' a 'much improved innovation'.[21] The advertisement spotlighted a lady hairdresser washing the hair of an anonymous female client. With her face downward in the washbasin – the standard practice through the latter nineteenth century – Truefitt's illustrated advertisement preserved the privacy of even the fictitious client-subject. For this new space not only created 'splendid suites' to entice women, but carefully mapped gender demarcations onto what was only recently a singularly masculine enclave of homosociability.

New spatial arrangements of gendered commercial space consequently altered the consumer experiences of male clients. By the construction of separate entranceways for women, customers of either sex were assured they would not cross paths, as ladies would 'not be subjected to the inconvenience of having to pass through or in fact see the gentlemen's room'.[22] As the main provider of female-to-female services, Douglas went so far as to divide his two Bond Street addresses by gender: number 23 was converted into the new ladies' shop, while number 21 was devoted exclusively to pre-existing male clients.[23] These two buildings operated completely independently of one another. In fact, the arrangement of the building demanded that a visitor to the ladies' parlour descend back to the ground floor and exit onto Bond Street in order to enter the men's saloon at the back of number 21.

The management of space and trade accoutrements accommodated the desire for discretion and concealment, despite client services taking place in open, populated spaces. The 'Ladies' Room' at Douglas's shop consisted of a long, wide single room marked along one side with private alcoves; each of these 'very small apartments' accommodated a single female client and was 'replete with every known (and to the male sex *un*known) appliance for adding lustre to the female complexion and toilet'. Contrasting the privacy seemingly afforded by these individual alcoves was the stately room in which they were nestled. An accompanying illustration depicted a relatively indiscreet public space, reminiscent of other nineteenth-century communal institutions like museum galleries or reading rooms, which promoted what historian Erika Rappaport terms 'public privacy' by engendering within visitors a false sense of seclusion.[24] And yet, according to one female columnist, 'each lady enjoys entire privacy', which seemingly protected 'those who are waiting their turn catching hairs upon their clothes'. In spite of the grand space 'furnished with every possible requisite for every branch and stage of the toilet', Douglas's room was insufficient in one respect. 'The room is not large enough to accommodate the customers that flock to the saloon in the season.'[25]

As recent additions, some ladies' hairdressing parlours were located on the second floor directly above gentlemen's hairdressing rooms. Gendered demarcation of space was further reinforced by diverse decorating schemes on the two levels. At Nestor Tirard's shop at 39 Curzon Street, the décor in the main men's saloon featured a 'vein marble chimney piece' and 'moulded doors paper[ed] with white and brown'. Increasingly luxurious fittings appeared as one moved upstairs, 'statuary marble pieces' presiding over the ladies' parlour, whose rooms were 'papered with paper and gilt moulding'.[26] For his female clients, Douglas constructed 'a waiting-room, with rich Persian carpet, beautiful fire, and a table heaped with fashionable newspapers and magazines suitable for lady-like waiting moments'.[27] In the cutting room, women were greeted by 'handsome grained panels' and 'snug green curtains', which gave 'a tantalising appearance to the place peculiarly suited to the supposed (or imagined) operations carried on therein'.[28]

Saloon proprietors attempted to protect feminine privacy in the early days of elite female shopping, as well as preserve the masculine comforts typically afforded existing male patrons.[29] Douglas's renovated gentleman's saloon subsequently presented 'the appearance of a comfortable reading room, with large fire, green baize covered table spread with newspapers, glass gasoliers, and many other appliances for comfort', many of which replicated male spaces in the middle-class home, like the personal library or den. Glass panels on each wall gave the illusion of enlarged, open apartments. Similar to the lady's department, its principal features were 'unique alcove boxes', paved with encaustic tile and lined with semi-opaque glass sides. Thus the illusion of privacy in the very public act of luxury consumption and bodily management was a primary concern for both male client and proprietor, as it was 'in private comfort' that the consumer could 'make those purchases which most conduce to individual effect'.[30]

Trade Critiques

Trade journals written for barbers scoffed at the transformation of the shaving experience into a private bodily ritual, as material culture and space positioned clients as active consumers of a luxury service rather than passive recipients of a quotidian necessity. An oft-criticised development was the provision of individual mirrors, so that male clients could observe the haircut and shave as they transpired. Trade columnists complained that this upset the traditional spatial configurations and communal practices of conventional barbershops:

> Instead of the one well-remembered looking-glass, with its black wooden frame, suspended by a nail near the clean jack towel, or fixed above the homely chimney-piece, each patient found himself before a great mirror, which became for the time his own peculiar property, and enabled him to witness his appearance under all the various expression imparted to it during the progress of the operation.[31]

Amplifying the mirrors' focus on the individual male body were decorative details encouraging clients' consumption of personal beauty wares. For the privacy afforded by spatial configurations seems to have also facilitated new forms of male beauty consumption. Decorative shelves became a common feature in upper- and middle-class barbershops. Flanking barber chairs, these shelves were 'filled with gleaming flasks and gorgeous vases, containing choice unguents and costly waters, presented temptations which were urged with bland civility by the obliging "artist"'.[32] The prominence of such goods for sale betrayed the influence of a commodified consumer culture that emerged from the mid-nineteenth century. Rather than concoct their own wares, barbers would increasingly sell manufactured goods to their clients: Rowlands' Macassar Oil, Rimmel's Bear's Grease, Lloyd's Shaving Euxesis, Pear's Soap. These ointments, tonics, and balms were also available for purchase at local chemists and perfumers, but hairdressers urged clients to purchase them at the time of haircut, thereby securing a handy commission. Some enterprising hairdressers and barbers continued to manufacture and wholesale their own goods for use in their shops or for clients to take home. Whether they prepared them on site or elsewhere, hairdressers and barbers had to offer an expansive range of wares to be competitive in the urban market.[33] Other shops expanded their items beyond the standard offerings, peddling masculine knickknacks like watches, chains, umbrellas, and stationery.[34]

In addition to new goods available for purchase, trade journals bemoaned elaborate new practices offered by 'pretentious' coiffeurs. 'Even in remote streets', observed one trader, 'handbills were given away, advertising a "perfumed shower bath", which experience interpreted to mean sprinkling the head with rosewater, from an implement like a flour-dredger'. In other circles, diamond-edge razors reportedly attained widespread popularity. Also popular was the 'Oxford style' of shampooing, having first appeared in the university's student toilet clubs. Echoing the 'American style', which would come to dominate the industry, the practice differed in the barber's use of two or three eggs in lieu of soap.[35] According to one columnist at *The Hairdressers' Chronicle*, the service demanded what was, for him, an uncomfortable level of physical contact with the barber. His 'head, seized from behind by the expert practitioner, was bowed over the receptacle, and in a moment the viscid preparation was poured upon it, while a pair of hands *slithered* (if we may coin a word) hither and thither over his unresisting skull'.[36]

Other more successful technologies designed to enhance the efficiency of hairdressers made for dramatic changes to the material space of the barbershop. Mechanised hairbrushing machines became fixtures in many West End and City saloons, not to mention their being important signifiers of the technological wherewithal of their owners.[37] The contraption consisted of a round, double-handled brush attached by wire pulleys to the barbershop ceiling. With its simple rotary function, hairbrushing by machinery permitted the unhindered turning of the brush in the hairdressers' hands. Reportedly 'a lazy, pleasant, soothing sort of operation', the brush revolved slowly until it was given 'a pull' by its operator. This would send hairdressers into a 'series of gymnastics on the leathern driven band' that secured the contraption.[38] While such contemporary descriptions suggest a chaotic experience, these technologies made for a rational ordering of barbershop space, as well as a standardisation of customer experience. Contrasting with the congenial informality of the working-class barbershop, the middling and elite establishment created a uniform experience for its male customers, who underwent elaborate grooming services in a regimented, carefully choreographed fashion.

The reorganisation of space with the addition of hairbrushing machinery comes to the fore in an 1875 advertisement for Hennig's haircutting rooms in

Figure 6.3   Hennig's Hair Cutting Rooms (1875), John Johnson: Beauty Parlour 1(25), Bodleian Library and ProQuest LLC.

Bloomsbury (Fig. 6.3). Like Professor Browne's room of the 1850s, the décor is relatively elaborate and suggestive of domestic comforts. A fire burns at the far end of the room below a mantel bedecked with a handsome clock and other ornaments, befitting the middle-class standing of the establishment. However, new technologies have reconfigured the organisation of the shop space, emphasising the standardisation of client experience. Most striking is the structuring of the space into very distinct 'stations'. While these stations do not divide customers to the extent of Douglas's individual alcoves, there is a clear delineation between clients that is bolstered by the lack of communal equipment shared amongst hairdressers and their patrons. Indeed, each station features its own hairbrushing machine, with the rotating hairbrush attached to a complex network of cables installed along the saloon's ceiling. Hennig's saloon also features individual sinks, seen in use by one assistant. The hairdresser douses the back of his client's head with a stream of water, which aligns with nineteenth-century practices of placing clients face down in the sink when shampooing. This was an unpleasant experience; not only was there the problem of downward streaming water, but many customers complained that a stench arose from waste in the streets, travelling through the pipes and directly into their nose and mouth.

Those lacking sufficient hair to undergo a shampoo or hairbrushing by machinery could find respite in Britain's booming wig and peruke industry, which surged through the mid-1860s.[39] New women's periodical publications contributed to the incredible popularity of fashionable hairpieces amongst England's elite and middle classes, and between 1855 and 1868, sales of false hair increased some 400 per cent.[40] Hairdressers and barbers profited from new consumer demands; one 1872 inventory registered the most valuable stock of London's leading beauty wholesaler as £3,809 worth of manufacturing hair, which he in turn sold to West End hairdressers and wigmakers.[41] But it was not merely elite and middle-class women who indulged in this trend. Some sources suggest a broader demand for false hairpieces that extended to men as well. This was due in part to exigencies of the Victorian labour market, which meant that youthful workers garnered the most work. Artificial hairpieces and dyes subsequently became a strategy for some Britons to minimise the appearance of age and physical debility. This included middle- and upper-class men, and, by 1893, London's leading wigmaker claimed that in the last year he had sold some 2,500 men's wigs.[42] False hair subsequently became a material fixture in some of London's leading barbershops, arranged in 'cases full of [wigs], and in lace edge boxes' decorating plate-glass windows and interior alcoves. Upon visiting Joseph Lichtenfeld's Oxford Circus barbershop for a shave, one columnist marvelled that he had 'never [seen] such an array of false hair in [his] life'.[43]

Despite frequent complaints by trade leaders about the expansion of grooming practices and goods, the provision of new, discreet grooming services for elite and middle-class men seems to have garnered considerable success for London establishments. A German barber visiting London in 1878 observed that Englishmen advocated frequent if not daily visits to the hairdresser for 'haircutting, singeing – which is done with wax candle ends – shampooing and shave'.[44] By the 1890s, some male West End patrons (or 'victims', as they were dubbed by one assistant) were purported to pay as much as five shillings and six pence per shave, compared with the standard 'ha'penny' or penny treatments in working-class saloons.[45] Extra services not offered in standard barbershops became indispensable to some male customers. One West End assistant described a client who visited the shop up to three times a week. Each time, he purchased 'a special soap and a fresh cake', not to mention a small, expensive bottle of eau de cologne, with which the assistant 'spray[ed] his face over and over until the perfume [was] exhausted'. The process took over a half-hour to perform. Another customer rejected new commercial wares and asked assistants to prepare a traditional wash 'of bay rum, mixed with white of egg, half an ounce of French perfume, and a few drops of lemon juice'. Meanwhile, another client demanded the assistant perform fifteen minutes of 'rubbing his face after shaving' so as to 'beautify the skin'.[46] Upon concluding the shave, assistants would typically offer some brilliantine for the moustache and a dab of perfume for the handkerchief. Finally, there would be a brush of the client's suit and hat, an offering of an umbrella, and an escort through the shop to the front entrance.[47]

Despite trade journals' opposition, similar albeit less ostentatious establishments soon appeared in urban railway stations including Charing Cross.[48] From the early 1870s, enterprising contractors like Eugene Thiellay (1838–1901) established private rooms offering haircutting and dressing, shaving, washing, and boot cleaning. To this, proprietors 'added the sale of small toilet requisites, corn and nail cutting, receipt of letters, delivery of messages, and, in one or two instances, foot-baths, sponge baths, and private dressing rooms'.[49] As one trade columnist argued, these services in many ways replicated those of traditional barbershops, where barbers received and forwarded messages and sold small jars of pomade and brilliantine. Yet the columnist definitively situated these developments within a 'new system', one that removed the congenial familiarity of the local barbershop, replacing it with a polished commercial façade of discreet, genteel grooming services.

Conclusion

Once new and innovative, particular material additions to British barbershops became increasingly standard: individual mirrors, shampoo systems, hairbrushing machinery, sumptuous goods for sale. Nonetheless, small-scale and working-class shops continued to shave local men without such accoutrements, creating a significant divide between them and well-equipped saloons. In this way, the elaboration of elite and middle-class men's experiences in high-end luxury saloons reduced the ease with which they had once solicited modest utilitarian barbershops, although it remains unclear the extent to which men abandoned lowlier shops. The divide was significant enough, however, to draw the attention of trade publications, which highlighted the growing class gulf. An 1883 satirical series, in *The Hairdressers' Weekly Journal*, detailed the exploits of anonymous columnist 'A Drone' on his visits to barbershops across the metropolis: on Regent Street, in the City, in Whitechapel. Traversing London's socioeconomic and imagined topography, the self-proclaimed 'willful idler' described both the services and facilities of local hairdressing businesses, noting at various junctures his attraction to the West End's 'very pretty windows' or his delight at being served by Englishmen 'instead of the eternal foreigner'.[50] Having visited many of London's upper- and middle-class establishments, he declared his surprise at finding 'so many places, all carrying on the same trade, [but] conducting it so differently'.[51]

However, 'The Drone' drew such conclusions before he had ventured to working-class barbershops, and it was in London's plebeian East End that he realised the significant material divisions separating different classes of barbershops. Forced to wait at one working-class establishment alongside another customer, the columnist was appalled by displays of sociable familiarity between the barber and his clientele. Aghast, 'The Drone' described how the proprietor, a 'half-dressed youth express[ing] his disgust very audibly', served a customer who 'actually divested himself of coat, collar, and necktie … chatting on things theatrical at the same time'. Fortunately, the charm of a subsequent shop provided the columnist welcome relief, and he deemed it 'in its way quite as complete as anything up West, excepting, perhaps, that [he saw] no appliance for brushing the hair by machinery'. Far removed from the luxurious privacy of West End establishments, he theatrically lamented his desire for upper-class shops, with their innovative machines and careful preservation of individual space.[52]

That is not to say elite and middle-class men's saloons were completely devoid of homosocial interaction.[53] To be sure, proprietors promoted West End saloons as a site of congenial encounters between peers, but only those of similar class standing. Members of parliament and the gentry solicited Douglas and Truefitt, and patrons were encouraged to take advantage of their presence. According to *The Hairdressers' Chronicle*, 'to meet at Douglas's [was] nearly as common an appointment as the West-end affords'. In no way did these measured encounters resemble the boisterous homosociability characterising London's utilitarian barbershops. Rather, Douglas's saloon was touted as an extension of the West End's Clubland, all the while affording 'every requisite likely to be required for a gentleman's hair – notably, pomades, washes, brilliantine, cosmetics, astringents, lotions, etc.'[54]

In many ways, shifting spatial configurations and the elaboration of grooming services amongst London's elite and middle-class men suggest a growth in luxury male beauty consumption. This development challenges perceptions of men's move away from beauty consumption through the late nineteenth and early twentieth centuries. As we will see in Chapter 7, this included the ways in which the industry's growing focus on female customers amplified beauty commodities' associations with deviant male sexuality. However, late Victorian male beauty consumption took a very specific form that prioritised individualised, increasingly mechanised rituals and bodily privacy. The new commercial spaces opened up by nineteenth-century grooming establishments meant that elite and middle-class patrons no longer had to undergo quotidian shaving practices in public, sociable forums like the local barbershop, which laid bare the vulnerabilities of the classed male body. While we do not know the extent to which middle-class men abandoned their local barbershops it is clear that, for many elite men, bodily self-fashioning was increasingly practised in the confines of the home or the feigned privacy of London's elite hairdressing saloons, a development that both engendered and limited the possibilities for male beauty consumption into the twentieth century.

Notes

1. 'Past and Present', *The Hairdressers' Chronicle*, 3:31 (1 May 1869), p. 50.
2. See Susan Vincent's chapter (Chapter 3) in this collection.
3. See, for example, C. Breward, *The Hidden Consumer: Masculinities, Fashion, and City Life, 1860–1914* (Manchester: University of Manchester Press, 1999); P. R. Deslandes, 'The Male Body, Beauty and Aesthetics in Modern British Culture', *History Compass*, 8 (October 2010), pp. 1191–1208; D. Kutcha, *The Three-Piece Suit and Modern Masculinity: England, 1550–1850* (Berkeley: University of California Press, 2002); and B. Shannon, *The Cut of his Coat: Men, Dress, and Consumer Culture in Britain, 1860–1914* (Athens, OH: Ohio University Press, 1996).
4. Breward, *Hidden Consumer*, pp. 55, 57.
5. To be sure, some elite men continued to rely on servants to shave them and trim their hair at home, and there is no doubt that ladies continued to do this. Indeed, a common practice in urban shops was the renting out of hairdressers to visit clients in their home and render their services in the comfort of a client's boudoir.

6. C. Oldstone-Moore, 'The Beard Movement in Victorian Britain', *Victorian Studies*, 48 (2005), pp. 7–34; G. Ofek, *Representations of Hair in Victorian Literature and Culture* (New York: Ashgate, 2009), p. 37; and S. Walton, 'Squalid Impropriety to Manly Respectability: the Revival of Beards, Moustaches and Martial Values in the 1850s in England', *Nineteenth-Century Contexts*, 30 (2008), pp. 229–245.

7. Many nineteenth-century print representations of hairdressers and barbers were decidedly unfavourable. One characterisation of the 'Average Barber', featured in the satirical journal *Tit Bits*, claimed he was 'in a state of perspiration and is greasy … wear[ing] a paper collar', as 'he snips and snips away, pinching your ears, nipping your eyelashes and your jaw until you think he must have cut off enough hair to fill a mattress'. Quoted in 'En Passant', *The Hairdressers' Weekly Journal*, 5 (3 June 1882), p. 73.

8. W. Andrews, *At the Sign of the Barber's Pole* (Cottingham, Yorkshire: J. R. Tutin, 1904), p. 8.

9. D. Herzog, *Poisoning the Minds of the Lower Orders* (Princeton, NJ: Princeton University Press, 1998), and 'The Trouble with Hairdressers', *Representations*, 53 (Winter 1996), p. 26.

10. Census returns from 1851 registered some 2,338 hairdressers in London, outnumbering metropolitan hatters but still significantly less than numbers of fashionable traders like tailors. *Annual Report of the Registrar-General of Births, Deaths, and Marriages in England* (London: George E. Eyre, 1855), p. 148.

11. Writing on mortality rates amongst hairdressers and barbers, Dr J. T. Arlidge noted, 'The occupation is unfavorable to vigorous development and muscular activity, whilst it rather favors effeminacy … Moreover, the character of the occupation recommends it for adoption by the weaker members of society.' See J. T. Arlidge, *The Hygiene, Diseases, and Mortality of Occupations* (London: Percival, 1892), p. 176.

12. 'Recollections of a Poor Barber', *The Hairdressers' Chronicle*, 11:283 (15 September 1877), p. 145.

13. *The Hairdressers' Chronicle*, 1:3 (1 January 1867), p. 5.

14. For other representations of barbershops, see Lewis Walpole Library, 789.0.59 BMC at 7605, Thomas Rowlandson, *A Penny Barber* (London: William Holland, 1789); and Metropolitan Museum of Art, 59.533.1658, Thomas Rowlandson after Henry William Bunbury, *A Barber's Shop* (1803).

15. C. Booth (ed.), 'Inner South London', *Life and Labour of the People in London*, 4 vols (New York: Macmillan, 1902), IV, p. 189.

16. The Charles Booth Archive at the London School of Economics and Political Science, Notebook B160, Hairdresser & Wigmaker Interviews, p. 79; Booth Archive, B160, p. 87.

17. See Chapter 8 in this collection.

18. Before their appearance at his new ladies' parlour at 23 New Bond Street, *coiffeuses*, or female hairdressers, were reportedly unheard of. In 1864, campaigner Jessie Boucherett claimed it 'hardly possible to introduce' women as ladies' hairdressers. See J. Boucherett, 'On the Cause of the Distress Prevalent among Single Women. A Paper Read at the Social Science Congress', *English Woman's Journal*, 12:72 (1 Feb. 1864), pp. 400–409; and 'The Present Fashions in Hair', *The Graphic*, 26 (28 May 1870), p. 603.

19. On the strike, see 'Trade Misunderstanding', *The Hairdressers' Chronicle*, 2:22 (1 Aug. 1868), p. 5; and 'Mr. Douglas and his Assistants', *The Hairdressers' Chronicle*, 2:23 (1 Sept. 1868), p. 5.

20. *The Hairdressers' Chronicle*, 12 (2 Mar. 1878), p. 37.

21. Advertisement in Leonard de Vries and Illonka van Amstel, *Victorian Advertising* (London: Murray, 1968), p. 45.

22. 'Trade Enterprise', *Hairdressers' Weekly Journal*, 1:5 (3 June 1882), p. 48. These developments echo the amenities offered by the department store in the late nineteenth century. Many scholars argue that the emergence of these stores facilitated the expansion of West End consumption and pleasure to increasingly mobile upper middle-class women. See, for example, W. Lancaster, *The Department Store: A Social History* (London: Leicester University Press, 1995); W. R. Leach, 'Transformations in a Culture of Consumption: Women and Department Stores, 1890–1925', *Journal of American History*, 71:2 (September 1984), pp. 319–342; M. Nava, 'Modernity's Disavowal: Women, the City, and the Department Store', in M. Nava and A. O'Shea (eds), *Modern Times: Reflections on a Century of Modernity* (London: Routledge, 1996); and E. D. Rappaport, *Shopping for Pleasure: Women and the Making of London's West End* (Princeton, NJ: Princeton University Press, 2001), especially chapters 3 and 5.

23. 'A West-End Hairdressers' Establishment Described', *The Hairdressers' Chronicle*, 14:351 (17 July 1880), p. 109.

24. Rappaport, *Shopping*, p. 124. See also R. Hoberman, 'Women in the British Museum Reading Room during the Late-Nineteenth and Early-Twentieth Centuries: From Quasi- to Counterpublic', *Feminist Studies*, 28 (Fall 2002), pp. 489–512.

25. 'A West-End Hairdressers' Establishment', p. 109. The men's rooms also featured private boxes, although the columnist found that '"gentlemen" scorn even to be shaved in "camera", and the snug green curtains in each and every box remain undrawn, while each and every operation is performed on manly heads'.

26. LMA, O/108/014/001, 'Lease for 21 years, counterpart', Henry White Hitchins and Jean Nestor Marie Tirard for 39 Curzon Street, Mayfair, Middlesex, 26 June 1865.

27. 'A West-End Hairdressers' Establishment', p. 109.

28. 'A West-End Hairdressers' Establishment', p. 109.

29. See J. R. Walkowitz, 'Going Public: Shopping, Street Harassment, and Streetwalking in Late Victorian London', *Representations*, 62 (1998), p. 1.

30. 'A West-End Hairdressers' Establishment', p. 109.

31. 'Then and Now', *The Hairdressers' Chronicle*, 3:32 (1 June 1869), p. 55.

32. 'Then and Now', *The Hairdressers' Chronicle*, 3:32 (1 June 1869), p. 55.

33. 'A West-End Hairdressers' Establishment', p. 110.

34. 'Our Correspondent, "A Drone", in the City', *Hairdressers' Weekly Journal* (31 March 1883), p. 206.

35. According to the *Oxford English Dictionary*, 'shampoo' did not function as a noun until 1838. Developed in New York, the American process was purportedly introduced to Britain by Alfred Tugwell of Scarborough in the late 1870s. 'Celebrities Connected with the Trade: No. 15 – Alfred John Tugwell', *Hairdressers' Weekly Journal*, 3:106 (17 May 1884), p. 315.

36. *The Hairdressers' Chronicle*, 3:32 (1 June 1869), p. 55.

37. 'Our Correspondent, "A Drone", in Whitechapel', *Hairdressers' Weekly Journal* (28 April 1883), p. 264.

38. 'Regent Street Hairdressers', *Hairdressers' Weekly Journal* (24 February 1883), p. 125.

39. Booth Archive, B160, p. 87.

40. 'Artificial Hair', *Lady's Treasury* (1 October 1868), p. 53. Quoted in Ofek, *Representations of Hair*, p. 37.

41. The 1872 returns reveal Robert Hovenden's total capital at £36,000. The stock in manufacturing hair was matched only by the combined worth of perfumery and foreign perfumery, some £2,453. The haircutting or 'trimming' department was valued at only £696. See S. Jones, 'R. Hovenden & Sons, Ltd.', *Business Archives*, 56 (1988), p. 29.

42. 'How Nature's Mistakes are Put Right', *Pearson's Weekly* (21 October 1893), n.p. According to wigmaker Willy Clarkson, the wigs were made so well that it was 'not possible, except for a coiffeur, to tell the difference between a wig and a real head of hair'. 'Trilby Feet and Svengali Wigs', *Westminster Budget* (13 December 1895), n.p.

43. 'Our Correspondent, "The Drone", with the Regent Street Hairdressers', *Hairdressers' Weekly Journal* (10 March 1883), p. 159. For more on Lichtenfeld, see his *Principles of Physiognomical Hairdressing, with Illustrations* (London: The Author, 1883).

44. '"The Hairdressing Trade in London" from *Der Friseur*', *The Hairdressers' Chronicle*, 12 (2 March 1878), p. 37.

45. Booth (ed.), *Life and Labour of the People in London*, vol. 13, p. 275. In utilitarian shops, which charged approximately 2*d*. or 3*d*. for a haircut and 1*d*. for a shave, the wage of a live-in assistant ranged between 6*s*. and 14*s*. per week. Booth Archive, B160, p. 59.

46. 'Such Luxuries are Costly', *Cassell's Saturday Magazine* (6 April 1898), p. 628.

47. 'Regent Street Hairdressers', *Hairdressers' Weekly Journal* (24 February 1883), p. 125.

48. *Kelly's Directory of Trades*, 1869; 1870; 1872; 1874.

49. *The Hairdressers' Chronicle*, 6:135 (1 June 1872), p. 46.

50. 'Our Correspondent, "The Drone", with the Regent Street Hairdressers', p. 159. By the late nineteenth century, a contemporary examination of trade directories found that of 1,696 master hairdressers, 518, or 31 per cent, were 'obviously foreigners'. See Booth (ed.), *Life and Labour of the People in London*, III, p. 277. On London's 'reductive and illusory' East/West divide, see L. Nead, *Victorian Babylon: People, Streets, and Images in Nineteenth-Century London* (New Haven, CT: Yale University Press, 2000); J. R. Walkowitz, *City of Dreadful Delight* (New York; Yale University Press, 1991), p. 38; J. R. Walkowitz, 'The Indian Woman, the Flower Girl, and the Jew: Photojournalism in Edwardian London', *Victorian Studies*, 42 (October 1998), pp. 3–46; and J. Winter, *London's Teeming Streets, 1830–1914* (London: Routledge, 1993).

51. 'Our Correspondent, "The Drone", with the Regent Street Hairdressers', p. 159. One of The Drone's stops included Professor Browne's Saloon. By 1883, it was reportedly 'an old-fashioned place' that had been 'gradually altered a piece at a time to meet the requirements of the advance of the age; but there is a want of thoroughness in the look of it'.

52. 'Our Correspondent, "A Drone", in Whitechapel', p. 264.

53. Neither did they create the level of privacy suggested by the construction of new, discreet spaces of grooming. Ultimately, these services and material goods improved the *public* appearance of men. There is subsequently a tension between private and public performance. The barbershop mediated this conflict, making male grooming acceptable for a new generation of consumers.

54. 'A West-End Hairdressers' Establishment', p. 110.

7

Queer Things: Men and Make-up Between the Wars

Matt Houlbrook

In January 1925 the weekly journal *John Bull* called the attention of William Joynson-Hicks, the Home Secretary, to an 'appalling miscarriage of justice' – 'a young man languishing today in jail who ... ought not to be there'. There was nothing unusual in this. Since its launch two decades earlier, *John Bull* had outspokenly defended the British everyman. Populist in tone, muckraking in style, it acted 'without fear or favour' to expose the dangers of over-bearing political and financial elites, a rising tide of immorality, and the insidious depravations of various 'foreigners'.[1] This story was more unusual, however: Thomas B., a twenty-three-year-old railway porter from Rhondda, had been imprisoned for three months by the Bow Street magistrate for 'importuning male persons for an immoral purpose'. Plainclothes police had observed Thomas 'accosting' men as he walked between the Tivoli Theatre, Lyons Corner House, and a nearby urinal, then arrested him on the Strand. He was 'searched and on him was found a few pounds in money and, certainly a remarkable thing, a lady's powder puff, powder and a small mirror'. Presented as evidence in court, the case against Thomas hinged upon these objects. Merely possessing a powder puff seemed to establish Thomas's offence, providing a material sign of his deviant character and transgressions. The contents of his pockets, police suggested, indicated that Thomas was the sort of man who would look for sex in London's streets. To 'prove' his guilt, their case interwove the effeminised male body, sex between men, the traces of commodity culture, and the operations of the law. According to this logic, the man who owned a powder puff was effeminate; the effeminate man possessed illicit sexual desires; such a man was of the 'male importuning type'.[2]

There was no explicit suggestion that Thomas had powdered his face, but his body had been symbolically, if not physically, marked as transgressive through the contents of his pockets. When *John Bull* came to Thomas's defence they did not challenge this logic. They acknowledged the presence of 'hardened and impudent blackguards long inured to their shameless traffic' in London – the sort of men who might rouge their cheeks. Yet Thomas, they suggested, was not part of this world. Having outlined his background and 'exemplary' character *John Bull* asked: 'is this the type of young man who becomes a social pest in the West End of London?' The answer, apparently, was no. Thomas had visited London only seven times. On this occasion he was visiting the British Empire Exhibition with his mother. This was 'no case hardened West End pest but a simple country visitor' – a rural innocent abroad in a city where glittering pleasures coexisted with moral perils and vice. *John Bull* extricated Thomas from the case against him. The powder puff:

> *belonged to his mother!* She was carrying it in a lady's vanity bag, with keys and money. The jet link handle broke ... the mother took out the powder-puff, the mirror, the keys and her money, and asked her son to carry them for her on the journey to Wembley.

Thomas was not a 'social pest', but a dutiful son. *John Bull* implored Joynson-Hicks to intervene to 'remove from this unhappy youth, not only the restraint upon his liberty, but the dreadful brand of shame that is eating into his heart'.[3]

The object found in Thomas's pockets (and the debate over its significance that followed) drove the story of the 'man with the powder puff'. More than a mundane trace of interwar commodity culture, the powder puff had a symbolic meaning that resonated on London's streets, in the courtroom, in a popular newspaper and in the minds of the reading public. Taking Thomas's story as a starting point, this chapter explores the relationship between gender, sexuality and things. In so doing, it draws upon recent theoretical and historiographical work on materiality to challenge dominant approaches in the history of sexuality. Following Frank Trentmann's conceptualisation of the relationship between material culture and history, I am interested in the powder puff not simply as a commodity (an object defined by consumerism and understood as a personal possession). Instead I understand it as an object that connects public and private life, and subjectivities or identities, with the material world in which they take shape.[4] While we are often used to thinking of sexuality as natural, innate and fixed, following an object like the powder puff from its production, marketing and retail through its use by a man to its appearance in court affords different perspectives on that assumption. First: it suggests how ideas of sexual difference and normality were historically specific and changed over time. As Karen Harvey suggests in her chapter in this volume, focusing on material culture suggests how fashioning identities of gender and sexuality was an ongoing and contested process. Second: it allows us to see how the material world was itself sexualised and gendered – understood as masculine or feminine or associated with particular kinds of sexual transgression. Around the same time that Thomas was arrested, the London County Council locked or removed the cast iron urinals that dotted the city's streets and alleyways. Elsewhere they added white tiles and full-length doors to toilet cubicles and introduced powerful new electric lights. The fabric of the city was changed to stop men meeting and to express dominant ideas of sexual difference and normality. This points to the third way that this essay challenges dominant assumptions in the history of sexuality: like the use and regulation of the urinal, the way that police looked for the powder puff is a striking example of the agency of things. Items like the powder puff carried meanings that could not easily be controlled by the individuals who possessed or sought them. Thinking queer about material culture, I conclude by showing the capacity of things to disrupt dominant ideas of sexual difference and normality and established modes of social classification.

The Powder Puff: Cosmetics as More than Commodities

Thomas's case is significant because it was not isolated: powder puffs and cosmetic products were used as evidence in dozens of prosecutions for importuning between the wars. These apparently innocuous objects nonetheless established links between the effeminised male body, sexual transgression, and criminality that could send men to prison. How could this be the case? Tracing the cultural, commercial, technological and legal foundations of a distinctive material culture of law enforcement, I place such objects within the intersecting histories that gave them meaning. Removing a powder puff from a man's pocket to use as evidence in court depended upon the growing salience of the effeminate 'painted boy' to public understandings of sexual difference in the 1920s. Cosmetics became integral to many queer men's self-presentation because of a pervasive assumption that same-sex desire was contingent upon an essentially woman-like character. While, as Jessica Clark shows in her chapter in this volume, new products and spaces for male personal grooming developed quickly in the late nineteenth century, by the interwar period men could use make-up to render their desires visible because of rapid changes in the production, advertising, and retail of cosmetics, and the emergence of a vibrant beauty culture that made make-up cheap, accessible, and an essential attribute of fashionable femininity.

Why did police officers and legal officials become obsessed with make-up? Looking for material evidence in importuning prosecutions allowed officers to address deep public distrust in their integrity in the 1920s. Other observers found cosmetics a fascinating yet troubling sign of how men could cross or blur boundaries between masculine and feminine just by manipulating their appearance. The use of cosmetics as evidence was braced by and contributed to anxieties about the Great War's disruptive effects on society and culture. Placing 'the man with the powder puff' against parallel debates over women's use of cosmetics, I show how changing ideas of fashionable femininity made the meanings of rouge or lipstick more unclear at the same time as men's make-up was becoming an acknowledged sign of sexual transgression. Thomas's defence was only part of an expansive debate over the meanings of make-up in interwar Britain.

In the lists of exhibits presented during prosecutions for importuning or keeping a disorderly house, the powder puff and other cosmetic products were a ubiquitous presence, as the Met turned a magpie-like gaze on arrested men's pockets and the floors of bars and nightclubs. In 1924 the hotel porter William K. was sentenced to nine months' hard labour after being arrested on Piccadilly. 'When searched', the Old Bailey heard, 'face powder, scented handkerchiefs, and two photographs of himself in woman's costume were found'.[5] London's courts often seemed captivated by the ephemeral traces of queer material culture. In one sense, cosmetics were equivalent to the material evidence used in other kinds of prosecution: the jemmy, for breaking and entering, for example. Yet while such objects were used to force open a door, the powder puff was less clearly linked to an offence. Rather than a criminal act, it stood for a criminal type, evoking powerful public images of the kind of man who might importune on London's streets. In 1936 one solicitor described 'a type of moral pervert who seemed to delight in imitating persons of the opposite sex, not only in dress and speech but in regard to the use of powder *and the carrying of such things as powder puffs and rouge*'.[6] When police officers presented 'such things' in court they rarely explained what they meant. They might describe arrested men's 'bad character', but were surprisingly curt when talking about their possessions: 'when [Alfred] was arrested he had upon him some rouge and a powder puff', one commented in 1922.[7] The objects were left to stand on their own, as if they possessed an intrinsic verbosity that needed no elaborating. Men themselves recognised the dangerous significance attributed to their possessions, discarding lipsticks, rouge and powder compacts when facing arrest. The most compelling evidence of queer material culture was left on the floor.[8]

Make-up's meaning was bitterly contested in court, as legal officials and defendants struggled to define the significance of commodities like the powder puff. Facing public suspicion and the threat of prison, arrested men tried to explain why they possessed such objects and evade the association between cosmetics and sexual transgression. Some emphasised the medicinal qualities of beauty products. In 1922, Lewis H. was tried before the Tower Bridge magistrate. Police testified to the tin of cold cream and face powder in his possession and suggested that these items embodied his deviant character. Supported by his mother, Lewis argued that he used them to relieve pain after shaving 'as [his] skin is so tender'.[9] Other men argued that the cosmetics in their pockets were necessary for their occupation. That was particularly the case for those who worked in the theatre or music hall, where cosmetics were used to create characters and address the effects of modern stage lighting.[10] In 1924, DS Harris arrested the actor Frank N. in a pub in Brixton: 'on him he found two powder puffs and some grease paint'. In cross-examination, Frank's solicitor emphasised the importance of cosmetics in his client's profession. Harris had to admit 'he knew that actors used grease paint, but he did not know that they powdered their face after making up'. Frank's mistake, his solicitor suggested, was only carrying those products out of the theatre and into the pub where they could gain very different meaning.[11]

These cases are not quite unique to the interwar period, but they are characteristic of it. Newspapers noted the presence of 'painted boys' in central London and police drew attention to arrested men's appearance, in the late nineteenth century, but there is no record of cosmetics being used as evidence in court.[12] That process had begun by 1912: arrested in the West End, Alan Horton's 'face and lips ... appeared to be artificially reddened and in [his] pocket ... was found a powder puff with pink powder on it'. This object, commented Lord Chief Justice Alverstone, was 'not unimportant in connection with an offence of this kind'. If the importance of cosmetics in importuning trials was acknowledged before the Great War, there were few recorded cases. It was in the 1920s and 1930s that such practices became most common, generating an unprecedented number of examples in legal files and newspaper reports. After the Second World War, the powder puff again vanished from the courtroom.[13] The courtroom history of cosmetics has a distinctive chronology.

Sexuality, Gender and Transgression

The use of cosmetics as evidence first suggests how ideas of sexual difference and normality were historically specific. The significance of the powder puff reflected an assumption that male 'effeminacy' was a sign of transgressive sexual desires. Challenging a pervasive contemporary assumption that sexual practices and identities have always been organised around the opposition between 'homosexual' and 'heterosexual' or 'gay' and 'straight', over the past three decades historians have drawn attention to the ways in which sexual identities have a history; they change over time and are shaped by divisions of gender, class, age, race, ethnicity and place. The 'man with the powder puff' story was underpinned by ways of thinking in which difference and 'normality' were embodied in the distinction between flamboyantly camp 'queans' and 'men', rather than in modern categories of homo- and heterosexual. Within working-class culture in the first decades of the twentieth century, this distinction offered both a mode of self-understanding and a way of interpreting other men's behaviour. Quentin Crisp recalled: 'the same exaggerated and over-simplified distinction that separated men from women ... ran like a wall straight and impassable between ... roughs and ... bitches'. Sexual difference was associated with effeminacy: Crisp 'was over thirty before I heard someone say ... that he did not think of himself as masculine or feminine but simply as a person attracted to other people with male sexual organs'.[14] Sexual desires were thus understood as an inherent attribute of gender, embedded in an innate physiology or psychology. Set against the 'exaggerated' distinction between men and women, male and female bodies were assumed to be 'sexed' in particular ways. The desire for a woman was considered inherently masculine. The desire for a man was a priori womanlike. The gendered opposition between 'quean' and man meant men neither understood themselves, nor were labelled by others, through their choice of sexual partner.

These ideas shaped how all contemporaries interpreted same-sex practices between the wars. They were codified through sexological case histories and theories.[15] They were most important in shaping how working-class men made sense of their lives. 'We were queer,' John Alcock recalled, 'so we were much more like women than we were like men.'[16] For Alcock, and others, the idea that his desires reflected his womanlike nature gave them meaning, shaping both how he talked about himself, and his erotic, affective, and social life. When same-sex desire was understood as contingent upon a broader deviation from normative masculinities, the basis for labelling someone a 'quean' was not who a man had sex with but his gendered character. Sam remembered: people 'might call you queer, but ... only ... because they thought you was a bit girlish ... not because of the sexual act'.[17] Terms like Nancy-boy and pouf denoted gendered patterns of behaviour rather than sexual behaviour and were used to describe those who failed to do what was expected of a man at work, on the streets, or at play.[18]

Men were labelled as different because their behaviour approximated to practices culturally ascribed to women, but the effeminised male body was thought to be sexed in specific ways. In 1922 the metal worker William S. was arrested for importuning on Waterloo Road. Seeking information about his background, police visited William's workplace in Hoxton. As workmates tried to understand William's behaviour, his failure to meet the demands of working-class masculinity acquired deeper significance. He was, they noted, 'rather womanish in habits'. Set against hegemonic masculinities, the man whose 'habits' were 'womanish' could not but desire men.[19] In 1933, similarly, the *Morning Advertiser* reported the trial of sixty men arrested at a Holland Park Avenue drag ball under the headline 'MEN DRESSED AS WOMEN'.[20] Reports of the case, and the comments of the Recorder, Ernest Wild, suggested that the men were thought to have done more than cross-dressing. Wild linked appearance and sexual character, and praised the police for exposing this 'nest of sodomitical haunts'. Treating male gender inversion as a sign of sodomy, he assumed that transgressive sexual desires could be read off the male body.[21] This represented a distinct shift in understandings of sexual difference that explains the absence of cosmetics from the courtroom before the Great War. Historians have highlighted the 'indeterminacy' of the associations between gender and sexuality in the nineteenth century. Male 'effeminacy' was not automatically read as a signifier of sexual practice or as an essential character trait of the 'homosexual'.[22] This meant that powder puffs had negligible power to 'prove' a defendant's 'guilt'. In the early twentieth century, however, the regular prosecutions reported in the press and a series of spectacular 'pansy cases' eroded this 'indeterminacy'. By the 1920s, the effeminate 'quean' was the dominant image of queer urban culture: exactly the sort of man who would look for sex with other men in London's streets.[23]

The use of cosmetics as evidence also allows us to see how material culture was itself sexualised and gendered – understood as masculine or feminine, or associated with particular kinds of sexual transgression. The opposition between 'quean' and man thus underpinned the second process through which cosmetics entered the courtroom: the emergence of the 'beauty industry' and a new mass market in cosmetics in the 1920s. Young women's increasing spending power and cinema's influence on ideas of fashionable femininity were the context within which 'selling beauty as a product became much more systematic, self-conscious and widespread'.[24] From being an expensive and dissolute preserve of performers and fallen women in the mid-nineteenth century, through modern industrial production, marketing and retail cosmetics became integral to a consumer culture that encouraged young women to buy into changing norms of self-presentation.[25] The growth of the international empires built by Elizabeth Arden, Helena Rubinstein and Max Factor between the wars was founded partly on their commitment to experimental research. A dialogue with the physical sciences led to the discovery of new colouring and therapeutic agents and precise chemical formulae for cosmetic products.[26] New processes like the 'Modern Face Powder Machine' depicted in Redgrove and Foan's *Paint, Powder and Patches* (1930) allowed cosmetics to be mass produced cheaply.[27] Commitment to innovation and technological advances meant new products appeared on the market at a remarkable rate in the early twentieth century – mascara, pressed powder and compacts, vanity cases, nail varnish, and twist-up lipstick. By the 1930s, the cosmetics industry was an international concern, with giant factories like that of Cheesbrough-Pond's on the Great West Road or Boots in Nottingham using the latest industrial techniques, scientific research and development and agreed standards of health and safety.[28]

These changes made lipstick or powder compacts an increasingly familiar presence in advertising and shops between the wars, as companies sought to encourage women to wear make-up and buy their products through sophisticated publicity campaigns that confronted young women with images of 'desirable' forms of femininity. Desperate to maintain their female readership and attract the lucrative advertising revenue provided by cosmetics companies, columnists gave advice on 'becoming visibly feminine' and offered guidance on applying cosmetics.[29] More than respectable, cosmetics became almost a social imperative for fashionable women. In the *Daily Express* in 1929 actress Clare Hardwicke commented: 'makeup is a modern necessity. No woman can do without it'.[30] If mass production made make-up cheap and advertising made it a 'modern necessity', changes in retail made cosmetics more accessible. Although salons had sold beauty products since the late nineteenth century, they had been neither publicly displayed nor widely available. The 'American' retail practices associated with the expanding chain and department store sector changed this. In 1909, Selfridges in London's Oxford Street became the first store to display powder and rouge openly. By the 1930s, their customers could sample products and 'learn secrets of the skilful and artistic treatment of the complexion' from trained experts.[31] The growth of the cosmetics industry was thus intertwined with the reinvigorated consumerism of the 1920s, exemplified by the success of companies like Woolworth's, selling affordable mass produced commodities.

In the 1920s, for the first time, items like the powder puff were thus cheap, readily available, and promoted as an essential attribute of modern womanhood. This was the context in which Taylor Croft observed that 'the use of cosmetics has become general' among queer men.[32] Buying into consumer cultures of femininity allowed working-class men to fashion a public persona through commodities available in the local department store. What was labelled 'effeminacy' reflected how they drew upon the gender culture in which they were socialised, to make their bodies publicly intelligible. Powder puffs, lipstick and eye shadow embodied what men understood as their essential nature. As a young man in the East End, Terry Gardener 'went to Woolworth's for a stick of make-up ... If you were posh you bought Leichner powder ... A threepenny stick of make-up ... a sixpenny box of powder and I was equipped for anything.'[33] Alex Purdie, similarly, 'was a swine for make-up ... We used to have a velouti on the ecaf ... thought we looked absolutely marvellous.'[34] The shops and products are recognisable and every-day. Men plucked and pencilled their eyebrows; they wore lipstick, eye shadow, rouge and powder; they painted their fingernails.[35] The material culture of fashionable femininity allowed them to create an arrestingly colourful and striking public persona. In a gendered consumer market, the use of cosmetics was unambiguously coded as womanlike. It was thus make-up that visibly distinguished the 'quean' from 'normal' men. Common phrases like 'men of the powder and paint calibre' suggest the importance invested in the condition of men's faces in defining their transgressions.[36]

The development of the beauty industry thus transformed the visual and material signs in which observers located queer men's deviance. By the 1920s police officers clearly assumed that transgressive sexual desires and criminal behaviour could be read off the effeminised male body. In 1927 representatives of the Street Offences Committee asked PC Handford 'have these male importuners ... anything distinctive about them?' Handford replied immediately: 'yes. Painted lips, powder'.[37] It was, the committee concluded, likely that a man would have 'outward indication of his nefarious habits'.[38] The 'painted boy' offered a working definition of the perpetrator of a sexual offence, his body a sign of deviant intent and his pockets subject to scrutiny. The cosmetics industry's spectacular success in ensuring its products were indelibly linked with femininity, beauty and appearance, in the 1920s meant that older forms of male body management, particularly the use of antiseptic powders after shaving, became problematic – increasingly considered incompatible with 'normal' masculinities, they now risked drawing suspicion.

The powder puffs produced in London's courts thus represented and shaped a change in how sexual difference was understood. Their use as evidence still depended on changes within the cosmetics industry, however. Consider the restaurant scene witnessed by A. B. Walkley in 1922. Watching a young woman 'plying her lipstick as frequently as her knife and fork' he was struck by 'the unabashed publicity of the whole affair. Women used to 'make-up' in private ... Now they powder their noses and redden their lips with a flaunting publicity in the street, on the top of the bus, at the restaurant ... everywhere.'[39] Applying powder on a bus required 'confidence' and the assumption that the fashionable modern woman had to maintain the illusion of beauty. It also required new technologies that allowed her to do so: portable cosmetic commodities that could be carried in a purse or pocket. In 1922, police displayed the 'face powder in a machine' found on Lewis H. To succeed, this use of evidence depended upon the associations between effeminacy and criminality. It could only be adopted because companies like Stratton had begun to manufacture mechanical powder compacts that men like Lewis could buy and carry after the Great War.[40]

The Agency of Things

As this suggests, the use of the powder puff as evidence in court is a striking example of the agency of things. Cosmetic items carried meanings that could not easily be controlled by the individuals who sought them. This process reflected and fuelled wider anxieties surrounding the erosion of social boundaries after the Great War. Describing London as a 'modern Gomorrah' in June 1925, *John Bull* drew attention to,

> a well-known teashop and public house in Coventry Street ... where painted and scented boys congregate every day without molestation of any kind ... sit[ting] with their vanity bags and their high-heeled shoes, calling themselves by endearing names and looking out for patrons.

This was a disturbing sight: 'we … conquered the Germans and now in London there is an outbreak of this deadly perversion … which will surely rot us into ruin unless we recover our sanity and fight it to the death'. Linking national identity and sexual morality, *John Bull* defined this visible gender transgression as un-British – a 'German' 'perversion' that threatened to accomplish what the Kaiser's armies had failed to do.[41] The 'painted and scented boys' enjoying themselves in the teashop 'shamed the name of England' and threatened its existence.[42]

This developed into a concerted attack on what *John Bull* called the 'painted boy menace'.[43] Their campaign drew upon established images of sexual difference and interwove traditional languages of racial degeneration and moral decline – evident in the allusions to Rome and Greece, and the fears that the British Empire would suffer a similar fate if vice went unchecked.[44] Yet these 'rouged rogues' were 'one of the worst menaces of modern times', embodying fears and anxieties triggered by the challenges of war.[45] The war was often experienced as a moment of profound dislocation that destabilised boundaries between classes, sexes, and races on which Britain's stability depended.[46] In particular, it was thought to have disrupted established gender roles. As women gained opportunities in the workplace, political power, and a degree of personal freedom, men were, supposedly, emasculated and feminised. Set against this upheaval, Susan Kingsley Kent suggests, postwar reconstruction tried to re-create a more ordered world, a desire 'nowhere more evident than in the realm of gender identity and relations between men and women'.[47] In reconstructed Britain, social stability and racial survival depended upon reasserting traditional ideas of masculinity and femininity and a domestic ideal embedded in the rigid division between gender roles. This made the 'painted boys' a terrifying threat, focusing concerns that boundaries between men and women were being eroded. Touring London's night haunts in 1920, Sydney Moseley was unnerved by 'a crowd of young men so made-up that it is not easy to guess their sex'.[48]

In showing how the male body could be transformed and identities manipulated, the powder puff thus symbolised the instability of the social body at large. In the late nineteenth century, Michael Roper suggests, 'manliness was judged largely in terms of external qualities: it was from a man's comportment, his physical appearance and performance, that inner qualities were judged'.[49] The legacies of war meant pervasive anxieties around the instability of categories of gender or class acquired greater resonance in the 1920s, as such assumptions figured the queer's make-up – like the hysterical victim of shell shock or the shattered body of the disabled – as a challenge to traditional notions of masculinity and character. Each embodied a dangerous feminisation of the British man; together they generated concerns over the degeneration of the male body through the traumatic experience of modern warfare. Found in men's pockets or seen on the face of the 'West End pouf', cosmetics were a reminder that the male body – supposedly the repository of masculinity – was never natural or stable.[50]

In this sense, objects like the powder puff had the capacity to disrupt ideas of sexual difference and normality and established modes of social classification. Produced in court, they exemplified a dangerous transgression of the 'natural' boundaries between men and women and suggested that it was impossible to truly know an individual's place. In allowing men to cross social boundaries the powder puff suggested just how fragile they were. This was an electrifying threat to an ordered society. More than this: the police were obsessed with finding material objects to support prosecutions. Searching men's pockets was only the tip of the iceberg. After a club or bar had been raided, officers scrutinised the floor, cloakroom and furniture. Men like William K., arrested on Piccadilly in 1938, could undergo the humiliating ritual of having their bodies tested for powder with a piece of cloth – later produced in court.[51] The lengths to which officers went to secure 'evidence' highlight the paranoid character of the material culture of law enforcement. If it was assumed that transgressive sexual desires were indelibly marked upon the male body, desperate attempts to retrieve powder puffs or lipsticks suggested the opposite: the queer body was not immediately legible. In 1936 one officer thus described youths with 'cosmetics on their faces, which had been skilfully made up and was not easy to detect'.[52] This was often deliberate: make-up was only temporary and could be easily removed, allowing men to move invisibly and avoid danger. Many used make-up carefully. Alex Purdie used Lipsyl – 'that colourless stuff you put on when you got sore lips' – rather than lipstick because 'you couldn't have it too dark'. Before going out, his friends checked each other's appearance: 'If you had too much slap on … your mates say too much slap on your ecaf. Yeah. Oh really girl? Yes … Go in the lavs here and have a look.'[53] The 'painted boy' did not always look distinctive. Boundaries between 'difference' and 'normality' were ambiguous and often indiscernible. This made the effeminate 'queans' and their make-up a potent threat to dominant moral codes.

These anxieties crystallised in violent debates over police practices in dealing with 'street offences' after the Great War. Like the 'soliciting' charges used to regulate female prostitution, the offence of 'importuning male persons for an immoral purpose' was used to suppress the use of public space by men looking for sex. Unlike prosecutions for gross indecency or public indecency, which usually arose after officers had witnessed a sexual act, making an arrest for importuning or soliciting meant attributing meaning to gestures or movements that could be ambiguous. Focusing on the visual signs that allowed them to differentiate the importuning man or soliciting woman from the crowd, officers thus scrutinised the appearance, location and movement of the body. To succeed in court, they had to convince the magistrate they had got it right.

In the 1920s, however, the Met's ability to read these signs was subject to intense scrutiny. As arrests for 'street offences' increased, several high-profile cases in which 'respectable' men and women had been wrongly arrested undermined the Met's credibility. In importuning cases like Frank Champain's 1927 trial, magistrates expressed disquiet with police practices, particularly their submission of testimony uncorroborated by the public, the fabrication of evidence and the use of *agents provocateurs* to entrap suspects, discharging defendants or passing sentence reluctantly. The ensuing furore generated Home Office and Met inquiries into the gap between working rules and legal conventions, culminating in the Street Offences Committee (1927) and the Royal Commission on Police Powers and Procedures (1928).[54]

Within this volatile climate some men challenged police actions in court and in print. Writing in *The Continued Extension of the Criminal Law* (1922), the sexual reformer George Ives noted with bitter irony how 'so little ... seems needed to constitute an offence that an alleged smile or wink, or look may cause an arrest ... any young person is at the mercy of any two detectives hunting in couples'.[55] Using cosmetics as evidence was one response to these criticisms. In 1919, the barrister W. J. H. Brodrick was cross-examined by the Association of Moral and Social Hygiene's committee of enquiry into sexual morality. Speaking of 'male prostitution', they asked, 'is the same type of proof demanded as in the case of a woman?' Brodrick replied:

> it is much easier ... These people are well-known to the police and much slighter evidence is accepted in their case than in the case of a woman. As a rule the evidence consists of rouge and powder puffs and things of that kind. It is quite easy to get. You never fail in a prosecution for want of evidence.[56]

Brodrick's optimism was misplaced, but suggests how unease over police procedures underpinned the material culture of law enforcement. If the queer body was never immediately visible and officers were unreliable, then the burden of proof was displaced onto items with a tangible existence. The 'rouge and powder puffs' found in suspects' pockets gave material form to untrustworthy personal testimony. The powder puff's meaning may have remained contested, but in the right circumstances the associations it carried could be enough to mark the criminal body and meet the demands of the legal process.

The powder puff's position within London's criminal justice system reflected a broader interwar fascination with individuals who 'faked it' or masqueraded to cross boundaries of class, gender, race, ethnicity or age. This was not a new phenomenon, but it became more pervasive: accounts of such lives were everywhere in the press, descriptions of metropolitan 'vice', and popular novels and films throughout the 1920s. It was manifested in concern over relationships between white women and black or Chinese men and through a growing number of cases of cross-dressing. The transgressive individual was presented variously as a source of massive anxiety and a figure of humour and intrigue.[57] Concerns over the use of cosmetics thus extended beyond the 'painted boy menace': we can understand the 'man with the powder puff' better if we also consider debates over women's use of make-up in the 1920s. Along with other 'cheap trappings of glamour', cosmetics were, for many young women, an exciting sign of modernity.[58] Yet one result was growing concern about make-up's effect on ideas of class, femininity and morality. Consider J. B. Priestley's disdainful comment on consumerism's demotic effects – provincial 'factory girls looking like actresses'. Here make-up was dangerous, because it allowed working-class women to pretend to a glamour and beauty inappropriate to their station. It made it impossible to know an individual's place since, 'for the first time in history, Jack and Jill are nearly as good as their master and mistress ... Jill beautifies herself exactly as her mistress does.'[59]

The link between cosmetics and performance made many observers wonder what women's make-up concealed. Set against the assumption that appearance was directly related to character, cosmetics were understood as 'symbols of arti-fice, deception and masking'.[60] Mrs Chesterton thus watched a young woman 'industriously making up her face' in a hostel in 1926. The transformation was amazing and immediate: 'powder, rouge and lipstick repair the ravages of fatigue ... she sets forth again looking like a rose refreshed'.[61] Making-up could mean faking it – a kind of deception. Particularly in the early 1920s, women's pages regularly warned readers against using 'camouflage' like this. True beauty was a natural beauty, reflecting a woman's inner being rather than the mask she wore.[62] By the middle of the decade, however, manufacturers used the transfor-mative potential of cosmetics to sell products: achieving the illusion of beauty held the tantalising prospect of excitement, social cachet and romantic fulfil-ment.[63] This signalled a shift in the meaning of selfhood. By the 1920s identity was increasingly thought of as a kind of performance, manifested in external signs and styles – dress, posture, and make-up – rather than being fixed in the body. 'In promising transformation', Kathy Peiss suggests, 'the cosmetics indus-try blurred the distinction between the made-up face as revealing a woman's inner self and the made-up face constituting that self'. Rather than authen-tic, stable, and immediately discernible, subjectivity was – as the 'painted boys' realised – something to be constructed through modern consumer culture.[64] That cosmetics could allow women to transcend their social position or exercise power over men unnerved some observers.[65] Others found opportunities for humour. 'There ain't so much mystery about [women] now', observed Charles Pooter in the *Empire News* in 1920, 'we knows all about wot they wears ... and 'ow they makes themselves beautiful':

> every woman nearly kids 'erself she's beautiful, but she puts a bit of face cream an' powder, an' rouge an' things on 'er face jest to make 'erself more beautiful, and then tells yer that she don't care wot anybody thinks about 'er, an' don't want ter attract the attention of men.[66]

The final anxiety surrounding women's use of cosmetics also reflected concerns surrounding the 'painted boy'. The signs used to identify men's sexual trans-gression echoed those in which contemporaries located women's immorality. Like queer men, women managed their bodies to enhance their visibility and desirability. Like queer men, their make-up was thought to symbolise a danger-ous independent femininity and unruly sexuality. Such assumptions shaped the organisation of policing, provision of social welfare, exposés of metropolitan vice, and forms of popular entertainment. In 1919 the association between cos-metics and sexual transgression was dramatised in D. W. Griffiths' film *Broken Blossoms*. Fifteen-year-old Lucy Burrowes escapes the violent attentions of her brutal stepfather onto the streets of Limehouse. First cautioned against the drudgery of marriage by a neighbour, Lucy is then 'warned as strongly by the ladies of the street against their profession'. The character of the two young women depicted in this scene is suggested through a set of powerful visual signs. One woman draws powder and a puff from a small vanity bag and ostentatiously 'makes-up'.[67] The meanings of these items appeared self-evident. As *John Bull* claimed, when discussing prostitution in 1925, 'the most unfledged yokel may distinguish the tribe at a glance: [from] the rouged lips and painted face [which] ... speak as plainly as the boldest aggression and most shameful of words'.[68]

Yet when women of all classes were embracing the exciting modern femininity associated with cosmetics, it was increasingly unclear which 'tribe' could be distinguished by their 'rouged lips': make-up was no longer an axiomatic sign of prostitution. Prostitutes, flappers, shop girls, and fashionable women all became 'women of the painted class'.[69] Boundaries between the respectable and the immoral collapsed. In the 1920 prosecution of the unlicensed Dalton's Club in Leicester Square, observers struggled to decode female self-presentation. 'Look[ing] around the crowded court', one journalist saw 'women whose faces are thick with rouge and whose eyebrows are thinly pencilled'. He assumed this meant they were 'of the unfortunate class'. Other witnesses struggled to ascribe meaning to make-up. Horace Prior explained: 'it is quite impossible to tell the character of a woman from her appearance alone'. The defence counsel agreed: 'of course it is. They don't wear the scarlet brand of shame on their brow' – or, he might have added, on their cheeks.[70]

This meant it became increasingly difficult to read women's class, status or morality from the condition of their face. In 1928 Mrs Chesterton described the confusion this might cause: '"In the old days you knew where you were by a girl's make-up", men have said to me, "but now all of them seem to look the same ... *there doesn't seem any clear dividing line.*"'[71] Lipstick or powder did not necessarily signify prostitution or sexual immorality. Simultaneously, a young woman's use of cosmetics might signal a glamorous and fashionable modernity, youthful individuality, erotic daring, or participation in an illicit sexual trade. These coexisting meanings gave the female body a disturbing instability of meaning. As with the 'painted boy', make-up focused anxieties about the disruption of gender roles and social boundaries after the Great War.

Conclusion

John Bull's story of the 'man with the powder puff' is a productive starting point from which to explore the relationship between gender, sexuality and material culture in interwar Britain. Why is the case characteristic of the 1920s rather than the 1890s or 1950s? What historically specific conditions had to be in place for Thomas's story to be told in court or a popular newspaper? One way to think about this is to construct an imaginary biography of the powder and puff found in Thomas's pockets. New scientific and industrial processes made these items cheap and ubiquitous; magazines and cinema made make-up an essential attribute of fashionable femininity. A young man, trying to make sense of desires labelled womanlike and construct a persona consistent with his inner nature, bought a powder puff at his local Woolworth's. On the Strand he was arrested, his pockets emptied, and the puff produced in court by police negotiating vociferous criticisms of their conduct and looking for material support for their actions. Thinking in these terms highlights the intersection between discrete historical processes – the emergence of the 'cosmetics industry', a particular understanding of sexual difference, the contentious politics of policing, and worries over the stability of social identities – which made such cases so common after the Great War.

In interwar Britain the powder puff became a fetish object. Produced in court it emblematised a society (and police force) under stress. Fetishism, Anne McClintock argues, constitutes 'the historical enactment of ambiguity itself', 'mark[ing] a crisis in social meaning as the embodiment of an impossible irresolution'. The powder puff came to stand for the disorderly nature of modern life, embodying the permeability of social boundaries, the impossibility of maintaining a stable system of sexual difference and normality and the illegibility of the body. It acquired symbolic resonance that belied its everyday status.[72] The powder puff's ambiguity was furthered through ongoing debates over its significance, for if cosmetics could provide material evidence of a man's criminality, their meaning was never entirely clear. Men challenged the meanings invested in their possessions, arguing that powder was acceptable and necessary rather than a sign of moral depravity: they might have applied powder to approximate the appearance of femininity, soothe sensitive skin or perform in London's theatres. This meant the police had to work hard to suppress alternative understandings of cosmetics' significance and contain the powder puff's 'disruptive or undecidable power'.[73] If successful, this evidence established a rigid distinction between queer and normal bodies. Crucially, however, this could often only be achieved by focusing on objects like the powder puff; it required a material commodity to establish the truth of a man's transgression. As officers searched men's pockets, they simultaneously tried to stabilise the boundary between difference and sameness. Even at the moment of finding, however, ambiguity persisted. The powder puffs remained a forceful reminder that no one need ever be who they seemed.

Notes

This chapter has drawn upon Matt Houlbrook, 'The Man with the Powder Puff in Interwar London', *Historical Journal*, 50(1), pp. 145–171 © 2007. Reproduced with permission.

1. S. Felstead, *Horatio Bottomley: A Biography of an Outstanding Personality* (London: John Murray, 1936); J. Symons, *Horatio Bottomley* (London: Cressett Press, 2001).
2. For the 'male importuning type', see The National Archives [hereafter TNA]: CRIM 1 387, *Rex* vs. *Robert B. and others*, keeping a disorderly house: 1927.
3. All quotes are from 'Grave Miscarriage of Justice: Branded with Shame by Circumstantial Evidence: the Man with the Powder Puff', *John Bull*, 24 January 1925, p. 11.
4. See, e.g., F. Trentmann, 'Materiality in the Future of History: Things, Practices and Politics', *Journal of British Studies*, 48 (2009), pp. 283–307.
5. TNA: CRIM 1 1041, *Rex* vs. *William K. / L.*: importuning, 1938; 'One of a Gang', *News of the World*, 3 October 1926, p. 3; 'Nine Months "Dard" and the "Cat" for a West End Pest', *Illustrated Police News*, 18 December 1924, p. 3. See also 'Charge against Army Captain', *The Times*, 24 April 1918, p. 2; 'Male Dancer's "Make-up"', *The Times*, 9 October 1919, p. 7; 'Convict's Cocaine', *Empire News*, 9 February 1919, p. 5; 'Clerk's Four Days', *Empire News*, 14 November 1920, p. 3; 'Powder, Rouge and Revolver', *People*, 5 April 1931, p. 9; London Metropolitan Archive [hereafter LMA]: A PMC 41, Public Morality Council, patrolling officer's report: December 1941.

6. 'Raid on Club', *The Times*, 27 November 1936, p. 4.
7. 'Smart Sentences for Disgusting Practices', *Illustrated Police News*, 18 May 1922, p. 3.
8. TNA: CRIM 1 639, *Rex* vs. *Austin S. and (33) others*: keeping a disorderly house, 1933: copy depositions, CI Smith.
9. LMA: PS TOW B01 049, Lewis H. and William S., importuning: 24 December 1922. See also, 'Numbered Prisoners on their Defence', *News of the World*, 24 January 1937, p. 19; TNA: MEPO 3 405, Francis Champain, importuning: attachment 35a, Street Offences Committee, report of the sub-committee, 28 January 1928.
10. H. Chalmers, *The Art of Make-up: For the Stage, the Screen and Social Use* (London and New York: D. Appleton, 1925); E. Ward, *A Book of Make-up* (London and New York: Samuel French, 1930).
11. 'Serious Charge against an Actor', *Illustrated Police News*, 10 April 1924, p. 7.
12. H. Cocks, *Nameless Offences: Homosexual Desire in Nineteenth Century England* (London: I. B. Tauris, 2003); M. Cook, *London and the Culture of Homosexuality, 1885–1914* (Cambridge: Cambridge University Press, 2003).
13. L. Moran, *The Homosexual(ity) of Law* (London and New York: Routledge, 1996), p. 137. The earliest case seems to be 'Impersonating a Woman', *The Times*, 24 April 1906, p. 4. See also 'West End Pest', *People*, 11 January 1914. The only postwar case I know of is TNA: CRIM 1 2424, *Regina* vs. *Cecil W.*, importuning: 1954.
14. Q. Crisp, *The Naked Civil Servant* (London: Jonathan Cape, 1968), p. 61.
15. Anomaly, *The Invert and his Social Adjustment* (London: privately printed, 1927), p. 9.
16. National Sound Archive [hereafter NSA]: C456 03 02, John Alcock.
17. J. Weeks and K. Porter (eds), *Between the Acts: Lives of Homosexual Men, 1885–1967* (London: Routledge, 1999), p. 125.
18. E. Partridge, *The Dictionary of the Underworld* (Ware: Wordsworth Editions, 1995), pp. 462, 496, 524–525, 527.
19. LMA: PS TOW B01 049, Lewis H. and William S., importuning: 24 Dec. 1922.
20. 'Numbered Prisoners at Old Bailey', *Morning Advertiser*, 21 February 1933, p. 3.
21. 'West End Nest of Vice Smoked Out', *News of the World*, 5 March 1933, p. 18.
22. A. Sinfield, *The Wilde Century: Effeminacy, Oscar Wilde and the Queer Moment* (New York: Columbia University Press, 1994); J. Bristow, *Effeminate England: Homoerotic Writing after 1885* (New York: Columbia University Press, 1995); C. Upchurch, 'Forgetting the Unthinkable: Cross-dressers and British Society in the case of the *Queen* vs. *Boulton and others*', *Gender and History*, 12 (2000), pp. 128–129.
23. M. Houlbrook, 'Lady Austin's Camp Boys: Constituting the Queer Subject in 1930s London', *Gender and History*, 14 (2002), pp. 31–61.
24. K. Peiss, 'On Beauty … and the History of Business', in P. Scranton (ed.), *Beauty and Business: Commerce, Gender and Culture in Modern America* (London and New York: Routledge, 2001), p. 12.
25. In 1930, 30% of women wore lipstick; by the 1940s 90% of women under 30 were making-up. S. Alexander, 'Becoming a Woman in London in the 1920s and '30s', in Alexander (ed.), *Becoming a Woman and Other Essays in 19th and 20th Century Feminist History* (New York: Virago, 1995), p. 311; A. Bingham, *Gender, Modernity and the Popular Press in Interwar Britain* (Oxford: Oxford University Press, 2004), p. 174.
26. T. Koller, *Cosmetics: A Handbook of the Manufacture, Employment and Testing of all Cosmetic Materials and Cosmetic Specialities* (London: Scott Greenwood, 1920), p. v.
27. H. S. Redgrove and G. Foan, *Paint, Powder and Patches: A Handbook of Make-up for Stage and Carnival* (London: William Heinemann, 1930), p. 31.

28. This discussion of the cosmetic industry draws upon K. Mulvey, *Decades of Beauty: The Changing Image of Women* (London: Checkmark Books, 1998), pp. 20, 56–57, 67, 74–75, 93; N. Shuker, *Elizabeth Arden: Beauty Empire Builder* (New York: Silver Burdett Press, 2001); K. Peiss, *Hope in a Jar: The Making of American Beauty Culture* (New York: University of Pennsylvania Press, 1999); M. Leveau-Fernandez, *Helena Rubinstein* (Paris: Flammarion, 2003).

29. See Chalmers, *Art of Make-up*, pp. 143–148; P. Tinkler, *Constructing Girlhood: Popular Magazines for Girls Growing Up in England, 1920–1950* (London: Taylor and Francis, 1995), pp. 152–160.

30. Bingham, *Gender, Modernity*, p. 174.

31. 'Beauty Adorned', *The Times*, 12 March 1932, p. 10; L. Woodhead, *War Paint: Miss Elizabeth Arden and Madame Helena Rubinstein: their Lives, their Times, their Rivalry* (London: John Wiley and Sons, 2003), pp. 71–73, 124–125.

32. T. Croft, *The Cloven Hoof: A Study of Contemporary London Vices* (London: Denis Archer, 1932), p. 67.

33. A. Jivani, *It's not Unusual: A History of Lesbian and Gay life in the Twentieth Century* (London: Indiana University Press, 1997), p. 22.

34. NSA: C444 03 30a-32a, Alex Purdie.

35. TNA: CRIM 1 633, *Rex* vs. *Laurence B.*, gross indecency: 1933; TNA: MEPO 3 758: DS Mogford: 25 August 1934; TNA: MEPO 2 4485, Running Horse public house: permitting drunkenness / disorderly conduct of undesirables: minute 63a: PS Gowen, 6 March 1937.

36. T. Burke, *The London Spy: A Book of Town Travels* (London: Thornton Butterworth, 1922), p. 303.

37. TNA: MEPO 3 405: transcript of proceedings, 5 January 1928: Q233, Q462.

38. Ibid.: Q459–467.

39. 'Lipsticks: their Use and Abuse', *The Times*, 11 October 1922, p. 8.

40. LMA: PS TOW B01 049, Lewis H. and William S., importuning: 12 December 1922; J. Edwards, *Powder Compacts: A Collector's Guide* (London: Miller's Publications, 2000), pp. 6–33.

41. P. Hoare, *Wilde's Last Stand: Decadence, Conspiracy and the First World War* (London: Arcade Publishing, 1997); L. Bland, 'Trial by Sexology? Maud Allan, Salome and the Cult of the Clitoris Case', in L. Bland and L. Doan (eds), *Sexology in Culture: Labelling Bodies and Desires* (Oxford: Blackwell, 1998), pp. 183–198.

42. 'A Modern Gomorrah', *John Bull*, 13 June 1925, p. 18.

43. 'Brazen Blackmail Gang', *John Bull*, 30 May 1925, p. 13.

44. See R. Luckhurst and S. Ledger (eds), *The Fin de Siècle: A Reader in Cultural History, c. 1880–1900* (Oxford: Oxford University Press, 2000).

45. 'Wickedest Gang in London', *John Bull*, 25 July 1925, p. 11.

46. S. Hynes, *A War Imagined: English Culture and the First World War* (London: Pimlico, 1992); P. Fussell, *The Great War and Modern Memory* (Oxford: Oxford University Press, 2000).

47. S. Kingsley Kent, *Making Peace: The Reconstruction of Gender in Interwar Britain* (Princeton, NJ: Princeton University Press, 1993), p. 2. See also, J. Bourke, *Dismembering the Male: Men's Bodies, Britain and the Great War* (Chicago, IL: University of Chicago Press, 1999); S. Grayzel, *Women's Identities at War: Gender, Motherhood and Politics in Britain and France during the First World War* (Chapel Hill: University of North Carolina Press, 1999); N. Gullace, *'The Blood of our Sons': Men, Women and the Renegotiation of British Citizenship during the Great War* (Basingstoke: Palgrave Macmillan, 2002); M. Kohn, *Dope Girls: The Birth of the British Drug Underground* (London: Granta, 1992).

48. S. Moseley, *The Night Haunts of London* (London: Stanley Paul, 1920), p. 43.

49. M. Roper, 'Between Manliness and Masculinity: the 'War Generation' and the Psychology of Fear in Britain, 1914–1950', *Journal of British Studies*, 44 (2005), pp. 347–348.

50. See I. Zweininger-Bargielowska, 'The Culture of the Abdomen: Obesity and Reducing in Britain, c. 1900–1939', *Journal of British Studies*, 44 (2005), pp. 239–273; A. Carden-Coyne, 'From Pieces to Whole: the Sexualization of Muscles in Postwar Bodybuilding', in C. Forth and I. Crozier (eds), *Body Parts: Critical Explorations in Corporeality* (Lexington, KY: Lexington Books, 2005); S. Koven, 'Remembering and Dismemberment: Crippled Children, Wounded Soldiers and the Great War in Great Britain', *American Historical Review*, 99 (1999), pp. 1167–1202; E. Showalter, *The Female Malady: Women, Madness and English Culture, 1830–1980* (New York: Virago, 1985).

51. TNA: CRIM 1 1041, list of exhibits, 11 October 1938.

52. TNA: MEPO 2 4485, Minute 23b, Insp. Gavin: 9 September 1936.

53. NSA: C444 03 30a - 32a, Alex Purdie.

54. Champain was initially convicted for importuning in urinals around the Adelphi. The public furore surrounding his successful appeal forced Joynson-Hicks to refer the case to the Street Offences Committee. TNA: MEPO 3 405: attachment 35a, report of the sub-committee; 'Another Case Dismissed on Appeal', *Birmingham Daily Mail*, 21 September 1927; 'Where Justice Erred', *News of the World*, 25 September 1927. See also, TNA: CRIM 1 547, *Rex* vs. *Harold R.*, importuning: 1931; TNA: MEPO 3 992, Hugh C., persistent importuner: 1935; TNA: MEPO 3 990, use of plainclothes officers in detecting indecency offences: 1933. I discuss these debates in Matt Houlbrook, *Queer London: Perils and Pleasures in the Sexual Metropolis, 1918–57* (Chicago, IL: University of Chicago Press, 2005), ch. 1.

55. G. Ives, *The Continued Extension of the Criminal Law* (London: J. E. Francis, 1922), p. 8.

56. The Women's Library, formerly London Metropolitan University, Association for Moral and Social Hygiene, Box 49, 'Committee of enquiry into sexual morality': testimony of W. J. H. Brodrick, 1 Dec. 1919. The Women's Library Archive has been moved to the London School of Economics since this research was undertaken.

57. On cross-dressing, see J. Vernon, '"For Some Queer reason": The Trials and Tribulations of Colonel Barker's Masquerade in Interwar England', *Signs*, 25 (2000), pp. 37–62; P. Gurney, '"Intersex" and "Dirty Girls": Mass Observation and Working-class Sexuality in England in the 1930s', *Journal of the History of Sexuality*, 8 (1997), pp. 256–290; A. McLaren, *The Trials of Masculinity: Policing Sexual Boundaries 1870–1930* (Chicago, IL: University of Chicago Press, 1997). On miscegenation, see L. Bland, 'White Women and Men of Colour: Miscegenation Fears in Britain after the Great War', *Gender and History*, 17 (2005), pp. 29–61; L. Tabili, 'Women "of a Very Low Type": Crossing Racial Boundaries in Late-Imperial Britain', in L. Frader and S. Rose (eds), *Gender and Class in Modern Europe* (Ithaca, NY: Cornell University Press, 1996).

58. Alexander, 'Becoming a Woman', pp. 222–223.

59. J. B. Priestley, *English Journey* (London: Victor Gollancz, 1934), pp. 376, 401–402.

60. K. Peiss, 'Making Up, Making Over: Cosmetics, Consumer Culture and Women's Identity', in V. de Grazia and E. Furlough (eds), *The Sex of Things: Gender and Consumption in Historical Perspective* (Berkeley and Los Angeles: University of California Press, 1996), p. 314.

61. Mrs C. Chesterton, *In Darkest London* (London, 1926), p. 84.

62. *Daily Mirror*, 24 May 1921, quoted in Bingham, *Gender, Modernity*, p. 173.

63. Tinkler, *Constructing Girlhood*, pp. 158–160.
64. Peiss, 'Making Up', p. 323.
65. H. C. Fischer and E. X. Dubois, *Sexual Life during the World War* (London: Francis Aldor, 1937), p. 109.
66. 'Marcus on Woman', *Empire News*, 28 March 1920, p. 6.
67. *Broken Blossoms*, dir. D. W. Griffiths (1919).
68. 'A New Peril to Women', *John Bull*, 10 January 1925, p. 16.
69. Moseley, *Night Haunts*, pp. 47, 150.
70. 'Visit to a Nightclub', *Empire News*, 18 January 1920, p. 5.
71. Mrs C. Chesterton, *Women of the Underworld* (London: Stanley Paul, 1928), p. 161.
72. A. McClintock, *Imperial Leather: Race, Gender and Sexuality in the Colonial Contest* (London and New York: Routledge, 1995), p. 184.
73. Ibid., p. 184.

8

Manly Drinkers: Masculinity and Material Culture in the Interwar Public House

Stella Moss

The English public house has long been perceived as a significant masculine social space.[1] A central feature of the English popular cultural landscape in the 1920s and 1930s, the pub was recognised by a host of social commentators as a venue central to the cultivation and expression of masculine identities. This chapter illuminates constructions and experiences of manliness in the 1930s by exploring the material world of the public house. Seeking out sources for such a study poses methodological challenges, not least since everyday working-class artefacts were often not preserved for posterity. In exploring how the built spaces and objects of the pub were variously imagined, understood and used, I draw on interwar social survey commentary. The works of Mass Observation, an influential social research organisation, offer perhaps unparalleled nuance in their discussion of the materiality of the public house. Alongside these documentary sources, I also draw on visual evidence in the form of photographs. As part of Mass Observation's research project, a notable photographer of the late 1930s, Humphrey Spender, was commissioned to capture the everyday life of the pub. This methodological connecting of different types of source offers opportunities to construct a material cultural history of the pub from diverse perspectives.[2] As with Chapters 3 and 6 in this volume, the discussion seeks to uncover the construction and contestation of masculine identities through the exploration of spatial and material worlds.

In considering masculinity and material culture, this chapter opens up new scholarly terrain. Historians of twentieth-century drinking cultures have tended to focus on issues of licensing regulation and the control of alcohol consumption.[3] Paul Jennings, among others, has considered the social significance of the interwar public house, emphasising its importance in forging social ties through recreational culture.[4] Women's drinking has begun to attract greater scholarly attention, including from Claire Langhamer, who has explored attitudes towards female presence in public houses in the era of the Second World War.[5] Andrew

Davies has called attention to the socio-cultural significance of pub-going as one of the core recreational practices available to working-class men, especially in their middle and later years, though crucially he has emphasised the ways in which unemployment and poverty often curtailed regular patronage.[6]

While existing scholarship has uncovered various aspects of the pub's appeal, little attention has been paid to its particular significance as a site of gendered performance. The public house was a socially vibrant and culturally influential space. As in other social worlds, like the family home, men were active agents in the production and contestation of masculinity via material culture.[7] Masculinity in the pub was linked to specific embodied practices and performative cultures; that is to say, particular practices and habits were considered as both constituting and reflecting manliness, and as such were widely practised.[8] Here contrasts might be drawn with the masculinities explored by Matt Houlbrook in Chapter 7: the masculinities typically displayed in the majority of working-class public houses in the interwar years would have been recognised by many contemporaries as representative of a hegemonic heterosexual norm. More broadly in recent years, innovative research has begun to reveal the multiple and varied representations and experiences of masculinity in twentieth-century England.[9] Consideration of key themes such as work, war, homosexuality, youth and family life has illuminated influential norms and practices through which manliness was variously understood and performed.[10] This scholarship has, for instance, underlined the influence of all-male, homosocial practices in forging cultures of masculinity, a theme central to this chapter, since the pub was a major forum for all-male recreational gatherings in interwar working-class communities.[11] Drawing on this scholarship, exploration of the everyday world of the pub will open up new ways of understanding how masculinity was represented and experienced in interwar England.

This chapter centres on a close study of pub life in the Lancashire industrial town of Bolton, drawing on the findings of Mass Observation [hereafter MO].[12] Founded in 1937, the MO venture was, at its heart, an ambitious attempt to conduct a social survey of the everyday lives of ordinary citizens, and so develop an 'anthropology of ourselves'.[13] Consternation about standards of methodological rigour was voiced from MO's early days, especially in relation to the somewhat haphazard sampling common to many surveys. Today, scholarly discussion tends to focus on how, not whether, MO's research findings can be analysed most productively.[14] As Vivienne Richmond discusses in Chapter 5, exploration of the everyday material culture of working-class lives can pose methodological challenges when source material is limited in volume or scope, and so it follows that the richness and range of MO sources offers much potential for historical investigation. A major aspect of the organisation's research was an in-depth exploration of working-class life in Bolton, which it styled as 'Worktown'. A key facet of this research, conducted in 1937–1939, involved the study of drinking cultures and the development of extensive participant-observer surveys of the town's three hundred public houses.[15] Observers spent many hours in licensed premises, noting the range and variety of pub sub-cultures, including, for instance, smoking, musical entertainment and gambling, as well as drinking.[16] The outcome of these surveys was *The Pub and the People*, published by MO

in 1943. This highly nuanced study remains one of the richest available historical sources on modern drinking cultures. Overall, the materiality of drinking
cultures emerged as a pre-eminent concern within MO's research. *The Pub and
the People* discussed at length the different rooms of the pub and their varying
social codes, and the objects and goods that formed the material fabric of the
pub, through and from which patrons derived meanings and understandings of
what it was to be a man.

In drawing on MO's research, this chapter seeks to interrogate the organisation's interpretive assumptions and assertions about masculine drinking practices. For MO, the public house was a vitally important space for the construction
of male identity, for it asserted that older forms and practices that had shaped
perceptions and experiences of manliness were, by the late 1930s, increasingly
under threat. MO contended that in the wake of the Great Depression, work, and
especially manual labour, were no longer the formative practice through which
masculinity was defined, experienced and understood by many men. Added to
this was the pervasive influence of new forms of popular culture, such as cinema
and radio, which MO considered to have a politically and culturally stultifying
influence. Thus, in a period when male labour markets (especially in the staple
heavy industries) were increasingly under threat, and ever more predominant
cultures of mass leisure and consumption were considered to induce a feminis-
ing effect, the pub was perceived as a site of assured authentic masculinity.[17] It
followed that MO's depiction of the Worktown drinker was typically positive,
as well as essentialised. *The Pub and the People* tended to articulate the male pub
drinker as a working-class, middle-aged, married breadwinner, for whom the
pub was a highly valued centre of community life, and where involvement in
tightly-knit networks of kinship and friendship both shaped and reflected manly
status.[18] It is notable that MO's emphasis on drinking, and indeed drunkenness,
as constitutive of working-class masculinity was in sharp contrast to temperance
discourses that had long praised abstinence from alcohol as a manly virtue.[19]

Alongside MO's textual analysis, this chapter considers Humphrey Spender's
photographs of pub life. Spender took hundreds of photographs of Worktown,
many of them now available online via a website hosted by Bolton Council.[20]
MO's intention was for a selection of pub photographs to be included for publication in *The Pub and the People*, but plans were scotched in the wake of wartime
privations, and it was not until a 1970 edition that a selection of ten photographs was finally published. By the late 1930s, Spender was established as a
talented up-and-coming social documentary photographer. In discussing the
photographic elements of the Worktown project, MO emphasised its purpose
as providing an impartial and objective visual record. Spender was later to claim
that he photographed in 'secret', trying to ensure his camera remained hidden
from view. He asserted that he had 'believed obsessionally that truth would
be revealed only when people were not aware of being photographed. I had
to be invisible.'[21] Though such claims invoke a discourse of objectivity, in any
reading of Spender's photographs it is important to take account of artistic
intent. Spender was a professional photographer and, perhaps inevitably, many
of his images reveal expert composition and a connoisseurial eye for the sympathetic portrayal of the everyday dynamics of working-class life.[22] Spender's

photographs lend much to a material cultural exploration of interwar pub life. If considered with awareness of Spender's aims and artistic intentions, the images offer striking visual representations of the built space of the pub, the objects it contained, and the manifold ways in which drinkers inhabited and used both.[23]

Drinking Rooms in the Public House

MO's Worktown study focused on 'traditional' public houses: that is, premises built in the Victorian and Edwardian periods, catering to a largely urban working-class clientele.[24] Found in both town centre and residential areas, most 'traditional' pubs had a loyal customer base, with many visiting their 'local' more than once a week. Often located on street corners, pubs in residential areas tended to draw patrons from the immediate surrounding roads, with the result that customers would ordinarily be well known to each other.[25] As with 'traditional' premises elsewhere in the country (and in contrast with the more 'open plan' drinking rooms usually found today), Worktown premises featured a number of small bars and drinking rooms. The chief rooms were: the vault, an all-male drinking room; the taproom, often used by male customers for games-playing; and the lounge or parlour, perceived generally as a more socially refined drinking room known for the presence of women as well as men, and often the site of activities like communal sing-songs.[26] As *The Pub and the People* made clear, the different rooms of the pub were characterised by particular cultural norms, with both social status and gender being formative influences. It is important to note that MO devoted attention to discussing masculinity in the context of men drinking in the company of women, but discussion of these themes is regrettably beyond the scope of this chapter.[27] Instead I focus on the all-male rooms of the pub, the vault and the taproom.[28] Such an approach allows us to consider why and how MO found homosocial drinking especially important to the creation and contestation of masculine identities, and to uncover why material culture was seen as integral to performing and enacting gender in the pub.

MO recognised the centrality of the vault to the everyday life of the public house.[29] Also known as the 'public bar', or simply the 'bar', for many men this was the chief, and often the only, room they patronised. MO contended that in many ways the vault was the most significant room in the pub, not least because of its marked cultural influence over its patrons. According to MO, in addition to heavy drinking (especially at the weekend, following payday on Friday), the vault was known for its vibrant cultures of comradeship and conversation.[30] Central to MO's analysis of the vault was its contention that this was a space where cultures of social status and gender were formed and contested. The assertion of *The Pub and the People* that 'the vault is working class [and] masculine' spoke to MO's wider interest in claiming this particular room as an important space where 'authentic' popular masculinity might be more fully cultivated and expressed.[31] MO placed particular emphasis on the prevailing 'taboo' against female customers, noting that 'only men are allowed in the vault.'[32] While numerous interwar social commentators reflected on the vault as an all-male space, given MO's marked interest in uncovering gendered drinking cultures, its emphasis on the vault as a masculine space was imbued with special resonance.[33] If the pub was a space where working-class manliness might be developed and consolidated, the vault was considered to offer particular and perhaps unparalleled opportunities for the unfettered manifestation of this masculinity. As *The Pub and the People* contended: 'the vault is the place where men are men'.[34]

The vault was plain and often worn, even shabby, with MO claiming it was the 'most inconvenient and uncomfortable' of pub rooms.[35] In marked contrast with upper- and middle-class men's clubs, where comfortable, salubrious features were *de rigueur*, sparse fittings and minimal decoration were as standard. Floors were often of plain wood, or even bare stone. In a few premises could be found 'worn brown lino'. Walls were similarly plain: one pub featured panelled sections with 'dark brown painted wood half way up, the rest covered with dingy, dull, red wallpaper'.[36] For MO at least, enthusiasm for decoration belonged in the spaces of the pub, chiefly the lounge, where women drank: interest in, and engagement with, aesthetic and decorative appeal was seen as a feminised sensibility, redolent of consumerist preoccupations, and as such, corrosive to the 'authentic' manliness prevalent in the vault.[37]

According to MO, a leading characteristic of the vault was the emphasis on standing, rather than sitting, to drink. Seating was typically limited, in both provision and style, with just a single wooden bench commonplace.[38] Crucially, benches and any chairs provided would, by convention, usually remain unoccupied. Vault customers would stand, either at the bar itself, or around the rooms (often near tables, if they were provided). Clearly still common in many pubs today, this practice of standing was known by interwar social commentators as 'perpendicular drinking'. MO paid this issue considerable attention, including making detailed reports of the time taken to consume pints of beer when customers were standing and sitting respectively. These surveys confirmed what licensing experts had argued since at least the late nineteenth century: that standing increased the pace of consumption and therefore led to greater levels of drinking and a higher incidence of drunkenness.[39] Thus, for MO, 'the fact that the vault is the place where you [...] stand [was] important'.[40] Standing to drink was an embodied masculine practice, since standing for even minutes, and usually hours, in the pub was perceived as a physical expression of manly vigour. That many vault customers were employed in physically demanding jobs, including in the local key industries of cotton spinning and coal mining, made this practice all the more striking. It followed that the vault was 'the place where the male comes to relax mentally, though not so much physically'.[41]

Like standing, spitting was perceived as an expression of masculinity central to the prevailing culture of the vault. Often associated with male sports, in the context of the public house, to spit in front of other men was to participate in a cultural practice understood as symbolic of masculine physicality. In many mid- to late Victorian pubs vault floors were covered in a layer of sawdust, sometimes leading to the popular description of it as a 'sawdust parlour'.[42] By the late 1930s, this layer had been reduced to a narrow ditch of sawdust by the bar counter in some Worktown vaults. Occasionally, this ditch was demarcated by a strip of wood screwed to the ground.[43] MO asserted that sawdust ditches were used widely and with gusto: *The Pub and the People* remarked that in one vault an evening's drinking was punctuated by the regular shooting of 'tidy gobs of spittle across the sawdust'.[44] In addition to, and sometimes instead of, a ditch publicans provided customers with spittoons; that is, receptacles designed specifically for the collection of spit. MO noted the variety of spittoons: in some premises they were 'round green china bowls, about six inches across, filled with sawdust'.[45] Others included: blue and brown china, cast iron, white enamel and polished copper.[46] Elsewhere, however, spittoons were absent and sawdust sometimes neglected in favour of the floor itself.[47] MO contended that it was in the pubs in the poorest areas of Worktown where 'maximum spitting' was to be witnessed.[48] In one 'rough' pub, 'shabby condition[s]' prevailed: while there were five spittoons in the vault, customers were seen to prefer instead to spit 'all over the floor' and even 'on the counter'.[49] For MO, spitting was an integral aspect of the strident machismo of the vault, with spittoons, for instance, considered to assume a 'far more important role than simply being spit receptacles'.[50] For MO, the importance of spitting lay partly in its restriction to the vault.

MO's emphasis on the materiality of the vault was rooted in a rough masculinity where embodied gendered norms were described as finding visceral expression. *The Pub and the People* noted: 'you may spit on the floor or burn the bar with a cigarette and the barmaid won't reprove you. Indeed, as one pub-goer remarked, "You can do almost anything you bloody well like in the vault, short of shitting on the place."'[51] The notion of the vault as a space connected with the basest of functions spoke to MO's attempt to represent this room as an anti-domestic space. *The Pub and the People* contended that: 'there is something of the gent's lavatory in a vault. [It] is nothing like home.'[52] It is significant that Spender's photography offered a parallel sense of the vault as a rough space, as encapsulated in his image of a sawdust ditch (Fig. 8.1). Here Spender offered a visual interpretation of the unrefined appearance of the vault, the sawdust ditch clearly visibly between the wooden bar and the stone-flagged flooring. Considered within the context of the broader cultural significance of spitting, this photograph gave a striking representation of the materiality of the vault: the image revealed a roughness which MO saw as central to the vault's status and character. The sawdust ditch formed part of a cultural matrix of objects in the vault whose use by drinkers was central to the importance of this particular room in fostering codes of masculine conduct. With an appreciation of this context, Spender's photograph might be located within the broader framework of social commentary about the pub and its centrality to working-class masculinity. His composition also spoke to the ideas of cultural authenticity that were central to MO's interpretation of pub life. The 'traditional' public house, with its rough sawdust, was part of an older culture now often undermined. Read with this cultural context in mind, Spender's photograph of the sawdust ditch can help reveal the spatial configuration and material world of the pub, as well as its significance in relation to gendered performativity.

By contrast with the vault, the taproom was a less rowdy room. Here masculinity was rooted less in coarse machismo and more in cultures of associational sociability. Prevailing norms of manliness were fostered and expressed through

Figure 8.1   Sawdust Ditch (Courtesy of Bolton Council).

associational habits; chiefly through conversation and games-playing among pub regulars who knew one another well. The taproom, MO contended, was 'more of a club room than the vault'. Customers were of the same working-class status as those in the vault – 'same people, same clothes' – but this was a room where regulars would gather. Indeed, *The Pub and the People* contended that, though tolerated in the vault, occasional strangers were resented and ostracised in the taproom.[53] That these rooms were adjacent renders their contrasting social norms all the more noticeable.

MO argued that, in material terms, the taproom was comparatively comfortable and more aesthetically appealing than the vault. Flooring tended to be linoleum, and wallpaper was predominant, as opposed to plain wood panelling.[54] Decorative tiling, especially around fireplaces, was common. Ornamental objects such as clocks and mirrors were often placed on mantelpieces, clearly echoing the domestic cultures of display that prevailed in the parlours and 'best rooms' of many working-class homes. For MO, however, the appeal of the room lay partly in its physical distinction and cultural differentiation from the home.[55]

MO drew attention to taproom seating arrangements: 'unlike the vault it is entirely a sitting-room [with] wooden benches round the wall and wooden stools'.[56] In some premises, benches were 'built-in [and] leather covered'. [57] The taproom, then, was the site of a contrasting culture of masculinity, where, unlike in the vault, sitting to drink was not frowned upon as effete, but rather indicative of a site of associational practices. In this space, conversation between regulars and games-playing were situated in a physical context of seated leisure, rather than standing rowdiness.

MO characterised the taproom as a place of belonging. It was a room where individuals considered themselves to be 'part of an institution [...] like the members of a political organization to their party, or a congregation to its church'. Underpinning the 'close relationship between the pub and the drinker' found in the taproom were the twin influences of familiarity and regularity, with patrons in many premises occupying 'the same places every night'.[58] MO noted with interest the 'degree to which the regular pub-goer can come to look upon the pub as a kind of second or alternative home'. Particular emphasis was placed on the ritualised habits of regulars. *The Pub and the People* noted the practices of one man who went to his local every day at seven thirty: 'When he comes into the taproom he goes to a cupboard in the wall, opens it, and takes out his spectacles. Then he puts them on, spreads the evening paper out on the table and reads it. He always stays until closing time.'[59] Here MO perceived the willingness of the landlord to allow a regular to keep a personal possession in the pub as evidence of an entrenched culture of belonging. Though the man did not always converse at length with other customers, he played an integral part in the life of this particular taproom. Overall, MO presented a vision of the taproom and its material culture as playing an intimate role in the formation and consolidation of social bonds and a closely-knit sense of community. While such an emphasis doubtless reflected MO's own underlying enthusiasm for a socially democratic working-class culture and politics, the fact that the material culture of the taproom helped foster a sense of belonging was seen as significant.

Also part of MO's exploration of the forging and sustaining of social bonds was a discussion of the taproom as a place of remembrance and commemoration. MO noted the presence in one Worktown taproom of 'a hand-painted Roll of Honour of customers who died in the war of 1914–18, the list of names surmounted by water-coloured representations of the Allied flags'.[60] Though by no means ubiquitous, this kind of commemorative memorial, a material manifestation of a collective memory of deceased pub regulars, was indicative of the deeply-rooted culture of homosocial bonds that might be formed in the public house, and the taproom especially. Given its more routinised culture, which was certainly less raucous than the vault, the taproom was the most likely of spaces for such a memorial. For MO, the memorial was a stark reminder that the losses of the Great War would have been made absolutely apparent in the social space of the taproom: in a room typically occupied by small numbers of men drawn from a local community, the deaths of regular patrons would have been felt keenly. Moreover, for MO, there was a sense here of the war's continuing influence in shaping popular practices and understandings of masculinity, given the suggestion that the deceased were not soon forgotten. Thus the material culture of the taproom could be intimately connected to much wider legacies of the war, and the impact of national and community loss on constructions of popular masculinity.[61]

MO considered games-playing as integral to performances of masculinity in the taproom. Though sometimes found in the vault, the playing of games in small groups was central to the culture of the taproom. Indeed, MO contended that some customers were 'more interested' in games than in drinking.[62] The appeal of games-playing was thought to lie in the manly companionship derived from conversation and banter, together with a spirit of competition that was often spurred on by the placing of small bets.[63] While cards were relatively common, dominoes was emphasised as 'the most popular pub game', being played in 'two-thirds of the local pubs'. In some premises particular facilities were available for the playing of dominoes, including special tables with 'raised edges to prevent the pieces falling off'. MO recorded the localised practices that shaped dominoes-playing: 'The face of the pieces is divided in half; on each half are a number of dots. In the form played almost everywhere else in the country, the dots number from one to six. Worktowners, however, play with dominoes whose dots range up to double nine.'[64] Such observations reflected MO's interest in localised material cultural practices. Darts had been gaining in popularity in Worktown since the Great War. Local practice dictated that each player had three darts, 'wooded and/or brass-shafted'. Most Worktown games were played 'round the board': that is, players had to score one, two, three and so on round the board up to twenty, and finish on the bull's eye. Darts was played sometimes by individuals or by small groups, but mostly in pairs.[65] Overall for MO, games-playing was part of a culture of masculinity in that it both promoted 'prestige' for the winner, but also fostered a 'democratic' impulse rooted in a mutual culture of belonging.[66] Taking part in games-playing was to assume one's place as a man in the pub, and it was through participation in these activities, and by using the objects associated with them, that customers made manifest their masculine identities.

Capturing a sense of the cultures of sociability in the taproom was a source of some fascination for Spender. Among the photographs he produced was an evocative image of domino-players (Fig. 8.2). In contrast with the photograph

Figure 8.2   Games-playing in the Taproom (Courtesy of Bolton Council).

of the sawdust ditch, there is a rather different compositional intent, with a sense of Spender's ambition in capturing players' concentration and focus on the game. The viewer's gaze is directed towards the pieces on the boards and (especially) the players' hands. The men's clothes represented vivid cultural referents, their flat caps, mufflers and jackets symbolic of the breadwinning, associational working-class masculinity seen by MO as central to taproom culture.[67] It follows that Spender's photograph and MO's analysis of the taproom might be read side-by-side here, each forming part of the same broad discourse on working-class masculinity and pub culture.[68]

Pint-drinking Cultures

Linking MO's discussion of the vault and taproom was a preoccupation with the material culture of drinking vessels, and specifically glasses, in these spaces. MO was fascinated by pint-drinking as a performative culture central to the cultivation of masculinity in the public house. Not surprisingly, there were numerous material cultural practices, including smoking, for instance, which MO emphasised as constitutive of gendered identities in the pub, but pint-drinking was assigned particular significance. MO's discussion of drinking glasses and masculinity focused almost exclusively on beer consumption, this being perceived as the manliest, as well as the most ubiquitous, of pub drinks.[69] The most common kind of drinking vessel was the pint glass, made from plain glass, with no decoration. Those who drank from these glasses were known as 'pinters'.[70] MO conducted numerous surveys into the pace of pint-drinking in Worktown pubs, confirming that the speed of consumption was fastest among those standing to drink in the vault. It also maintained that the average beer consumption among pub regulars was just over three pints per night. The pint glass was thought by MO to be the most 'manly' of vessels because it was 'unrefined': the combination of maximum size and uncomplicated utility were thought to account for its appeal.[71]

Though less common than plain vessels, glass and sometimes china pint mugs, featuring a handle, were also in evidence in Worktown.[72] MO asserted, for example, that following their recent introduction in one pub, beer mugs had proved 'very popular', according to the landlord.[73] The appeal of the mug, MO contended, stemmed from the fact that the handle gave the drinker 'something to grip on to'.[74] Half-pint measures of beer were sold, and served in plain glasses, again with no decoration. It is significant that, owing to its focus on pint-drinking as a manly habit, MO in fact downplayed the importance of half-pint drinking in Worktown: there is a telling discrepancy between some of MO's raw survey reports and data on drinking vessels and the analysis published in *The Pub and the People*. Indeed, numerous survey reports (as well as other types of evidence such as autobiographies) confirm that while certainly secondary to pint consumption, half-pints were by no means unusual. A key factor here was economic prudence, since some could only afford to drink halves of beer.[75] Overall, however, MO reflected an ambition to draw on and extend the notable cultural norms which linked pint-drinking with masculinity. This discursive preoccupation could be observed, for instance, through MO's discussion of the 'habit' whereby drinkers would pour a half-pint of beer into a pint glass, rather than consume it from the smaller glass in which it had been served, so concerned were they by the effete associations of the smaller vessels.[76] The consumption of beer from pint glasses was thus a performative culture which both shaped and contributed to masculine identity: as MO asserted, 'when one has attained the degree of a pinter, a half pint seems insignificant'.[77] Thus, the 'size of the pint glass' was seen as symbolic of a particular masculine culture. MO reflected on the culture of machismo that privileged the drinking of pint measures, noting numerous conversations among Worktown drinkers about the extent of their pint consumption. One man claimed, for instance, to have drunk up to eighteen pints a night and 'noan ben any the worse for it'.[78] For MO, such boasts were indicative of the ways in which consuming considerable quantities of alcohol were considered part of a particular masculine culture which often condoned heavy drinking and even valorised drunkenness as evidence of unfettered virility. Ultimately, for MO there was a strong sense that there was 'something "manly" about pint drinking'.[79]

Particular emphasis was laid on perceived links between pint-drinking and the male worker. In part this stemmed from deeply-rooted ideas of beer as both a pleasure and reward for hard work. Pint-drinking was described as most common among 'labourers' and those employed in 'heavy manual work'.[80] MO recorded one conversation among working men who had called into a pub for a midday pint: '2 men in vault [...] Order pints, drink them in 4 mins. [Mass] Observers are having shandy. Chaps express contempt. One says "Beer's the stuff". The other, "Six pints a day do a man good." They go, drive off in municipal dust-cart number x.'[81] Given its emphasis on the public house as a hub of authentic working-class culture, MO was at pains to elaborate on these close links between a man's status in terms of his role as worker and breadwinner, and his identity as a regular drinker and pub patron.

Strongly associated with the material culture of pint-drinking was the practice of buying drinks in rounds; that is, individuals taking turns to buy drinks for other men with whom they were socialising. This was considered to be not merely common practice, but a 'ritual [...] because of strong social compulsion for its observance'.[82] Drinking in rounds was especially common among those participating in games like dominoes and darts, with the winner often obliged to purchase drinks for those who had lost.[83] In discussing the social influence of this culture, MO noted that it was younger men who were 'most self-conscious' about this ritual for they recognised the importance of successfully adopting this practice in ensuring acceptance in their local pub, thereby consolidating their masculine status in the wider community. Notably, 'pub etiquette' required that if a man knocked over another's glass, he was required to buy a replacement drink, even if the glass had been 'nearly empty'.[84]

A further strand of MO's discussion of pint-drinking cultures related to the act of toasting. Though typically less prevalent, and less elaborate, than in the eighteenth and nineteenth centuries, a brief toast was commonplace in Worktown.[85] Drinking to the health of companions was considered not 'altogether dead yet, although it is not enforced by the strong social sanctions that make the non-observance of standing rounds a serious matter'.[86] A toast usually involved 'a perfunctory gesture of lifting the glass in front of the mouth a moment before the first sip; and sometimes the gesture is omitted, and the words alone used'. Sometimes glasses were tapped lightly together, as remains common today.[87] Via the materiality of the pint glass, the verbalised greeting and the gendered performance of consumption, the practice of toasting, and pint-drinking more broadly, played a key role in the material cultures which were constitutive of prevailing social bonds of masculinity in the pub.

Conclusion

The 1930s public house was a site where cultures of masculinity were forged, consolidated and contested. For MO, there was a sense of belonging unique to the pub. Away from the burdens of work, and the responsibilities of family and home, the pub offered prized opportunities for the bonds of kith and community to mature. Codes of manliness were inextricably linked to men's engagement with, and understanding of, the material culture of the pub. It was through the occupation of the social spaces of the vault and taproom, and via practices like pint-drinking, that performative gendered cultures were practised, imagined and represented both by drinkers themselves, and by social commentators like MO and Spender.

The appeal of the pub as an imagined source of 'authentic' popular culture continued to hold influence beyond the interwar years. In a review of *The Pub and the People*, George Orwell praised MO's finely nuanced discussion of the 'elaborate social ritual' and 'creative communal' sociability of the public house.[88] In a well-known newspaper article of 1946, Orwell penned a vivid portrait of his ideal imagined pub, the Moon Under Water. Given the author's political and social inclinations, it is not surprising that the pub he described bore a striking resemblance to the kinds of premises MO had investigated before the war. Orwell's fantasy boasted the major hallmarks of a Worktown pub, including, for instance, Victorian architecture, darts and pint-drinking in plain glasses.[89] Across the mid- to late twentieth century and into the twenty-first, authenticity has been a highly prized, if often chimerical, aspect of pub culture. Widespread interest in the preservation of 'heritage' premises is rooted to a significant degree in an enthusiasm for the historic material culture of public houses as constitutive of a lost authenticity – though often chronological precision is not prioritised in these popular imaginings.[90] Moreover, MO was not alone in its conceptualisation of the male drinker as the apotheosis of a certain form of manliness. As anthropologist Daniel Miller has recently commented, the 'masculine worker propping up the bar at the pub' has remained an influential totem of a popular masculinity.[91] As MO contended in the late 1930s, the pub has long been an influential forum for the cultivation and expression of manliness, and as this chapter has demonstrated, it is often at the intersections of spaces, objects and bodies that this gendered culture is made manifest.

Notes

1. While much work remains in uncovering the history of masculinity and drinking cultures, for useful commentary on the nineteenth century, for instance, see the seminal B. Harrison, *Drink and the Victorians: The Temperance Question in England, 1815–1872* (London: Faber, 1971).
2. On combining documentary and visual sources, see G. Rose, *Visual Methodologies: An Introduction to Researching with Visual Methods* (London: Sage, 2012), pp. 189–226.
3. See, for example, J. Nicholls, *The Politics of Alcohol: A History of the Drink Question in England* (Manchester: Manchester University Press, 2009).
4. P. Jennings, *The Local: A History of the English Pub* (Stroud: The History Press, 2011), pp. 193–210.
5. C. Langhamer, '"A Public House is for All Classes, Men and Women Alike": Women, Leisure and Drink in Second World War England', *Women's History Review*, 12:3 (2003), pp. 423–443. My own work has also contributed to these historiographical developments: see, for example, S. Moss, '"Wartime Hysterics"? Alcohol, Women and the Politics of Wartime Social Purity', in J. Meyer (ed.), *British Popular Culture and the First World War* (Leiden: Brill, 2008), pp. 147–172. On performativity and the Victorian barmaid, see P. Bailey, 'Parasexuality and Glamour: the Victorian Barmaid as Cultural Prototype', *Gender and History*, 2:2 (1990), pp. 148–172.
6. A. Davies, *Leisure, Gender and Poverty: Working-Class Culture in Manchester and Salford 1900–1939* (Buckingham: Open University Press, 1992), pp. 30–54.
7. See J.-M. Strange, 'Fatherhood, Furniture and Inter-personal Dynamics in Working-class Homes, c. 1870–1914', *Urban History*, 40 (2013), pp. 271–286.
8. For helpful discussion of these and other concepts, see D. Hicks and M. C. Beaudry (eds), *The Oxford Handbook of Material Culture Studies* (Oxford: Oxford University Press, 2010).
9. M. Francis, 'The Domestication of the Male? Recent Research on Nineteenth- and Twentieth-century British Masculinity', *Historical Journal*, 45 (2002), pp. 637–652. On the history of masculinity more broadly, see S. Brady and J. Arnold (eds), *What is Masculinity? Historical Dynamics from Antiquity to the Contemporary World* (Basingstoke: Palgrave Macmillan, 2011).
10. Examples of this rich scholarship include: M. Roper, *Masculinity and the British Organization Man since 1945* (Oxford: Oxford University Press, 1994); J. Meyer, *Men of War: Masculinity and the First World War in Britain* (Basingstoke: Palgrave Macmillan, 2009); M. Houlbrook, *Queer London: Perils and Pleasures in the Sexual Metropolis, 1918–1957* (Chicago, IL: University of Chicago Press, 2005); M. Tebbutt, *Being Boys: Youth, Leisure and Identity in the Inter-war Years* (Manchester: Manchester University Press, 2012); L. King, 'Hidden Fathers? The Significance of Fatherhood in Mid-twentieth-century Britain', *Contemporary British History*, 26 (2012), pp. 25–46.
11. M. Roper and J. Tosh (eds), *Manful Assertions: Masculinities in Britain since 1800* (London: Routledge, 1991).
12. For recent discussion, see J. Hinton, *The Mass Observers: A History, 1937–1949* (Oxford: Oxford University Press, 2013).
13. C. Madge and T. Harrisson (eds), *First Year's Work 1937–38* (London: Lindsay Drummond, 1938), p. 100.
14. A. Pollen, 'Research Methodology in Mass Observation Past and Present: "Scientifically, About as Valuable as a Chimpanzee's Tea Party at the Zoo"?' *History Workshop Journal*, 75 (2013), pp. 213–235.

15. Mass Observation, *The Pub and the People: A Worktown Study* (London: Victor Gollancz, 1943), p. 17.
16. The Mass Observation (MO) Archive is held at the University of Sussex. Selected parts of the archive, including much of the Worktown Collection, are now available online. See http://www.massobs.org.uk/.
17. MO, *The Pub and the People*, pp. 217–219.
18. For discussion of pub subcultures and homosexuality, see Houlbrook, *Queer London*.
19. This was a key trope of the *White Ribbon*, the journal of the British Women's Temperance Association, from its establishment in 1896 and throughout the interwar years.
20. See http://boltonworktown.co.uk/.
21. H. Spender, *'Lensman' Photographs 1932–52* (London: Chatto & Windus, 1987), p. 15.
22. Spender also produced images of pub life for the popular magazine *Picture Post*, and in many cases there are striking stylistic parallels with his Worktown compositions. See Spender, *'Lensman' Photographs*, pp. 100–103.
23. For useful discussion of methodology, see P. Tinkler, *Using Photographs in Social and Historical Research* (London: Sage, 2013).
24. Numerous contemporary pub surveys classified pubs into two main types: '"traditional' and 'improved'. 'Improved' pubs were often located in suburban areas, and offered attractions such as food and gardens in an attempt to encourage moderate drinking. See D. Gutzke, *Pubs and Progressives: Reinventing the Public House in England, 1896–1960* (DeKalb, IL: Northern Illinois University Press, 2006).
25. MO, *The Pub and the People*, p. 109.
26. Ibid., pp. 95–97.
27. See, for example, MO, *The Pub and the People*, pp. 135, 143–148.
28. MO, *The Pub and the People*, pp. 94–95.
29. Ibid., p. 95.
30. Ibid., p. 105.
31. Ibid., p. 155.
32. Ibid., p. 105.
33. B. Nicholson, 'Drink', in H. Llewellyn Smith (ed.), *The New Survey of London Life and Leisure*, vol. 9: *Life and Leisure* (London: P. S. King, 1935), pp. 251–252.
34. MO, *The Pub and the People*, pp. 106–107.
35. Ibid., p. 95.
36. Ibid., pp. 21, 97, 95.
37. Ibid., pp. 95–97.
38. Ibid., pp. 21, 95.
39. Ibid., p. 174.
40. Ibid., p. 105.
41. Ibid., p. 105.
42. Ibid., p. 206.
43. Ibid.
44. Ibid., p. 23.
45. Ibid., p. 95.
46. Ibid., p. 206.
47. Ibid.
48. Ibid., p. 204.
49. Ibid., p. 152.
50. Ibid., p. 95
51. Ibid., p. 105.

52. Ibid.
53. Ibid., p. 95.
54. Ibid.
55. Ibid.
56. Ibid.
57. Ibid.
58. Ibid., p. 113.
59. Ibid., p. 133.
60. Ibid.
61. Scholars have devoted considerable attention to exploring the legacies of the First World War: see, for instance, M. Roper, 'Between Manliness and Masculinity: the "War Generation" and the Psychology of Fear in Britain, 1914–1970', *Journal of British Studies*, 44 (2005), pp. 343–363.
62. MO, *The Pub and the People*, p. 92.
63. Though illegal in pubs, betting and gambling were common: MO, *The Pub and the People*, p. 262. For discussion, see M. Clapson, *A Bit of a Flutter: Popular Gambling and English Society, c. 1823–1961* (Manchester: Manchester University Press, 1992).
64. MO, *The Pub and the People*, pp. 301–302.
65. Ibid., p. 299.
66. Ibid., p. 312.
67. Regrettably, broader discussion of clothing in the pub is beyond the constraints of this chapter. See MO, *The Pub and the People*, pp. 140–143.
68. Beyond the scope of this chapter is discussion of some of the dissonances between MO's text and Spender's photographs. For instance, Spender's Worktown collection includes a handful of images of men sitting in the vault, this offers a contrast to MO's pronounced emphasis on standing to drink as ubiquitous.
69. On the range of drinks consumed, see MO, *The Pub and the People*, pp. 30–37.
70. MO, *The Pub and the People*, p. 115.
71. Ibid., pp. 40–41.
72. Ibid., p. 23.
73. Ibid., p. 184.
74. Ibid., p. 183.
75. Ibid., p. 92.
76. Ibid., p. 184.
77. Ibid.
78. Ibid., p. 35.
79. Ibid., p. 184.
80. Ibid.
81. Ibid., p. 123.
82. Ibid., p. 177.
83. Ibid., p. 180.
84. Ibid.
85. Ibid., p. 181.
86. Ibid., p. 182.
87. Ibid.
88. G. Orwell, 'Review of *The Pub and the People*', *The Listener*, 21 January 1943.
89. G. Orwell, *Evening Standard*, 9 February 1946.
90. See G. Brandwood, *Britain's Best Real Heritage Pubs* (St Albans: CAMRA, 2013).
91. D. Miller, *The Comfort of Things* (Cambridge: Polity Press, 2008), p. 4.

Concluding Remarks

*Hannah Greig, Jane Hamlett
and Leonie Hannan*

This collection of essays showcases some of the many ways in which scholars are now using material culture to interrogate ideas about gender and using questions about gender to frame new studies of material culture. Long seen as the preserve of museum curators, surviving objects are increasingly coming into play in historical work. More than this, academics and practitioners (for instance, museum professionals, artists and makers) are working together to forge new ways of working with material culture and, in so doing, they are opening fresh perspectives on the material past. The purpose of this book has not been to map these fields in their entirety, but rather to provide the student with a variety of case studies illuminating current methodologies as well as the breadth and rich potential of differing analyses. In this way, this book does not seek to map a coherent narrative of continuities or changes over time. Nonetheless, placing these essays side by side reveals some common elements and shared agendas as well as suggestive differences.

To begin with, looking at what material things meant, and what people did with them, reminds us of the fluidity of gendered meanings and their cultural complexity. Material cultures do not always divide easily into things associated with men and things associated with women, and an examination of a material terrain ostensibly associated with one sex often brings the other into view. The early modern guild, for instance, might be presumed to be an exclusively male environment. However, as Helen Smith has demonstrated, scrutinising the guilds' material culture and material requirements, unexpectedly reveals a variety of women otherwise hidden from the guilds' histories: the female benefactors, craftswomen and servants who created and maintained such professional organisations. At the other end of this book's range and chronology, Matthew Houlbrook has revealed how an everyday object promoted as essential in defining the 1920s woman – the powder puff – was of key significance to contemporary conceptions of masculinity and used to articulate a new kind of queer identity that challenged the normative gendered assumptions of the day.

Indeed, the complex agendas and interpretations associated with the otherwise ordinary powder puff remind us that the material world can play an active and significant role in the transformation of identities, something that is similarly revealed by Karen Harvey's study of late eighteenth- and early nineteenth-century drinking vessels and their place in a story of changing ideas about masculinity. Harvey has shown us how a close reading of these objects and their decoration maps a story of male pride in artisanal prowess, one that emerged as ideas about manliness were transformed in the wake of industrialisation. Vivienne Richmond's search for the maker of an ordinary but incredibly rare pair of woman's calico drawers from the late nineteenth century took her not only to the needlewoman who made them but to a closer reading of contemporary ideas about gender, propriety, respectability and, also, individual identity and expressions of independence.

When we look at how ordinary objects were used in everyday practices, we often find that men and women did not stick to the rigid prescriptions of the day. People might make or use things in unexpected ways that sit uneasily alongside historians' expectations about the performance of gendered roles and behaviour in the past. Objects, then, communicate changing values and can offer historians barometers of shifting social mores. The ceramic vessels studied by Harvey carry such stories in their form and decorative details. In contrast, the powder puff tells us little through its material form alone. Instead, the history of gender and sexuality resonate through the meanings and symbolism attached to the powder puff when it was used, or merely carried, by an individual. The fact that the powder puff had entirely different social and sexual connotations as a commercially available commodity highlights the importance of context and the particular interaction between person, object and site.

Although it might not always be possible, contextualising objects can be key to understanding past material cultures. Many of the essays in this book consider context in terms of the relationship between objects and body, and the relationship between objects and environment (or what is often called space and place), placing these at the centre of their analyses. Of course certain practices, like shaving, bring bodies and objects into necessary and intimate contact. Susan Vincent's exploration of this practice over a long period of time demonstrates how eighteenth-century men began to place a new emphasis on being clean-shaven. That men persevered with this time-consuming and sometimes painful task is a testament to the importance of presenting the face of 'polite' masculinity to the outside world. Samuel Pepys's quest to find a convenient means of shaving himself, reminds us that the relationship between bodies and objects involved particular kinds of skills. And it is no surprise, then, that contextualising historical objects often involves understanding the skills originally required to make and use them – skills that may now be lost. Writing letters, for instance, demanded varied expertise, from making ink to creating a seal, feasibly honed over a lifetime. These skills were shared by many early modern men and women, yet, as Leonie Hannan's chapter explores, the product they created could be highly gendered. Women regularly wrote letters in particular places and for particular purposes that were often distinct from those of men. Yet, at the same time, letter-writing also provided women with access to an intellectual culture which (if explored entirely through the printed word) might too easily be presumed to be dominated exclusively by men. As Harvey notes, 'skills are body and place-specific', and attention to such specifics recurs throughout these chapters, often transforming our understanding of the material culture in question.

The specifics of place are key to many of the case studies included here, and this book has explored a range of different kinds of gendered spaces, from the formally male world of the early modern London guild to salubrious nineteenth-century women's hair salons and gentlemen's barbers. In both these cases, the gendered story is not the single-sex story we might presume. Smith finds women represented in the ostensibly male domains of the guilds. Jessica Clark notes that the hair salon cultivated an atmosphere that aimed to please the female customer but which was likely to have been designed entirely by men, whilst spaces for barbering catered to a changing type of man, one aligned to a new kind of masculine status associated with an emerging idea of social class. In her exploration of the 1930s public house, Stella Moss finds a similarly complex narrative of spatial and gendered distinction. With pubs built on a domestic scale, their owners felt the need to demarcate space in terms of its similarity to, or difference from, home.

The ability of material culture to shape behaviours, opinions and identities within particular historical contexts is vividly suggested by each contribution to this book. Notably, though, the material cultures examined in the book involved people and objects operating in networks and assemblages, with meanings forged through various relationships and interactions. In this regard, each chapter reminds us of the limitations of binary models within cultural history – be they binary divisions between male and female, or binary dichotomies of object and subject. Complex interactions are as evident in moments of habit and routine (shaving, writing or drinking) as they are in moments of performance (company celebrations, the production of prize-winning drawers or arrest on the streets of London). And the gendered stories that emerge from these fragments are not simply stories just about men or just about women. Rather they are expressions of multiple masculinities and femininities, forged and framed in relationship to each other. Indeed, many of the objects we examine here – and the ways those objects were used, shared and exchanged – express the connections and commonalities between masculine and feminine worlds and not just the divisions between them.

Resources

As we have discussed, research projects that focus on gender and material culture use artefacts themselves to a greater or lesser extent according to the approach taken and the availability (or survival) of appropriate objects. However, gaining direct access to historical objects can be critical for the researcher – in terms of both the material evidence they offer and the different historical questions they provoke. Below are the details of some resources that enable researchers to identify, locate and access objects and art works relevant to their studies. These resources relate primarily to collections of objects in museums and galleries. Many of the listed catalogues include images of the objects and can, therefore, provide really excellent information on individual artefacts. However, viewing objects online only offers a very limited interaction with material culture and initial research amongst these digital resources is best followed up by visits to museums, galleries and archives to look at objects in person.

Museum and Gallery Catalogues

You can often locate objects and images via publicly accessible online catalogues. Although these catalogues rarely represent a complete list of all holdings, they do reveal the kinds of objects that exist in particular collections. Once initial research has been conducted online through these resources, museum and gallery staff – such as archivists and librarians – are able to advise on how to access the collections in person.

V&A:
http://collections.vam.ac.uk – well over a million individual objects relating to the history of art and design.
British Museum:
www.britishmuseum.org/research/collection_online/search.aspx – over three and a half million objects from across the British Museum's vast collections, which reflect global histories.
The National Portrait Gallery:
www.npg.org.uk/collections.php – portraits (paintings, prints, sculptures, miniatures and photographs), searchable by sitter or artist.
Lewis Walpole Library:
http://images.library.yale.edu/walpoleweb/ – an extensive collection of eighteenth-century British prints.
The Wellcome Collection:
www.wellcomecollection.org/explore.aspx – a diverse collection including images, video and articles 'exploring what it means to be human'.
National Trust Collections Online:
www.nationaltrustcollections.org.uk – objects from a wide range of British historic houses, searchable by collection, category or period.
English Heritage Archives Online:
www.englishheritagearchives.org.uk – over a million entries detailing photographs, plans and drawings of English Heritage sites.

Museum of London Collections Online:
http://collections.museumoflondon.org.uk/Online/ – provides access to the Museum
of London's vast archaeological archive relating to finds excavated in the capital city.
Beamish: The Living Museum of the North, Collections Online:
http://collections.beamish.org.uk – photographs, oral history recordings, books and
trade catalogues recording life in the North from the early nineteenth century until
the 1940s.
The Fashion Museum Collections Online:
www.museumofcostume.co.uk/collections/collection_search.aspx – menswear, wom-
enswear, accessories, fashion photographs and more from 1600 to the present day.

Projects and Blogs

Blogs and project websites are a good way to keep up-to-date with scholarship in this
field. As the examples listed below show, researchers from a range of disciplines regularly
document their thoughts online, often months or years before their findings will appear
in full and in print.

The Material World Blog – a global hub for thinking about things, edited by Haidy
Geismar, Daniel Miller and Matthew Hockenberry amongst others: http://www.
materialworldblog.com.
THINGS: a CRASSH Seminar series – This is the blog for a seminar series running at
CRASSH, University of Cambridge, in 2011–2015. The series uses objects as common sites of study to bring together historians, historians of art, and historians of
science to look at the history of the early modern period: https://thingsc18th.word-
press.com.
Commodity Histories – a public forum where you will encounter stories from current historical research, pick up news from around the world and discover new
resources: http://www.commodityhistories.org.
BBC Your Paintings – a project that brings together digitised images of paintings
from across the nation, including images from small and rare collections that are
not available through the big galleries and websites: http://www.bbc.co.uk/arts/
yourpaintings/.

Key Texts

History

Glenn Adamson, *The Invention of Craft* (London: Bloomsbury, 2013).

Leora Auslander, 'Beyond Words', *American Historical Review*, 110:4 (2005), pp. 1015–1045.

Maxine Berg, *Luxury and Pleasure in Eighteenth-Century Britain* (Oxford: Oxford University Press, 2005).

Lorraine Daston (ed.), *Things that Talk: Object Lessons from Art and Science* (New York: Zone Books, 2004).

Anne Gerritsen and Giorgio Riello (eds), *Writing Material Culture History* (London: Bloomsbury, 2014).

Hannah Greig, *The Beau Monde: Fashionable Society in Georgian London* (Oxford: Oxford University Press, 2013).

Hannah Greig and Giorgio Riello, 'Eighteenth-Century Interiors: Redesigning the Georgian', special issue, *Journal of Design History*, 20:4 (2008), pp. 273–289.

Jane Hamlett, *Material Relations: Domestic Interiors and Middle Class Families in England, 1850–1910* (Manchester: Manchester University Press, 2010).

Tara Hamling and Catherine Richardson (eds), *Everyday Objects: Medieval and Early Modern Material Culture and its Meanings* (Aldershot: Ashgate, 2010).

Karen Harvey (ed.), *History and Material Culture: A Student's Guide to Approaching Alternative Source*s (London: Routledge, 2009).

Margaret Ponsonby, *Stories from Home: English Domestic Interiors, 1750–1850* (Aldershot: Ashgate, 2007).

Giorgio Riello, *Cotton: The Fabric that Made the Modern World* (Cambridge: Cambridge University Press, 2013).

Carolyn Steedman, 'What a Rag Rug Means', *Journal of Material Culture*, 3:3 (1998), pp. 259–281.

John Styles, *The Dress of the People: Everyday Fashion in Eighteenth-century England* (London: Yale University Press, 2007).

John Styles and Amanda Vickery (eds), *Gender, Taste and Material Culture in Britain and North America, 1700–1830* (London: The Paul Mellon Centre for Studies in British Art, 2006).

Frank Trentmann, 'Materiality in the Future of History: Things, Practices, and Politics', *Journal of British Studies*, 48:2 (2009), pp. 283–307.

Amanda Vickery, *Behind Closed Doors: At Home in Georgian England* (London: Yale University Press, 2009).

Lorna Weatherill, *Consumer Behaviour and Material Culture in Britain, 1660–1760* (London: Economic and Social Research Council, 1988).

Other Disciplines (anthropology, literary studies, art history and museum studies)

Arjun Appadurai (ed.), *The Social Life of Things: Commodities in Cultural Perspective* (Cambridge: Cambridge University Press, 1986).

Bill Brown (ed.), *Things* (Chicago: University of Chicago Press, 2004).

Elizabeth Edwards, Chris Gosden and Ruth B. Phillips (eds), *Sensible Objects: Colonialism, Museums and Material Culture* (Oxford: Berg, 2006).

Henry Glassie, *Material Culture* (Bloomington, IN: Indiana University Press, 1999).

Amiria Henare, Martin Holbraad and Sari Wastell (eds), *Thinking through Things: Theorising Artefacts Ethnographically* (London: Routledge, 2007).

Ian Hodder, *Entangled: An Archaeology of the Relationships between Humans and Things* (Malden, MA: Wiley-Blackwell, 2012).

Ann Rosalind Jones and Peter Stallybrass (eds), *Renaissance Clothing and the Materials of Memory* (Cambridge: Cambridge University Press, 2000).

Daniel Miller, *The Comfort of Things* (Cambridge: Polity Press, 2008).

Jules David Prown, 'Mind in Matter: An Introduction to Material Culture Theory and Method', *Winterthur Portfolio*, 17:1 (1982), pp. 1–19.

Christopher Y. Tilley (ed.), *Handbook of Material Culture* (London: Sage, 2006).

Index

Page numbers in *italics* refer to an illustration.